Reshaping Change

Reshaping Change features data collected from over twenty years of fieldwork and provides important insights into studying organizations and making sense of organizational change. It does much more than provide a simple overview of theory and change models and instead makes the processual approach comprehensible and accessible to both researchers and practitioners.

The book highlights the need to move beyond snapshot anecdotal accounts in drawing on case studies of radical and large-scale change in General Motors, Pirelli, Shell, Britax and Laubman and Pank. New conceptual developments and theoretical critiques are combined with critical reflections on the practice of doing research in organizations. Whether we are chroniclers, storytellers or analysts is just one of a set of questions raised about our role as consumers, actors and authors of change stories. This is an innovative and highly practical book that captures the truly complex processes of the changing organization and demonstrates the theoretical and practical value of using a processual perspective.

Patrick Dawson holds the Salvesen Chair of Management at the University of Aberdeen. He has published numerous academic articles and several books in the field of organizational change.

Understanding Organizational Change

Series editor:
Bernard Burnes

The management of change is now acknowledged as being one of the most important issues facing management today. By focussing on particular perspectives and approaches to change, particular change situations, and particular types of organization, this series provides a comprehensive overview and an in-depth understanding of the field of organizational change.

Titles in this series include:

Organizational Change for Corporate Sustainability
A guide for leaders and change agents of the future
Dexter Dunphy, Andrew Griffiths and Suzanne Benn

Reshaping Change
A processual perspective
Patrick Dawson

Reshaping Change

A processual perspective

Patrick Dawson

Routledge
Taylor & Francis Group

LONDON AND NEW YORK

First published 2003 by Routledge
11 New Fetter Lane, London EC4P 4EE

Simultaneously published in the USA and Canada
by Routledge
29 West 35th Street, New York, NY 10001

Routledge is an imprint of the Taylor & Francis Group

© 2003 Patrick Dawson

Typeset in Times by Wearset Ltd, Boldon, Tyne and Wear
Printed and bound in Great Britain by The Cromwell Press, Trowbridge, Wiltshire

British Library Cataloguing in Publication Data
A catalogue record for this book is available from the British Library

Library of Congress Cataloging in Publication Data
A catalog record for this book has been requested

ISBN 0–415–28409–0 (hbk)
ISBN 0–415–28410–4 (pbk)

To Rosie Mae Dawson

Contents

Figures

Series editor's preface

It is an accepted tenet of modern life that change is constant, of greater magnitude and far less predictable than ever before. For this reason, managing change is acknowledged as being one of the most important and difficult issues facing organizations today. This is why both practitioners and academics, in ever-growing numbers, are seeking to understand organizational change. This is why the range of competing theories and advice has never been greater or more puzzling.

Over the past 100 years there have been many theories and prescriptions put forward for understanding and managing change. Arguably, the first person to attempt to offer a systematic approach to changing organizations was the originator of Scientific Management – Frederick Taylor. From the 1930s onwards, the Human Relations school attacked Taylor's one-dimensional view of human nature and his over-emphasis on individuals. In a parallel and connected development in the 1940s, Kurt Lewin created perhaps the most influential approach to managing change. His planned approach to change, encapsulated in his three-step model, became the inspiration for a generation of researchers and practitioners, mainly – though not exclusively – in the USA. Throughout the 1950s, Lewin's work was expanded beyond his focus on small groups and conflict resolution to create the Organization Development (OD) movement. From the 1960s to the early 1980s, OD established itself as the dominant Western approach to organizational change.

However, by the early 1980s more and more Western organizations found themselves having to change rapidly and dramatically, and sometimes brutally, in the face of the might of corporate Japan. In such circumstances, many judged the consensus-based and incrementally-focussed OD approach as having little to offer. Instead a plethora of approaches began to emerge that, whilst not easy to classify, could best be described as anti-OD. These newer approaches to change were less wary than OD in embracing issues of power and politics in organizations; they did not necessarily see organizational change as clean, linear and finite. Instead they saw change as messy, contentious, context-dependent and open-ended. In addition, unlike OD, which drew its inspiration and insights mainly from psychology, the newer approaches drew on an eclectic mix of sociology, anthropology, economics, psychotherapy and the natural sciences, not to mention the ubiquitous post-modernism. This has produced a range of approaches to change, with suffixes and appellations such as emergent, processual, political, institutional, cultural, contingency, complexity, chaos, and many more.

It is impossible to conceive of an approach that is suitable for all types of change, all types of situations and all types of organizations. Some may be too narrow in applicability whilst others may be too general. Some may be complementary to each other whilst others are clearly incompatible. The range of approaches to change, and the confusion over their strengths, weaknesses and suitability, is such that the field of organizational change resembles more an overgrown weed patch than a well-tended garden.

The aim of this series is to provide both a comprehensive overview of the main perspectives on organizational change, and an in-depth guide to key issues and controversies. The series will investigate the main approaches to change, and the various contexts in which change is applied. The underlying rationale for the series is that we cannot understand organizational change sufficiently, nor implement it effectively, unless we can map the range of approaches and evaluate what they seek to achieve, how and where they can be applied, and, crucially, the evidence that underpins them.

Bernard Burnes
Manchester School of Management
UMIST

Acknowledgements

The research reported in this book has been drawn from a number of organizations over many years. From the initial fieldwork conducted on the uptake and use of computer-aided design in 1980 through to the collection of data on the use of advanced communication and information technology in organizations in the twenty-first century, the number of interview transcripts and observation notes has continued to grow. Making sense of all these data has not been an easy task, but acknowledgement must be given to the openness of many people in relaying their work experience and in being supportive of this type of longitudinal and time-consuming research. For being allowed to observe senior executive meetings, participating in discussions on strategy and change, and being given access to senior managements' thoughts and ideas – even when this has resulted in conducting interviews in various airline lounges around the world – I give them my thanks. Equally open and supportive have been middle managers and those at divisional and plant level, who are often active shapers and implementers of change. Close proximity and ongoing relations with this level of management have provided a rich source of data, and have certainly provided insight into political process and the practice of managing branch-level and shop-floor change. Over the years a number of these people have been ex-MBA students, who have been very helpful in providing sustained access to sites in order to engage in longitudinal processual research. Building these relationships has been critical to my fieldwork experiences, and their support is acknowledged here.

The long periods of time spent on the shop floor of manufacturing plants, in the branch offices of service companies and in marshalling yards examining freight-yard operations have provided abundant opportunities to reflect on the very different experiences of change by employees in organizations. This also draws you very close to the people you are studying and enables the collection of rich data in which contradiction, ambivalence and ambiguity are as evident as fixed positions and certainty. After establishing long-term relationships, I found it was not unusual to be invited outside the formal workplace to various social occasions; such opportunities highlighted the false divide between work and non-work activities, and the influence of our home life on how we experience change at work. At this juncture it is appropriate to thank those individuals who were willing to be interviewed and re-interviewed in their workplaces and in their homes. The home-based interviews provided a forum for useful discussion and debate, especially on how household decision-making influences employee experience of change at work. To all those people who gave their time so freely, I am deeply grateful.

Three other groups that have also been very open and congenial in discussing change issues have been collaborating agencies, consultants and trade unions. Union officials and their shop floor representatives have provided a useful lens through which to reflect on the management of change. Interestingly, they also drew attention to the organization of unions and the problems and issues that face all those who seek to steer or shape the change process. Although change consultants have generally been less open and far more reluctant to spend time in supporting this type of research, the Commonwealth Scientific and Industrial Research Organization (CSIRO) was one Australian group that significantly aided the process of gaining company access, made a wide range of official documents available for analysis, and provided a source of enthusiastic interviewees and contributors to research. Thanks must also be given to the various funding bodies, universities, Deans and Heads of Departments/Schools who have supported this type of research, which necessarily requires 'out-of-office' activity – especially when publications from fieldwork may be three or four years downstream from study commencement.

The material used in this book aims to explain the contribution that a processual perspective can make to understanding processes of organizational change. Data collected over 23 years are used to illustrate the theory and practice of processual research. Although the high administrative responsibilities of my present job preclude the possibility of full engagement in this type of research over the next few years, there remains a need for further processual studies on change. I would therefore like to acknowledge all the other researchers who have shown an interest in the processual perspective, and especially, those researchers who are at an early stage in their academic careers. I would also like to acknowledge the support of Gisela van Bommel, who, in managing our postgraduate programmes and my own busy schedule, managed to protect space for the completion of this manuscript when many other demands were being made on my time; Suzanne MacDonald for her support in administrative matters; and Lisa Pope for help with typing the appendices.

In carrying out fieldwork studies I have worked closely with a number of colleagues over the years. In particular, I would like to acknowledge the collaborative support of Cameron Allan, Sarah Buckland, Verna Blewett, Geoff Bloor, Ian McLoughlin, Gill Palmer, Niki Panteli, Margaret Patrickson and Jan Webb. I would also like to give special thanks to Jon Clark for his supervisory support during my early experiences in British Rail marshalling yards, and Liz Kummerow for useful discussions on how best to use processual case studies for teaching purposes. In reviewing chapters and commenting on the book, I would like to acknowledge the constructive and helpful academic comments of Geoff Bloor, David Buchanan, Jane Farmer, Jeff Hyman, Ian McLoughlin, Niki Panteli, Andrew Pettigrew and David Preece.

As this book draws on research that has been published elsewhere, as well as new empirical material, I would like to thank: Taylor & Francis for granting permission to republish case material from an article entitled 'Multiple voices and the orchestration of a rational narrative in the pursuit of "management objectives": the political process of plant-level change' (2002; *Technology Analysis & Strategic Management*, 12(1): 39–58); Routledge for permission to use and revise a chapter entitled 'Managing quality in the multicultural workplace' (in Wilkinson, A. and Willmott, H. (eds) *Making Quality Critical: New Perspectives on Organizational Change*); and Elsevier Publishing for permission to further develop the article 'In at the deep end: conducting processual research on organizational change' (*Scandinavian Journal of Management*, 13(4): 389–405).

As with all my books, I would like to give special thanks to Sue Thomson, who has been more than understanding for all the time I have spent at the computer when I should have been engaging in more social activities with the family (especially for my rather early departure from our New Zealand family holiday so that I could return to complete this book on time). I would also like to give a special mention to my teenage daughter Rosie Dawson and my youngest son Gareth Dawson. When work appears daunting and burdensome they remind me of the need to maintain balance and humour in my life. Finally, I would like to thank my eldest son Robin Dawson for spending two wonderful days with me snowboarding at Cadrona ski field in New Zealand – a place worthy of some longitudinal fieldwork.

1 Introduction

- Aims and objectives
- Structure of the book
- Predispositions: a processual view of change

> The very act of choosing concepts and distinguishing among events involves the researcher in the construction and interpretation of the events, and this is never a value-free or intellectually neutral process for the very fact that judgement is required . . . Inevitably, one measures according to one's theoretical predispositions, analyses the data accordingly, and thus, tends to produce support for the initial conjectures.
>
> (Pfeffer, 1982: 33–34)

Aims and objectives

The main purpose of this book is to highlight the theoretical and practical value of using a processual approach for studying and making sense of organizational change. It also aims to make this approach understandable and accessible to students and researchers who are interested in studying the way change unfolds over time and in context. It is particularly critical of studies that present rational linear accounts of change, as well as those who avoid practical fieldwork issues and yet are quick to offer theoretical critique. The context within which change occurs, the substance of the change in question, and the political behaviour of individuals and groups, all interact over time in the shaping and reshaping of organizational processes of change. This processual perspective is the focus of the book. As such, the main body of the text sets out to present an explanation and analysis of this approach that improves our knowledge and understanding. It is also intended to stimulate interest in the approach and to generate questions for debate and consideration that may lead to future developments in processual research.

The commitment to studying change over time and in context links theoretical and conceptual developments to a methodological allegiance to longitudinal field studies. The processual perspective is an inductive–deductive approach, which, whilst drawing on our existing body of knowledge in the formulation of research questions and the clarification of concepts, is also data-driven in allowing new insights and conceptual developments to emerge during the collection and analysis of data. Data collected from over twenty years of fieldwork in companies in Australia, Scotland, New Zealand and England are used to discuss conceptual issues and theoretical concerns, as well as spotlighting the practicalities of carrying out processual research on change in organizations. General Motors, Pirelli, Shell, Britax, and Laubman and Pank all provide useful data that demonstrate the reshaping of change in the uptake of a range of company initiatives. The case studies are presented in a readable way and are intended both to demonstrate certain dimensions of the processual perspective and to serve as material for debates on undergraduate and postgraduate courses on organizational change.

The book also provides useful case illustrations for shorter management development programmes that address theoretical issues through the use of practical examples. One intention is to provide an informative yet accessible book that is of both academic value and practical worth to students of management, trade unionists, change consultants, company managers and employees. Another target is the academic and research community, as well as students seeking to embark on longitudinal qualitative research in doing a masters or doctoral dissertation. Finally, students interested in research methods in business should find this book a useful reference in detailing the theory and practice of engaging in processual research.

The objectives of the book can be summarized as follows:

1   To outline the main conceptual dimensions of a processual framework for understanding change, and to clarify what is involved in developing and applying a processual approach to the study of organizations.
2   To provide readable case studies from a number of high-profile companies that serve to further our knowledge and understanding of the change process.
3   To examine research strategy and design, and to evaluate the methodological contribution of the qualitative longitudinal case study.

4 To identify and discuss how the results from processual research can be presented to academic, practitioner and student audiences, and to illustrate some of the advantages of using this approach.

5 To reappraise common interpretations of the processual perspective and to spotlight areas in need of further refinement and development.

6 To provide a critical yet innovative book that is accessible to students and practitioners concerned with organizational change issues and debates.

A central argument is that the processual perspective should be acknowledged as an approach in its own right and should not be collapsed under the broader divergent category of an 'emergent approach'.

Structure of the book

Chapter 2 examines what we mean by a processual perspective, and provides a historical overview of this approach through drawing on the work of Burns and Stalker (1961), Child (1972), Elger (1975) and Pettigrew (1985). Attention is focussed on clarifying and explaining the main orientation of the processual perspective, rather than a review of other major change theories and models (for a discussion of these alternative models, see Dawson, 2003). Moreover, while reference is made to other processual writers and research, the framework developed and described represents my own approach to studying change in organizations. The main dimensions of the context, politics and substance of change are all explained and later illustrated through leading company examples of the uptake and implementation of new technology and management techniques (see Chapters 3–5). During the process of organizational change, these dimensions are shown to overlap and interlock in shaping and reshaping workplace outcomes. Consequently, linear stage models of change are rejected and a more complex and dynamic conception of change is advocated. Also accommodated within this processual framework are the rationalized accounts and stories of change agents. It is recognized that *post-hoc* rationalizations often occur, and the construction of neat logical stories can provide useful political leverage in shaping decision-making on change. As powerful political tools these change stories are important, and there is a need to evaluate critically their influence on reshaping processes. In doing this, the concepts of multiple narratives and competing histories are included in the framework developed in Chapter 2. These concepts are used in the case study chapters and are further taken up in an examination of data analysis and publication, and in a discussion of future developments of the processual perspective.

After delineating and explaining the constituent elements of a processual approach, the empirical chapters that follow draw on company change data to illustrate the three key dimensions of context, politics and substance. In Chapter 3, the contextual dimensions to change are examined in the introduction of a quality management programme at three different plants of Pirelli Cables. It is shown how a strategy that was developed and employed successfully in one plant did not prove so successful in another context in the same company. Gender, ethnic divisions and the local culture and history of plant operations are all shown to influence the shaping and reshaping of workplace change.

Chapter 4 examines the political process of change within an automotive manufacturing plant. Longitudinal data are used to highlight how differing vested interest groups manoeuvred to steer, shape and resist change. A local management team (a change coalition) orchestrated shop-floor change through the active construction of a rational account of the process of change for the purpose of securing their own preferred outcomes. The substance of change is taken up in Chapter 5, which examines the uptake and use of video conferencing systems in Shell Expro in Scotland, and the movement towards cell-based teamwork arrangements at Britax Industries in South Australia. It is shown how the new work arrangements are open to local reconfiguration and how there is an ongoing reshaping process in the uptake of new operating procedures and in the use of new technology. The chapter usefully demonstrates not only the social shaping of technology, but also the way technical knowledge is constrained by training programmes that promote prescribed behaviours in their application and use.

The methodological chapters that follow turn attention to the practice of conducting processual research and the problem of making sense of rich qualitative longitudinal data. In reflecting on over twenty years of fieldwork experience, some of the 'realities' of doing this type of research are outlined and evaluated. In Chapter 6, the main focus is on the methodological orientation of processual studies and key issues in the design of longitudinal field research. The importance of maintaining a commitment to the smaller intensive longitudinal case study is stressed, and the need to accommodate constraints and opportunities in research design is discussed through a number of practical illustrations. Chapter 7 then examines the practice of doing processual research in organizations. The importance of spending time in organizations and the issues arising from sustained fieldwork activity are discussed. The need to accommodate multiple perspectives and the value of combining a range of data collection techniques are demonstrated through recounting fieldwork experience and the problems of data collection. The chapter concludes with an account of the difficult and time-consuming task of processual analysis. By drawing on past experience, an attempt is made to illustrate what it is like to engage in this type of processual research.

Once the fieldwork is complete in the collection of longitudinal data, there is the long, hard task of data analysis in the preparation of material for publication. The write-up of case study data may form part of a journal article, a conference paper or a book chapter. In addition, the researcher will need to present the case material to participating organizations so that they can check for 'factual' errors and issues of commercial sensitivity. Chapter 8 takes up these issues in a discussion of data analysis in the preparation of material for presentation and publication. It is argued that company change stories are often misleadingly constructed around a linear series of 'successful' events that serve to show the company in a positive light to any interested external party. This misrepresents the complex, murky and political nature of change, and as such it is suggested that the processual researcher has an important contribution to make in presenting findings that counterbalance the rational accounts common in the popular management literature. A critical appraisal is made on the relationship between author and audience, and the main forms of the written case study are summarized.

In the concluding chapter, it is argued that the in-depth longitudinal case study is a mainstay of processual research and that researchers should not equate more case studies with higher-level data. The chapter reconsiders the main aims of the book, and is critical of the growing call for increased systematization and codification. Procedural regulation and standardization are rejected, with critical self-reflection, innovation and creativity being identified as central to the future development of the processual perspective.

Predispositions: a processual view of change

The need to study change over time and in context steers the development of certain concepts and links theoretical concerns with methodological considerations. In the case of the processual perspective, there is a commitment to qualitative longitudinal field studies that can capture the dynamic processes of change 'as they happen'. Thus, our main concern is with a critical examination of the contribution of the processual perspective in studying and making sense of the shaping and reshaping of complex processes of change. These processes also engage with people's expectations about future possible scenarios and reflections on past experience. These elements of the past and expectations of the future remain open to reinterpretation and reconstruction, and their very existence can create tension and conflict. The ways in which various accounts, or views of the world, may vie for dominance highlights the importance of power and politics. This level of complexity in studying change raises a number of theoretical and methodological issues. In this book, it is argued that the strength of the processual approach is in capturing these multiple realities and experiences of change in context and over time.

Essentially, the book aims to provide insight and clarity on theoretical issues, conceptual developments, methodological and research design matters, data analysis questions and types of case study write-up, which are all part of the practice of doing processual research in organizations. Although this type of research is time-consuming and demanding, it is also very rewarding and is well suited to those who appreciate multiple and shifting views and reject the notion that it is possible to find *the* authentic account that explains organizational change.

2 A processual approach to understanding change

- A processual approach: reshaping change as an ongoing process
- A brief history of the processual perspective
- Discarding the emergent label and reinstating the processual perspective
- Conclusion

The processual perspective described in this chapter has evolved over time and speaks from over twenty years of fieldwork experience and research. It attempts to take into account some of the early criticisms levelled at the foundational work of Pettigrew (see Buchanan and Boddy, 1992; Knights and Murray, 1994; Alvesson and Willmott, 1996), in formulating an approach that is accessible and useful in studying change in organizations. Although reference is made to some of the original research associated with this school (Pettigrew, 1985), the focus is on my own particular conceptual framework for understanding change. The chapter commences with an outline of this approach, explaining the three main elements of the politics, context and substance of change. A number of conceptual differences, compared with earlier studies are then highlighted, and a brief history of the processual perspective is provided. It is argued that many of the roots to this approach can be traced back to empirical work conducted in the 1940s and 1950s. A summary of Pettigrew's (1985) landmark work in ICI is provided, and a number of criticisms of the study are discussed and evaluated. This historical overview of processual research also gives attention to the misrepresentation of the processual perspective as an 'emergent approach' to change management. The chapter concludes by calling for more critically reflective processual studies to further our understanding of organizational change.

A processual approach: reshaping change as an ongoing process

The processual approach developed here consists of three main elements, namely the politics, context and substance of change (see Figure 2.1). The politics of change is taken to refer to political activities outwith and

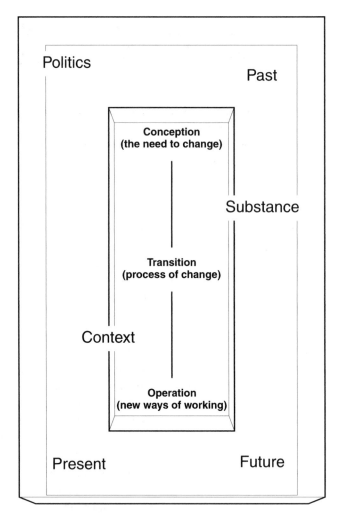

Figure 2.1 *Organizational change: a processual framework*

within the organization. The former may involve: senior business leaders or industry groups lobbying government; the formation of various strategic competitor alliances; governmental pressure brought to bear on corporate decision-making (for example, in the relocation or rationalization of European business operations); and the influence of overseas divisions of Multi National Corporations (MNCs) on local operations. Internal political activity can be in the form of shop-floor negotiations between trade union representatives and management, between consultants (working within the organization) and various organizational groups, and between and within managerial, supervisory and operative personnel. These individuals or groups can influence decision-making and the setting of agendas at critical junctures during the process of organizational change. This dimension is thereby seen to comprise the political activities of consultation, negotiation, conflict and resistance, which occur at various levels outwith and within the organization during the process of organizational change. The more covert forms of political process may be evident in the legitimization of certain norms and values that, while often remaining implicit, nevertheless serve to influence individual and group responses to change. Kamp (2000: 77), drawing on the work of Hildebrandt and Seltz (1989), refers to the social principles that shape norms and provide the 'lens through which external conditions of possibility are interpreted'. She refers to this as a layer of 'stiffened politics' (stabilized patterns of politics), which she argues explains how continuity rather than change marks shop-floor politicking where employees are 'often stuck in old marriages' unable actively to engage in the shaping and reshaping of change (Kamp, 2000: 89). As such, shop-floor responses characterized as reactive and resistant are often inappropriately described within the conventional change management literature as a 'legitimate problem' for management to resolve. However, it is argued here that shop-floor resistance is an integral part of political process that requires examination and analysis. Among other things, such an analysis offers an additional source of insight and knowledge on the change process. Essentially, the political behaviours of employees that are generally labelled as signifying 'resistance' to change will take many forms and emerge for many different reasons. As Schlesinger *et al.* (1992: 346) note:

> Political behaviour emerges in organizations because what is in the best interests of one individual or group is sometimes not in the best interests . . . of other individuals and groups. The consequences of organizational change efforts often are good for some people and bad for others. As a result, politics and power struggles often emerge through change efforts. Whilst this political behaviour sometimes takes the form of two or more armed camps publicly fighting it out, it usually is subtler. In many cases, it occurs completely under the surface of public dialogue.

Power relations and political process have been identified as central in steering company change programmes (Buchanan and Badham, 1999). For example, the commitment of middle management to strategy implementation cannot be taken for granted (see Porter *et al.*, 1976). As research has shown, variations in commitment can significantly influence the reshaping of change (Guth and MacMillan, 1989), particularly in cases where differing vested interests between management levels and functions do not align with strategic objectives (Wilkinson, 1983). Child (1997: 70) argues that the political drivers for change centre on first, the way in which we interpret our situation and in so doing reformulate our intentions; and second, the process of mutual negotiations, persuasion or imposition of preferred outcomes. As Buchanan and Badham (1999: 231) conclude:

> In the domain of practical action, as we noted earlier, management is a contact sport. If you don't want to get bruised, don't play. There is little to be gained by complaining about the turf game, its players, its tricks, its strategies, its tactics and its potential damage. Criticism of the existence of organizational politics is likely to have as much impact as criticism of British weather ... The main argument of this book is that the change agent who is not politically skilled will fail.

The second major concern of a processual approach is with the context in which change takes place. An historical perspective on both the internal and external organizational context is central to understanding the opportunities, constraints, and organizationally defined routes to change (Kelly and Amburgey, 1991: 610). As discussed in more detail later, the coexistence of a number of competing histories of change can significantly shape ongoing change programmes. In this sense, the contextual and historical dimension can both promote certain options and devalue others during the process of organizational change. Consequently, under this framework the contextual dimension is taken to refer to the past and present external and internal operating environments as well as the influence of future projections and expectations on current operating practice.

External contextual factors are taken to include: changes in competitors' strategies; level of international competition; government legislation; changing social expectations; technological innovations; and changes in the level of business activity. Internal contextual factors are taken to include Leavitt's (1964) four-fold classification of human resources, administrative structures, technology, and product or service, as well as an additional category labelled the history and culture of an organization. This latter category is used to incorporate both an historical perspective that can take account of competing histories and an understanding of organizational culture. By so doing, the framework is able to accommodate the existence of multiple narratives and competing histories of change. Essentially, it is argued that the history of past change projects may be rewritten to service present objectives, and in many companies *post-hoc* rationalizations of change are not uncommon. Both past reconstructions and future expectations are important in understanding the current contextual conditions under which change unfolds. In other words, during the complex dynamic of workplace change a company may move in and out of a number of states, sometimes concurrently, as the process of change is continuously influenced by the interplay and conflict between historical reconstructions, current contextual conditions, and future expectations.

The third and final area of concern relates to the substance of change. The four main dimensions are:

1 *The scale and scope of change.* This ranges along a continuum from small-scale discrete change to a more 'radical' large-scale transformation. A distinction can be made between change in small units of operation, the factory or branch office, divisional level change and corporate transformations.
2 *The defining characteristics of change.* This refers both to the labels attached to change projects and the actual content of the change in question. Companies embarking on change initiatives associated with, for example, total quality management or business process re-engineering can ultimately implement radically divergent changes in workplace operations (see, for example, Dawson and Palmer, 1995).
3 *The timeframe of change.* Timeframes are variable and can involve a rapid reaction to a critical juncture in market conditions through to changes that emerge over a number of years. Furthermore, change programmes are normally characterized by temporal fluctuation; for example, a change initiative that at the outset evolves incrementally may be followed by a fairly rapid and specified period of implementation. As such, the longer-term nature of these changes can go unnoticed in studies that focus on only one critical period in the process of workplace change.
4 *The perceived centrality of change.* This refers to the extent to which the change is viewed as being critical to the survival of the organization. If the change is viewed as central to the continual operation and competitive position of the company, then it can have major implications for the timescale, resource support and overall employee commitment to change.

Finally, it should be stressed that the group of determinants categorized under the substance of change are not static; rather, they change over time and overlap with contextual and political elements. For example, it is not uncommon for definitional confusion to surround the introduction of new management techniques and for the content of change to be redefined during the process of organizational adaptation. Moreover, knowledge of the substance of change and clarification of what the change means for a particular organization can in itself become a political process, influenced by external contextual views and the setting of internal agendas around the management of change. In this sense, there is a continual interplay between these three groups of determinants during the process of organizational change. In short, the processual framework outlined above is concerned with understanding: the political arenas in which decisions are made, histories recreated and strategies rationalized (politics); the enabling and constraining characteristics of change programmes and the scale and type of change (substance); and the conditions under which change is taking place in relation to external elements, such as the business market environment and internal elements, including the history and culture of an organization (context).

In examining processes of organizational change, it is recognized that in practice it is often difficult to identify any clear start or end of change. For example, although one consequence of the September 2001 terrorist attack in New York has been a shake-up and restructuring of the airline industry, a number of commentators have suggested that the need for change preceded this event that brought into such stark relief the need for and urgency for change. In the case of large-scale radical change programmes, it is often possible to identify a period over which the conception of the need to change occurs. During this time, discussions and debates may ensue about either the need to respond to external or internal pressures for change, or the perceived need for innovation and change to meet future, but as yet unknown, competitive conditions. This conception of the need to change may be reactive to a shifting contextual environment, reflect proactive decision-making on the need to change, or be some combination whereby the action of a competitor stimulates consideration of change and influences the development of proactive strategies in the adoption of certain preferred change initiatives. This type of initial awareness in the conception of the need to change is often viewed as the 'before' change period, although in practice it is clearly an important element within the change process. The different types of organizational change are shown in Figure 2.2.

In the case of large-scale radical change programmes, senior management engagement and the commitment of resources is usually required to

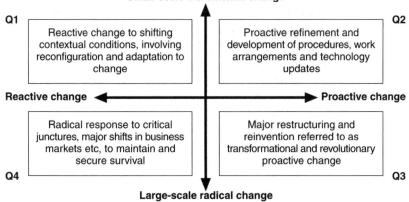

Figure 2.2 *Types of organizational change*

move from awareness of the need to change to the actual process of mobilizing people in the planning and implementation of change. Decisions also have to be made on the substance of change, and this will often involve the task of search and assessment. For example, certain individuals may be given the task of identifying and evaluating one of a range of change initiatives (technologies, new management techniques, ways of doing business) in order to inform decision-making processes. In many cases these decisions may have been made at the outset, and may undergo further revision as more information is collected on what is available in the marketplace, what costs are involved, and what the pay-back on investment is likely to be. The timeframe involved with this task may be relatively short, involving a quick analysis of options, or it may instigate a major evaluation exercise requiring a team to visit other organizations and/or suppliers operating in different states and countries. The timeframe, activities and analyses of options are of course also part of a political process in which certain preferred change options are likely to be promoted by certain individuals and/or groups who may also seek to discredit avenues of development proposed by others. Choice and decision-making is more about power and politics than it is about 'best options', although in retrospect the decision taken may well be rationalized as the best option.

The planning and implementation of change usually brings to the fore a range of occupational and employee concerns. During this process of change people will support, resist and attempt to steer the direction and outcomes of a number of different tasks, activities and decisions. In the case of General Motors, senior management identified the need for change but it was the employees within the plant who orchestrated the restructuring process (see Chapter 4). In contrast, a more top-down approach was used in the Pirelli Cables change programme (see Chapter 3), whereas Shell Expro identified a particular group to champion a smaller-scale change initiative (see Chapter 5). The way the substance of change is reconfigured over time, the importance of context as a factor influencing change and the political process of steering change, are all illustrated in the case study chapters that follow.

After the implementation of a major change, people continue to reconfigure and adapt work arrangements, and individual behaviours continue to be influenced by the culture and history of the factory or office. As new organizational arrangements and systems of operation begin to settle into regular patterns and routines, a relatively stabilized system of operation may be seen to exist. As noted elsewhere (Dawson, 1994: 40):

> Although in reality it is often unrealistic to talk of an 'endpoint' of change it does make sense to talk of the 'effects' of a particular type of change. In the case of large-scale operational change, it is possible to identify a period at some stage after implementation when the daily work routines of employees become part of the operating system (which is no longer regarded as 'new'). Whilst the ongoing process of change will continue, this is the period which can be used to identify the outcomes of change on organizational structures and traditional operating practices.

The approach thereby views change as a complex ongoing dynamic in which the politics, substance and context of change all interlock and overlap, and in which our understanding of the present and expectations for the future can influence our interpretation of past events, which may in turn shape our experience of change. Although the approach accepts that for analytical purposes it is often useful to identify and delineate as before (conception of the need to change), during (transition) and after change (routine operation), it rejects simple linear stage models and argues that there can never be a single authentic account of change. Although there may be dominant or public change account, there are always multiple versions of events and a range of competing histories that are themselves open to continual reshaping over time. This reshaping of change is a central element of the processual perspective.

The processual perspective developed in this chapter has many similarities to the framework proposed by Pettigrew (1985), and yet it also differs in a number of important ways. It is one processual approach within a broader set of studies that can be located under the processual perspective (see, for example, Clark *et al.*, 1988; Pettigrew *et al.*, 1992; Clark, 1995; Harrison and Samson, 1997; Collins, 1998a; Preece *et al.*, 1999). The section that follows provides a brief historical overview of the emergence and development of the processual perspective in order more accurately to locate and explain the contribution of this body of work.

A brief history of the processual perspective

There has been a longstanding interest in the processual dynamics of change, as illustrated by Dalton's (1959) study of the changing alliances, power-plays and the purposeful management of information by cliques in pursuit of advantages over others, and Gouldner's (1965) analysis of the dynamics of management–worker interaction and the influence of social processes during a succession of bargaining incidents. Roy's (1967) study from November 1944 to August 1945 on the process of quota restriction and goldbricking in a machine shop is a good example. This illustrates the process by which operators met their quota for 'gravy jobs' then 'knocked off', and how over time they restricted output on jobs they considered 'stinkers' and deliberately produced at lower rates. The workers sought to manage their earnings (determined by variations in hourly production piecework rates) and to ensure that the rates for 'gravy jobs' were not lost whilst engaging in work behaviours that would encourage the reconsideration of rates for 'stinkers'. As a fellow worker advised (Roy, 1967: 316): 'Don't let it go over $1.25 an hour, or the time-study man will be right down here!' As Elger (1975) indicates, many of these early empirical studies can be broadly placed within a processual school. As he notes (Elger, 1975: 114):

> The processual perspective emphasizes that the social structures of industrial concerns are patterned by negotiations and interpretation among participants with diverse interests and resources, so that analyses of variations and changes in such structures must attend to those sustaining and transforming processes.

In drawing on the work of Woodward (1958, 1980) and Burns and Stalker (1961), Elger outlines how these studies have often been too quickly ignored and misunderstood. He demonstrates how the case studies of Woodward draw attention to an ongoing process in which management ideology, established rhetorics and political manoeuvring, all serve to influence change outcomes. Similarly, in detailing the work of Burns and Stalker (1961), Elger (1975: 109) argues that whilst a systems typology is their starting point, 'they develop, in relation to a rich array of empirical materials, a processual analysis which treats actors' allegiances, perspectives and strategies as problematic features of organizational action'. His discussion highlights how major detailed empirical studies of innovation and change have historically drawn attention to *process* in the study of organizations. At this time, Child's (1972: 2) critique of systems orthodoxy also drew attention to the process by which power-holders make strategic choices. He highlights the role of agency and choice in the way that individuals and groups can influence the environment rather than simply being constrained by operational contingencies. As he states in a later reappraisal of the strategic choice perspective (Child, 1997: 44):

> Strategic choice articulates a political process, which brings agency and structure into tension and locates them within a significant context. It regards both the relation of agency to structure and to environment as dynamic in nature. In so doing, the strategic choice approach not only bridges a number of competing perspectives but also adopts a non-deterministic and potentially evolutionary position. Strategic choice, when considered as a process, points to the possibility of continuing adaptive learning cycles, but within a theoretical framework that locates 'organizational learning' within the context of organizations as socio-political systems.

The early work of Burns and Stalker (1961) and the perspectives of Elger (1975) and Child (1972) contributed to the political process perspective that forms part of the processual approach developed in this chapter. In addition, Child's (1972) concept of *strategic choice* focusses attention on the dynamics of change and continuity. He is critical of the tendency within organizational analysis to polarize between forms of determinism or voluntarism, and suggests that attention should be given to what he terms as 'the paradoxes of simultaneous choice and constraints, change and continuity' (Child, 1997: 70). This aspect of continuity and change is also picked up and developed by Pettigrew (1985) in *The Awakening Giant. Continuity and Change in ICI*. This book powerfully demonstrates the limitations of theories that view change either as a single event or as a discrete series of episodes that can be decontextualized. In a comparative analysis of five cases of strategic change, the study illustrates how change as a continuous incremental process (evolutionary) can be interspersed with radical periods of change (revolutionary). These major change initiatives are associated with major changes in business market conditions (such as world economic recessions) in which managers develop active strategies that build on these circumstances in order to legitimize and justify the need for change. For Pettigrew, 'change and continuity, process and structure, are inextricably linked' (1985: 1), and he argues that the intention is not simply to substitute a rational approach with a political process perspective, but 'to explore some of the conditions in which mixtures of these occur' (1985: 24). He also notes how empirical findings and theoretical developments are generally 'method-bound', and how studies on organizational change have tended to adopt the planned stage model approach of Organizational Development (OD). Pettigrew is highly critical of such approaches to change, which are seen to ignore the importance of *changing*. As he states (1985: 15):

> For as long as we continue to conduct research on change which is ahistorical, acontextual, and aprocessual, which continues to treat the change programme as the unit of analysis and regard change as an episode divorced from the immediate and more distant context in which it is embedded, then we will continue to develop inadequate descriptive theories of change which are ill-composed guides for action. Indeed as I have implied already there is still a dearth of studies which can make statements about the how and why of change, about the processual dynamics of change, in short which go beyond the analysis of *change* and being to theorise about *changing*.

In drawing on longitudinal contextual data (134 people were interviewed between 1975 and 1983), Pettigrew examines the interplay between internal contextual variables of culture, history and political process with external business conditions as factors that maintain continuity or bring about change. In providing what he terms an 'holistic, contextualist analysis', the approach provides both multilevel (or vertical) analysis, such as external socio-economic influences on internal group behaviour, and processual (or horizontal) analysis, for example in studying organizations 'in flight' with a past, present and future. In multilevel theory construction, attention is given to the way contextual variables in the vertical analysis link to those examined in horizontal analysis, and how 'processes are both constrained by structures and shape structures . . . both in catching reality in flight and in embeddedness' (Pettigrew, 1985: 37).

Pettigrew clarifies how this work builds on his PhD work (under the supervision of Enid Mumford) on the politics of organizational change (Pettigrew, 1973). He views political process as evolving from individual and group levels, in which interest groups may form for a range of reasons developing different rationalities that direct action and response (whilst a particular rationality may predominate at any one time, this is seen to be open to change). For Pettigrew (1985), change creates tension over the existing distribution of resources through threatening the position of some whilst opening up opportunities for others. As such, change stimulates power plays and heightened political activity. He notes how it is normally the case that the greatest political energy is released when the decision to change is being made, rather than during implementation when constraints have already been set (Pettigrew, 1985: 43). He also suggests that the political and cultural elements of change are likely to overlap in the management of meaning, especially in situations where individuals or groups seek to legitimize their own position and delegitimize others (see also Bloor and Dawson, 1994). As he explains (1985: 44–45):

> Key concepts for analysing these processes of legitimisation and delegitimisation are symbolism, language, belief, and myth . . . Myths serve also to legitimate the present in terms of a perhaps glorious past, and to explain away the pressures for change which may exist from the discrepancies between what is happening and what ought to be happening. In these various ways it may be possible for interest groups to justify continuity in the face of change, and change in the face of attempts to preserve continuity.

In his study of ICI, Pettigrew (1985: 438–476) demonstrates how strategic change is a continuous process with no clear beginning or end point, and how it often emerges with deep-seated cultural and political roots that support the establishment of a dominant ideology. As such, he usefully illustrates how these strategic change processes are best understood in context and over time, as continuity is often 'a good deal easier to see than change' (Pettigrew, 1985: 439). For example, insufficient commercial pressure, satisfaction with the *status quo*, lack of vision, and the absence of leadership are all identified as contextual factors constraining change. Drawing on the work of Kanter (1983), he supports the view that integrative structures and cultures are broadly facilitative of 'the processes of vision-building, problem-identifying and acknowledging, information-sharing, attention-directing, problem-solving, and commitment-building which seem to be necessary to create change' (Pettigrew, 1985: 456). On the other hand, segmentalist structures and cultures with clearly defined levels and functions are viewed as inhibitative of change. This dichotomy by Kanter (1983: 396) is a modification of the distinction of organic and mechanistic organizations made by Burns and Stalker (1961). They argued that a mechanistic system is most appropriate for an organization that uses an unchanging technology and operates in relatively stable markets. It is characterized by clear hierarchical lines of authority, precise definitions of job tasks and control responsibilities, a tendency for vertical interaction, an insistence on loyalty to the concern, and an emphasis on task skills and local knowledge rather than general knowledge and experience (Burns and Stalker, 1961: 119–120). Conversely, an organic form is deemed most appropriate to changing conditions, which gives rise to innovation, and the continual willingness to tackle fresh problems and unforeseen requirements. It is characterized by a network structure of control, authority and communication, a reliance on expert knowledge for decision-making, the continual redefinition of individual tasks through interaction with others, and the spread of commitment to the firm beyond any formal contractual obligation (Burns and Stalker, 1961: 121–122). Pettigrew's findings support this early work by Burns and Stalker (1961) and the later work by Kanter (1983) in concluding that leadership was critical to all five ICI cases in initiating strategic change and facilitating a movement from segmentalist to integrative structures and cultures (Pettigrew, 1985: 457).

This foundational work of Pettigrew has been widely referenced and discussed in the organizational change literature (see Collins, 1998b; Preece et al., 1999; Burnes, 2000). For example, in a critical review of Pettigrew's contextualist approach Collins (1998b: 71) concludes that:

> While most writers of a critical bent would tend to accept that Pettigrew offers a useful and valid framework for the analysis of change and its management, some have observed an imbalance in Pettigrew's work. It has been observed, for example, that whereas Pettigrew quite correctly observes that matters of theory and practice are inseparable and indivisible, the theoretical, conceptual and methodological elegance of Pettigrew's work seems to have been purchased at the expense of practical advice and practitioner relevance.

In a critique of the work of Pettigrew, Buchanan and Boddy (1992) also argue that the richness and complexity of a multi-level analysis does little to simplify or clarify processes of change and thereby renders the research largely impenetrable for the organizational practitioner. In other words, whilst the research findings adequately convey the complexity of organizational change, they have also tended to mask, mystify and create barriers of interpretation to a non-academic audience who may seek practical tools for action. As Buchanan and Boddy (1992: 61–62) conclude:

> We are asked in this perspective to accept an intuitive definition of change as strategic, to put to one side as unimportant the control agenda of the project manager, and to work with a complex multivariate and multi-layer model of process and context which, while of considerable interest to the researcher, does not constitute a 'user friendly' guide to practical management action. The logics of problem solving and ownership are subordinated by a preoccupation with the logic of legitimacy. The social and interpersonal dynamics of the processes Pettigrew addresses are not explored in a manner that facilitates the easy identification of practical advice.

Although they point out that it was not Pettigrew's intention to offer practical advice, they remain critical of this approach, both as a method for analysing data on change and as a perspective that serves to disable attempts to develop practical managerial advice (Buchanan and Boddy, 1992). To be fair to Pettigrew, the work has been used successfully in executive teaching and consultancy. In 2002, in recognition of his standing in the field, Pettigrew was asked by the Office of Public Sector Reform to summarize the main message of his research on change since 1985 (Pettigrew, 2002). In contrast, whilst the author's own processual research has been used openly to identify a number of practical guidelines (Dawson, 1994), these have been criticized for appearing 'almost as an afterthought' (Burnes, 2000: 295). Although there is some justification in the claim that these earlier guidelines were too restricted in their focus on managing change (Dawson, 1994), it is argued here that there is value in using this approach to identify practical dimensions to change. As shown elsewhere (Dawson, 2003), this practical advice should not be limited to a consideration of how managers can 'better' manage change; rather, it should have a broader agenda that extends beyond management and include advice to non-managers and others (such as trade unions, politicians, business development agencies) who seek a greater understanding of organizational change.

Accessibility and the practical dimension to understanding change are two further elements that have informed the processual approach developed by the author in this chapter. On this count, the structure of the ICI book makes it a difficult tome for new researchers and postgraduate students. For example, the final chapter seems to move away from the processes of strategic change discussed in Chapter 11 (which would be a more appropriate concluding chapter). In addition, whilst the interview programme covers people at various hierarchical levels there is a tendency to view strategic change from the perspective of management. Although clearly a major and worthwhile study, a greater use of observation and a fuller account of the lived experience and perspective of different employee groups would provide a useful counterbalance to the main thrust of Pettigrew's argument. On this count, Alvesson and Willmott (1996) have criticized this approach for supporting the *status quo* and avoiding any real critical scrutiny of workplace change through assuming established priorities and values to be legitimate (see also Bloor and Dawson, 1994). Knights and Murray in adopting a political processual perspective, also criticize Pettigrew's (1985) tendency to accept management strategy as unproblematic without questioning the political process of social construction. As they state (Knights and Murray, 1994: 183):

> Another sense in which our perspective differs from but contributes to a processual approach is in recognizing how technology and the market can be constructed by practitioners as either externalities over which the organization has little control or as open to negotiation internally. It is these constructions to which the strategic and the processual approaches respectively respond but in so doing; they take a particular management interpretation as given and thus reproduce it as reality, rather than reflect critically upon its power-infused construction.

Although the work of Pettigrew provides a useful counterbalance to rational textbook models, some commentators have argued that it does little to challenge conventional wisdom (Alvesson and Willmott, 1996). In combining some elements of Pettigrew's approach (the emphasis on context and process) with a more critical conceptualization of politics, Knights has moved towards what he terms a 'critical processual perspective'. In developing this position, Knights and Murray (1994) point out that although the processual perspective of Pettigrew recognizes socio-political processes, it tends to view conflict and resistance as potentially disruptive to the smooth and rational management of an organization. From their perspective, the effectiveness of management control is neither seen as legitimate nor is it demonized; rather, notions of rationality and effectiveness are questioned and the uncertainty of organizational outcomes highlighted. Organizational politics is seen as central to understanding the 'messy' processes of change, but not in seeking to identify a more 'politically sensitive' way for change agents to successfully implement more effective systems of management control

(Knights and McCabe, 1998). Although Pettigrew would claim that he does not view politics as pathology but as natural and everyday, his focus remains on higher levels of management where the major resource decisions are made. As he states in an interview with Ken Starkey (Starkey and Pettigrew, 2002: 22):

> If you have a simple barometer (or maybe I should say politicalometer) which could measure the amount of politics in organizations I think you would find high readings near the top of the organization in times of the prospect of, and the reality of, change.

The processual research used to inform the approach developed here also seeks to accommodate and account for the socio-political processes of conflict and resistance, but in pursuing this aim the research openly searches for and uncovers the different views and experiences of individuals and groups at all levels within organizations. Unlike the ICI study, the intention is to provide a framework for exploring the contemporary experience of workplace change for a range of different employees (Dawson, 2003), rather than focussing on the role of senior managers in managing strategic change (Pettigrew, 1985: xv). Essentially, it is about understanding processes of organizational change through using a compendium of data collection techniques including observational work and in-depth interviewing of, for example, trade unionists, senior managers, line managers and supervisors, change consultants, shop-floor workers and branch office personnel (see Dawson, 1994, 2003). However, before discussing these issues in more detail (see Chapters 6–8), the next section draws attention to the misleading representation of the processual perspective as an 'emergent approach to change management' (Burnes, 2000).

Discarding the emergent label and reinstating the processual perspective

In an article on positions and perspective in understanding organizational change, Palmer and Dunford (2002: 245–246) identify the processual perspective with what they categorize as a navigating approach:

> In the navigating approach to change, control is still seen as at the heart of management actions, although a variety of factors external to managers mean that while they may achieve some intended change others will also occur over which they have little control. Outcomes are often emergent rather than planned and result from a variety of

convergent influences, competing interests, and processes. The contextualist or processual approach typifies this position. Associated with the work of writers such as Dawson (1994) and Pettigrew and Whipp (1991), the approach shares an assumption with contingency theory that change unfolds differently over time and according to the context in which the organization finds itself. However, it parts company from contingency theory in assuming [quoting Burnes, 1996: 187] 'that change should not be and cannot be solidified, or seen as a series of linear events within a given period of time; instead, it is viewed as a . . . process that unfolds through the interplay of multiple variables'.

It is perhaps not surprising that the 'emergent' label has come to be attached to the processual perspective, as an important argument of this approach has been that radical large-scale change does not simply occur overnight (it is not an event) but takes time (Dawson, 1994). As Pettigrew and Whipp (1991: 108) state: 'the management of strategic and operational change for competitive success is an uncertain and emergent process'. And yet these approaches do not view change as necessarily being driven from the bottom up, as claimed by Burnes (2000: 278); nor do they ignore the role of change agents (see Dawson, 1996: 92–111). In a previous publication, the author used the computerization of British Rail's (BR) Freight Division to illustrate the processual nature of large-scale change programmes (Dawson, 1994: 48–69). In this instance there was considerable preparation and planning, and an autocratic top-down task force approach was used to circumvent organizational procedures and traditional operating practices. As such, it is argued here that this 'emergent' label is being inappropriately applied to this perspective that in the text of Burnes (2000: 280–314) is contrasted to the planned OD model.

Although Burnes (2000: 280–314) indicates that proponents of (what he terms) the 'emergent approach' are a 'somewhat disparate group', he places the work of the author under this category and then makes a number of claims that require further discussion and clarification. Whilst his books (Burnes, 1992; 1996; 2000) do provide a good overview and explanation of the growing body of change management literature, his analysis misrepresents the processual approach. Essentially, he argues that the planned OD approach that derives from Kurt Lewin's ice cube model of change (unfreezing, changing and refreezing) dominated thinking from the late 1940s to the early 1980s. He claims that since the 1980s there has been increasing criticism of this approach (Burnes, 2000), especially in the more contextual and processually oriented studies in the UK (see, for example, Dawson and McLoughlin, 1986; Child and Smith, 1987; Pettigrew, 1987a, 1987b; Clark *et al.*, 1988). The US-dominated OD approach also came under attack from the work of Dexter Dunphy and colleagues in Australia (Dunphy and Stace, 1990) and Kanter (1983) in the USA. As Kanter and her colleagues explain: 'organizations are never frozen, much less refrozen, but are fluid entities with many "personalities" . . . to the extent that there are stages, they overlap and interpenetrate one another in important ways' (Kanter *et al.*, 1992: 10).

According to Burnes (2000: 283), there are two common beliefs underlying what he terms as this new 'emergent' approach. First, change is viewed as an ongoing 'emergent' process with no finite end point. Second, change emerges from the actions and decisions of people in organizations; for example, as the outcome of conflicts between different vested interest groups (in attempts to adjust the organization to changes in the external environment, or through attempts to construct and implement a new social reality on the organization). As such, change is viewed as a continuous process and consequently attempts to impose a linear sequence of planned actions on what are untidy processes 'which unfold in an iterative fashion with much backtracking and omission' (Buchanan and Storey, 1997: 127) are heavily criticized (see also Wilson, 1992).

From a discussion of the central role of power and politics in the processual approach through to the role of knowledge management and change agency, Burnes (2000: 299–300) summarizes what he derives to be the main tenets of the emergent approach. Although some of these would map onto the processual perspective developed here, others would not, and hence it is worth commenting upon and differentiating between the more general assumptions that are seen to lie behind an emergent approach.

The main tenets that align with a processual perspective are: first, that an understanding of power and politics is central to an understanding of the processes of organizational change; and second, that small-scale incremental changes can over time lead to a major re-configuration of an organization. In contrast, the notion that this approach equates with a contingency perspective (Burnes, 2000: 285), in advocating that planned change is inappropriate in an uncertain environment, starts to highlight the problem with this more general 'emergent' label. The processual approach does not view the non-linear dynamics of change as only being in evidence in turbulent environments, and nor does it reject the notion of planning. The approach recognizes that there are often critical junctures that necessitate radical change – as illustrated by the Enron debacle – and that ongoing processes of change occur within organizations operating in relatively stable environments as well as those operating in dynamic business contexts (see also Bloor and Dawson, 1994; Dawson, 2003). Over the last decade, the increasing number and rate of organizational change initiatives (both proactive and reactive) has drawn attention to the inadequacy of a one best way approach (such as the rational participative approach of many OD consultants), and the need for a broader understanding of the complex untidy and messy nature of change. However, in so doing the processual approach is not making a statement against the importance of planning for change; rather, it is pointing out that change is unpredictable and therefore that there will be a need to accommodate and adapt to the unexpected, the unforeseen twists and turns, the omissions and revisions that are all part of managing the process of change over time. Furthermore, in seeking to make sense of the way change unfolds, the processual approach also provides insight into processes of continuity as well as the temporal reshaping of change. Although the approach enables us to distil out some practical dimensions to change, it is far less prescriptive than the work of Kotter (1996) – which is also characterized under the emergent label – and it is more analytical in seeking to achieve a broader understanding of organizational change.

The processual approach developed in this book sets out to supply guidance on how to study complex change processes as they happen (see Chapters 6 and 7) as well as providing a conceptual framework for understanding the way change is shaped and reshaped over time. It does not presume to present a definitive explanation of change; rather, the intention is to provide a framework for studying and making sense of change. As such, it does not argue that all change is slow and emergent and that there are not critical junctures or more radical rapid changes brought about by reactions to unforeseen circumstances. Nor does it assume that it is possible to write the single authentic account of change, as there will always be multiple stories and accounts of change. Finally, the claim by Burnes (2000: 297) that the processual approach 'whilst stressing the issue of process, tends to play down or ignore the role of the change agent' does not equate with the processual studies reported here. On the contrary, the role of change agents in orchestrating the change process is identified as a central element in the power plays and political manoeuvrings of individuals and groups during programmes of change (see Chapter 4).

Essentially, the processual approach outlined in this book aims to provide a way to study, analyse and explain change processes that broadens our understanding and promotes critical reflection. It does not set out to present any grand theory of change; rather, the phenomenon of interest is change and people in organizations. As such, it is interested in the way things emerge and reveal themselves over time, but it is also interested in critical junctures that may stimulate rapid change as well as processes that serve to maintain and sustain existing ways of doing things. It is a processual and not an emergent approach, and it remains open to further development and refinement. It assumes that change is an ongoing complex dynamic process that may be a management-stimulated reaction to business market shifts, it may come about through non-management initiatives, or it may reflect proactive planning and implementation of new technologies or techniques. Change may range from small-scale incremental change initiatives to large-scale radical change programmes that may be introduced with high employee involvement (collaborative approach), by more autocratic means (coercive approach), or somewhere in-between these two extremes. The processual approach developed here does not advocate one position or view over another; rather, it seeks to examine a wide range of change processes from a variety of different perspectives to broaden our understanding and knowledge. It examines change by focussing attention on the views and experiences of shop-floor or branch-office employees, trade unionists, middle managers, senior executives, change agents and outside collaborators, or through the lenses of gender, ethnicity or age. As such, the practical lessons to be drawn on change can be directed to one of a number of groups and need not centre on the common prescriptive theme of the 'successful management of change'. In short, the framework developed in this chapter seeks to aid our analyses of change processes through being accessible, of practical worth, promoting critical reflection and being analytically robust. It should be viewed as a perspective in its own right, and not be collapsed under a more disparate 'emergent' school.

Conclusion

The chapter has demonstrated the strengths of a processual approach for understanding organizational change. As Preece *et al.* (1999: 79) reflect:

Why is the focus on process so important? The answer in essence lies in the exigencies of implementing change for, even if the means of doing this could be clearly specified and controlled (which is extremely doubtful), the responses of employees are unpredictable – there are always new challenges emerging, unintended effects, complaints, commitment and opposition from all parts of the organization, and unexpected developments both within and outside the organization.

This common interest in studying the unpredictable nature of change over time and in context unites this body of research under the processual perspective. However, there are also a number of conceptual and methodological dimensions that differentiate the approach developed in this chapter from other processual studies, namely:

1 *Competing narratives* is used as a central concept. There is no attempt to reconcile outliers or different interpretations of change. As such, the approach seeks a more critical understanding of the change process by accommodating multiple perspectives. For example, stories (individual and group narratives) are viewed as powerful vehicles for resisting change as well as managing preferred change outcomes.
2 The concept of *multiple histories* is deemed important to understanding power plays and the political processes of change; for example, the way history is rewritten to fit the political objectives of differing vested interest groups.
3 The broader concept of the *substance of change* is used to capture not only the characteristics of a new technology or the principles of a new management technique (content), but also the scale and timeframe of change, as well as individual and group interpretation of the change phenomenon and the perceived centrality of the change.
4 *Practical advice and relevance.* This approach assumes that practical lessons can be drawn from processual studies of organizational change on, for example, managing, resisting, steering and making sense of change.

The processual approach advocated does not seek to elevate 'emergence' as the central organizing concept, nor does it reject 'planning' as something outside of the change process; rather, it seeks to develop a conceptual framework to further our understanding and insight into the complex non-linear processes of organizational change. Within this approach, interpretation and perception of 'the way the world operates', of individual and group attitudes to particular change initiatives, narratives and stories of past events and expectations of future outcomes and possibilities, all serve to influence this dynamic process. There are multiple narratives of change and competing histories that are themselves refined and developed in terms of current contextual conditions, the power- and political game playing of significant individuals and vested interest groups, future expectations and various interpretations of the substance and intent of change initiatives. As such, there is no room for simple apolitical prescriptive stage models other than in the minds of those who seek simple solutions to complex change issues. While rational models do provide currency for decision-making and justification for taking certain preferred change options over other possible alternatives, in practice they form part of a political change process and should not be viewed as a theoretical representation of change. In contrast, the processual approach does not take a normative stance in capturing processes of change, and nor does it promote a single model of how to manage change 'successfully'. The approach enables us to study change processes and allows for critical reflection and radical reappraisal of taken-for-granted assumptions about the nature and purpose of change. It also provides an opportunity to reflect on, for example, the reasons and drive for change, and to question whether change is in the career interests of certain individuals rather than the longer-term interests of the organization. In a world where the barrage of change initiatives consumes a large amount of resources as well as the time and energy of many individuals and groups, it is perhaps appropriate to consider the sociological, psychological and commercial implications of endlessly embarking on change initiatives. It is also worth reflecting that despite the growing number of books and consultant panaceas on how to manage change 'successfully', most major change initiatives still fail to achieve their objectives. What is needed are more critically reflective processual studies that can counterbalance the tendency for abstract academic pontificating or the endless search for universal ingredients of success. It is hoped that this chapter has gone some way to highlighting the value of a processual approach in understanding organizational change.

3 The context of change at Pirelli Cables

- The uptake of TQM in Pirelli Cables Australia: the Minto case
- Implementing TQM in cable processing in South Australia
- Implementing TQM in cable manufacturing in South Australia
- Comparative shop-floor issues and the context of change
- Conclusion

This chapter sets out to illustrate the importance of the contextual dimension to making sense of and understanding the process of workplace change. The example of Pirelli Cables is used to demonstrate the way change was shaped and reshaped in three different plants of the same company. A common strategy and approach to implementation was used on all three sites, and yet the experience of employees and the outcomes of change were markedly different. The focus on one company is useful, as it spotlights the importance of local contextual factors as shapers of change. As Morris and Wilkinson (1995: 728) conclude in a special edition of the *Journal of Management Studies* on the transferability of Japanese management techniques, whilst there has clearly been a worldwide uptake of some of the more basic principles of TQM such as the adoption of a continuous improvement philosophy in the search for waste elimination, there remains a need for further empirical research to identify and explain variations in the extent of teamwork and employee involvement in particular organizational settings. In other words, while there are external contextual factors that can help explain the company uptake and use of new management techniques, there are also important internal contextual conditions that provide insight into the way change unfolds and is reshaped within particular organizational and plant/branch settings. The Pirelli case used in this chapter illustrates how the very different operating contexts (the history and culture of the plants) and the dynamics of change implementation (the politics, substance and context of change) resulted in contrasting experiences of change (although the focus is on context, political process and the substance of the change remain intertwined as an integral part of the shaping process).

The uptake of TQM in Pirelli Cables Australia: the Minto case

During the 1990s, Pirelli Cables introduced Total Quality Management (TQM) into their Australian operations. The Managing Director viewed TQM as a practical approach that would help solve some ongoing operational problems (such as high scrap rates), and it would also fulfil corporate objectives of ensuring that TQM was taken up by all their operations worldwide. Although the Australian government offered seminars and part-funding to support the company uptake of TQM (through the National Industry Extension Scheme), the senior executive decided to fund their own programme and, following a series of presentations, appointed an outside consultant to manage the change process. With the high cost of material waste and process inefficiencies (with labour accounting for under 15 per cent of total operating costs), the financial justification of the programme was never in doubt.

The implementation of TQM was initially piloted in the Minto plant in New South Wales. A new position was created – the TQM manager – who, in collaboration with Blakemore Consulting, set about implementing TQM across the whole of Pirelli's business operations in Australia. Initially only three teams were formed, but as the programme progressed new teams were created to tackle particular manufacturing problems. The six phases normally associated with the formation of TQM teams were as follows:

1 An established steering committee would decide on a problem that needed investigating.
2 An appropriate facilitator was chosen for each particular TQM team.
3 Shop-floor volunteers – normally approached by the facilitator – were selected.
4 The facilitator set achievable targets for the TQM team.
5 The proposed objectives set for the TQM team were checked against worldwide standards of excellence provided by Pirelli's corporate headquarters in Italy.
6 The performances of the TQM teams were monitored as they worked towards achieving set targets.

During the period of initial operation a number of unforeseen problems arose. At this time, considerable emphasis was being placed on getting results in order to highlight shop-floor achievements at steering committee meetings. This emphasis on monitoring performance and achieving targets did not support the broader philosophy of the importance of trust in gaining employee commitment towards, and acceptance of, TQM. During the first six to nine months of the programme middle management adopted a low profile, and although a monthly review committee was set up interest soon waned, and as a consequence the review meetings were cancelled.

The problem of gaining middle management and supervisory commitment became a major issue that threatened the viability of the programme. Resistance to TQM was largely in the form of questioning its relevance to their area of operation. TQM, as a tool for solving process problems, assumes that problems exist, and that production workers are best placed for identifying solutions. However, the problem of dealing with unexpected operating contingencies, both technical and human, is central to the jobs of line supervisors, who tackle these problems as part of their daily work routines. Consequently, the introduction of a system that offers to take away the 'problem' of fire fighting also poses a threat to the jobs of front-line supervisors. In other words, if supervisors define their job (and their reason for being) in terms of dealing with disturbances in production, and if TQM is heralded as a new methodology for solving production problems through group employee participation schemes, then supervisory resistance is a reasonable response to a change that questions their position within the organization. The resistance of supervisory personnel to the TQM project may also be explained by a failure to integrate supervisors into the implementation programme. They remained the 'forgotten' employees, and their concerns were largely ignored during the planning and implementation of change.

In reflecting on Pirelli's early involvement with this programme and the response of the trade unions, the TQM manager commented that:

> In 1989, when we started our TQM programme, we had several problems that we needed to address. One was staff turnover, we had a quality problem, we had scrap problems and we wanted to improve our customer service. We went to the unions first before we started and we said, 'Look we're going to introduce TQM'. And they were very new to it in [19]89; it was a very new thing. And they said, 'Well what's it going to be, a three-month wonder?' And we said, 'No. We've got about a five-year plan and TQM's here and we want to do it, but we don't want to go through the hassles of having union problems'. We laid the whole project out and the unions were very cooperative. But in the latter part when we started to show some big profits, the union of course then starts to ask, 'Well, what's in it for us?' And our company now [1994] is looking at profit sharing and things like that.

From the perspective of employees at Pirelli's Minto plant, there was some concern that TQM groups were solving company problems, and yet there were no financial rewards for any savings their solutions achieved for production. The view that an operator would rather make a good product than a bad one forms part of the TQM philosophy, and it is assumed that this is its own reward. But shop floor personnel also sought active recognition of their contributions. A failure to recognize their contribution led to a shift in employee work behaviours that resemble some of the findings of Roy's (1967) study on quota restriction in a machine shop (see Chapter 2). In this case, rather than restrict output, employees discovered that they could legitimately reduce their production time by joining as many TQM teams as they could. This provided them with time off the shop-floor in a more pleasant office environment, debating problems and discussing possible solutions. In practice, many limited their active participation at such meetings and simply used the time as a break from shop-floor routines. However, as multiple teams developed, the time spent by shop-floor employees in TQM meetings increased whilst production output inevitably declined. This in turn put pressure on supervisors, who became increasingly frustrated in their attempts to manage schedules and reallocate labour during TQM team meetings. Some employees were members of four different TQM teams, all of which met once a week. In relaying their concern to management, a decision was made to restrict the number of TQM teams of which an employee could be a member to two.

In discussing senior management commitment and the formation of TQM teams at Minto (their cable manufacturing plant in New South Wales), Ross Willmott (the Group Project Manager) made the following comments:

> We were extremely lucky that our senior management were fully behind our TQM programme. In fact our managing director is chairman of the steering committee. We had that push all the way along from the top. We certainly had our share of problems. We tried to do too many things at once, we had far too many teams, and we were wasting a lot of people's time attending meetings. When we first started we just said, 'You, you and you, you're on a TQM team and away you go'. That wasn't very good. What we did is that we picked people that we knew would contribute to the project. Horses for courses, if you like to put it that way. And our choice of facilitators was very carefully done. We picked young active men who were very keen (or women, I mustn't forget that), who were very keen and very motivated. We are also very multi-cultural up there in Minto. And we

did have a problem. First of all we had to have English classes. We had to teach people to read the language. There's a few that sort of think that you are trying to get at them, for the need of a better word. But in fact we were amazed by some of the very brilliant suggestions we got from the shop floor.

In drawing on lessons from their experience of managing change at their Minto plant in New South Wales, Pirelli then went out to implement TQM more broadly throughout their Australian operations. However, the very different contextual circumstances of their plants elsewhere resulted in the reshaping of planned implementation processes in response to a number of unforeseen events. Management had a plan and a timeframe for the 'successful' management of change, but they were not prepared for the very different contextual conditions and local operating cultures of the two adjacent plants in South Australia. The cultural socio-political aspects of change turned out to be far more important and influential than had been anticipated, or accommodated for, in planning the process of change.

Implementing TQM in cable processing in South Australia

When management announced that TQM was going to be introduced into the Cable Processing Plant (CPP) in South Australia, employees were highly sceptical. Although they were informed about the benefits that had already arisen from the adoption of TQM at the Minto site, they remained very doubtful about claims for greater employee involvement. Local management advocated that TQM would enable shop-floor personnel to get involved in operational decision-making through group problem-solving meetings. Their aim was to get employees with detailed knowledge of shop-floor operations to contribute to, and be part of, employee teams that would tackle shop-floor problems in order to improve the work process and increase the efficiency of shop-floor production.

The increase in daily interaction between employees was one of the biggest changes to shop-floor operations as a consequence of TQM-related activities. TQM not only facilitated greater communication between shop-floor personnel, it also improved employee relations and promoted a climate of collaboration. For example, there is a greater willingness among operators to help each other out if there are problems in particular areas. Another change that has stimulated a move towards greater teamwork is the use of feedback statistics based on areas of operation rather than individual achievements. As one interviewee explained:

> Everyday our figures are done as a whole, not individually. Total scrap and downtime. Now they are telling people if it is ARTOS's (cutting and stripping machine) fault or a moulding fault. Now they are telling us to be careful of certain things in case length is different. It is much better now, although it took a while to change people's attitudes. Now they have to sit down and talk as a team. Instead of thinking as individuals they are exchanging views. We have a chart that shows how ARTOS is going and not the individual operators.

Within Pirelli, the use of TQM statistics was based on areas of operation rather than being focussed on the acquisition of individual performance measures. According to CPP employees, this promoted greater communication and interaction among staff, and highlighted the importance of teamwork. Although CPP employees generally supported the move towards teamwork, the labour process was still structured around one operator per machine, and hence teamwork activities centred on TQM groups that did not reflect a change in shop-floor working arrangements. In other words, although there has been a movement towards self-management on the shop floor – in the sense of employees regulating activities between themselves through monitoring operations and correcting faults – the organization of work remains largely as it was prior to TQM. What has changed is the nature of shop-floor control through attempts to develop high-trust relationships between operators, union representatives and supervisors. Management viewed collaboration between employees as an integral part of newly established routines, and central to the development of a more harmonious system of employee relations.

In part, the acceptance of TQM in CPP can be explained by the success of the original TQM team, which looked at the problem of downtime with the cable-cutting and stripping machines (known as the ARTOS TQM). This team was used as an exemplar by management to demonstrate the success of TQM in Pirelli Cables, and to illustrate what can be achieved with the right team tackling the right problem. In practice, however, it was impossible to predict the potential problems within teams (such as interpersonal conflicts), or whether the areas chosen to be tackled were going to lend themselves to group problem-solving techniques. In observing a number of TQM group meetings during their early establishment, it was noted how this group forum was used to vent some longstanding tensions that had remained hidden and unspoken on the shop floor. Although in one case this certainly provided the opportunity to 'clear the decks', it was more typically the start of protracted and acrimonious squabbles between vociferous individuals. Moreover, while the ARTOS TQM team was used as a 'success' story for TQM and shop-floor change, little attention was given to stories of 'failure', and conflict was viewed by management as an individual problem rather than an issue arising from the use of TQM. In other words, all 'successes' were attributed to TQM and the associated teams, whereas all 'failures' were attributed to particular individuals or groups. In the view of those interviewed, the ARTOS TQM was used as a flagship by management for the purpose of convincing shop-floor employees of the benefits of TQM. For example, a piece of internal correspondence from the production manager to all TQM teams in December 1990 was used to highlight the success of the ARTOS TQM. The document outlined the paid efficiencies for the last eighteen weeks (which averaged out at 103 per cent compared with 65 per cent for the first ten weeks of TQM) and then set about thanking individual team members for their contribution, concluding with a: 'Thanks to all the team, your efforts and ideas is what TQM is all about'. This support and attention from management has further served to boost the morale in CPP and, in particular, the benefits of TQM to 'successful' team members. These individuals in turn sought to support TQM and in so doing raise their own profile:

> People communicate. Before, they didn't say what was going wrong and you would look at their sheets and ask them what happened, and they wouldn't really say what was wrong. They thought it would reflect on them if they had a problem, rather than complain or say anything, they would put up with it. Everything is a lot more open than it was before.

Although the early 'success' in CPP promoted greater interaction among employees and more open discussions on the daily work problems they encountered, as already indicated, work remained organized on a one operator per machine basis. There was also a rate set for each machine, which operators were expected to meet, and thus the individual monitoring and evaluation of employee performance was still a central part of the managerial control mechanisms on the shop floor. While teamwork remained largely a function of the group problem-solving activities associated with TQM, CPP employees felt that there had been an improvement in interpersonal communication and that there was greater collaboration between employees in helping each other out. In short, the evaluations of TQM by CPP supervisors, operators and union representatives were all favourable and supportive of the more general move towards greater teamwork and collaboration on the shop floor. In the words of a shop-floor operator:

> Before you would do things and you weren't listened to. Usually, you do things and you aren't listened to. Now they write things down, and follow things up. The next week we will ask why something hasn't been done, and there is usually a good reason. You can say things objectively. If you aren't happy with something, they will take note. Before we would say something and you would have to chase it up. Now things are done for us, somebody always follows things up. Before it was just OK we'll look into it, and three weeks later nothing was done. That has changed now.

Implementing TQM in cable manufacturing in South Australia

The experience of TQM in the Cable Manufacturing Plant (CMP) contrasts in a number of significant ways with experiences of the adjacent Cable Processing Plant (CPP) and the Minto Manufacturing Plant (MMP) in New South Wales. First, while there was general support for the philosophy of TQM, criticisms were levelled at the way in which it was being used and 'abused' within CMP. Second, sectional and interpersonal conflicts were identified as major obstacles to collaborative teamwork and the development of less adversarial systems of operation. Third, the local management team and line supervisors were viewed as a major problem impeding the successful introduction of TQM. Finally, the industry was experiencing a major recession (external context) and a number of employees had recently been retrenched (fear of job loss). Thus, while issues of employment and job security were a major operator concern, many spoke at length about a general failure of management to act upon workers' recommendations:

> Total Quality Management – it doesn't exist here. You have people here who really have no idea what is going on. They are going along for the ride. A lot of those involved in management are in charge of the meetings and they go on their merry way giving the operators a little bit of paperwork. Their workload doesn't increase, but those on the floor have increased their workloads. They want information and the guys on the floor treat it as a joke . . . I dropped out of one [TQM team] because they listen to you, but nothing is done. You can only bang your head on a brick wall for so long before it starts to hurt. Like

I said, we started out with two pieces of paperwork and now it is eight pieces of paperwork, all through TQM.

There was a general feeling among shop-floor employees that action needed to be taken by management to make CMP more profitable so that customers could be retained and the further retrenchment of staff would not be necessary. On this count, the operators described the frustration they felt through working within a system (TQM) that had improved the communication between management and the shop floor, but had not changed management's willingness to act upon the recommendations made by operators. TQM was seen to have created more work for operators, and yet it had failed to deliver on the promise of employee involvement in management decision-making. Whilst it was recognized that TQM facilitated greater liaison between various occupational groups and hierarchical levels within the plant, it was claimed that management action remained the preserve of management. In practice, this meant that if a TQM team suggestion was made by a manager or supervisor then there was a good chance that it would be acted upon immediately, whereas if a suggestion was made by operators it would take a considerable time before any action was taken, and only then if continual support for the suggestion had been made by employees and the recommendation had been restated over a number of months. In short, the communication channels had been opened with TQM, but the monopoly on ideas for decision-making had remained in the hands of management. This 'split' between management and shop-floor employees was also seen to be reflected in the management of the TQM teams, which were largely structured on an hierarchical basis. As one operator recalled:

At the TQM meetings, I will say as much as I want to say, but I have to work here still. We had a meeting last Tuesday. They asked us to try things different ways, and we do, but the moment we ask them to do something, they say no, we can't do that. They expect us to give, but they won't do anything for us.

Many of the employees interviewed commented that operators should be given the chance to run TQM meetings. They claimed that the majority of supervisors did not have a detailed knowledge of the machines being operated on the shop floor, and therefore were not well placed to decide the best course of action. This perceived lack of knowledge about shop-floor operations among line supervisors created an additional antagonism among shop-floor personnel; namely, that their supervisors did not have an adequate knowledge base from which to 'trouble-shoot' in the case of machine breakdowns or operator difficulties. As a result, operators felt unable to go to the supervisor for help: 'if my machine went wrong, I couldn't go to a supervisor because they don't know a thing about it'. In short, one of the biggest failings of local management was seen to stem from their inability to relate to the routine problems and concerns of shop-floor workers.

The shop-floor perceptions and attitudes of management in CMP contrast with those in CPP, and in so doing highlight how similar implementation strategies may not have the same effects between plants located on the same manufacturing complex. They also indicate the importance of TQM team formation, and the early 'success' of TQM groups in stimulating further enthusiasm and support from the shop floor. In the case of CMP, both the supervisors and operators agreed that when TQM was first introduced they tried to achieve too much too soon and consequently achieved very little. Operators also indicated that they felt that TQM was a 'dead loss' when it was first introduced into the plant, and that within a couple of months they had developed a far more positive attitude towards it. After a further twelve months, the employees interviewed indicated that they had returned to their original view. They advocated that TQM was a 'waste of time' the way it was being practised in the cable manufacturing plant.

In evaluating the effects of TQM on shop-floor operations, interviewees claimed that many of the problems experienced on the shop floor were the result of management incompetence and their failure to ensure that trained operators were working reliable machines. They claimed that poorly-trained, ill-equipped operators will produce scrap no matter how many TQM teams management initiate. From a shop-floor perspective, training was therefore identified as a major issue that wasn't being tackled adequately by management. The common view on the shop floor was that employees should have comprehensive training provided for the machines that they were expected to operate. In addition, interviewees argued that the machines provided should be able to operate at the set standards. From an operator perspective, working conditions had deteriorated and morale had plummeted since the uptake of TQM. It was argued that management overlooked obvious solutions to problems, and simply blamed the workers for high levels of scrap.

Within this context, there was a worsening of employee relations and a heightening of conflict between local managers and shop-floor employees. TQM as an intended cultural change programme merely brought conflicts of interest into sharp relief and drew attention to the existence of various occupational groups with overlapping and competing value and belief systems. In examining the effects of TQM on employees' attitudes and beliefs, an important distinction should be made between surface and deeper level elements of organizational culture. Following Schein (1985), the surface level elements can be taken to refer to those things in an organization that are readily accessible and we can observe directly, such as espoused values articulated in company documents, office layout, and dress codes. In contrast, the deeper aspects of culture can be taken to refer to those underlying assumptions and beliefs that evolve as groups attempt to make sense of their collective experience within the work environment. In this case, the company (as with most organizations) was characterized by the existence of a broader Pirelli culture (a dominant organizational culture) in conjunction with a number of other competing cultures and local subcultures (see Bloor and Dawson, 1994) that may also take the form of countercultures. At the level of the plant, the dominant culture largely reflected the strategic positioning and political standing of particular group alliances and did not reflect the existence of long-term cultural norms that support homogeneity. The introduction of TQM within Pirelli's Australian operations was a misplaced attempt by management to establish cultural homogeneity (a dominant and common belief system). They mistakenly believed that the establishment of problem-solving teams would pull employees together in the common pursuit of agreed company objectives. They also believed that through using their position of power and influence to constrain or displace disruptive staff and reward those who conform to the newly prescribed set of values, they would be able to reduce inefficiencies and waste while improving employee morale and commitment. In the case of the cable manufacturing plant, the longstanding male-engineering subculture was critical of surface level changes and opposed the establishment of quality programmes through questioning the competency of management to tackle the 'real' issues on the shop floor. In the words of one operator:

> It has got worse. To try and save money and cut down on the scrap, they are pushing sick machines as hard as they can. They are running shorter jobs, they are keeping levels up but the scrap isn't really coming down . . . If the machine breaks down it is a relief. You don't see anyone unhappy when the machine breaks down. It is not just because of the time off, it is just relief. One broke down for four or five days, and the operator was over the moon.

Comparative shop-floor issues and the context of change

These three cases illustrate how the shop-floor experience of TQM can vary enormously both across and within different companies and industries. In the case of Pirelli Cables Australia, these differences are highlighted between three separate plants, two of which were operating within a single manufacturing complex located in South Australia. For example, within the Cable Processing Plant (CPP) TQM was generally seen as a positive development that improved the work environment of supervisors and shop-floor employees, whereas within the Cable Manufacturing Plant (CMP) TQM was criticized heavily by shop-floor staff. In the case of the Minto Manufacturing Plant (MMP), supervisory and employee concerns were also raised during the introduction of TQM. These 'problems' were largely explained by management as minor oversights in their implementation strategy, and were seen as part of the change management 'learning' process. It was assumed that the implementation of TQM in CMP and CPP would be fairly straightforward and uncontroversial. As it turned out, the different cultures and histories of the two adjacent plants, the very different work environments and labour composition, longstanding relationships with management and between employees, as well as issues of ethnicity and gender, all served to shape and reshape the process of change. For example, the opportunity for greater communication and interaction was viewed as a positive and non-threatening development by many of the female operators working at CPP, and contrasted with the feeling at CMP, where the male definition of 'worker value' was far more rooted in the technical and engineering elements of the labour process. In addition, the turnover of employees at CPP was greater than at CMP, and with the latter workforce the job was seen as a mark of social standing outside as well as within the work environment. In other words, the male operators (typically full-time) tended to define themselves by their job, in contrast to the female operators (a mixture of full-time and part-time), who viewed their work as one element within a matrix of roles. In CMP, the downturn in the market for manufactured products posed major problems for employees who had spent a working lifetime within the company and were being threatened with compulsory redundancies. In this plant, the fear of unemployment significantly reduced the morale of staff and heightened their resistance to TQM, which was perceived as a new management technique for reducing staff requirements through making operations more efficient. In contrast, redundancies were not imposed on permanent full-time operators in CPP, as the plant was largely able to absorb the downturn through the non-replacement of staff (what the company termed 'natural wastage'). Whether female operators would have been so accommodating to change if their jobs had also been threatened remains questionable, although the contrasting values placed on the job as defining social status would also seem to have influenced the response of employees to the change process.

Apart from the differences between the two plants there were a number of similarities, in particular regarding the question of English language fluency and ethnic origin as a factor facilitating and inhibiting employee involvement in TQM, and the problems of interpersonal conflict and poor communication between the different shift operators. As one interviewee recounted:

> We have problems with nationalities. We have got Portuguese,
> Yugoslavs, Maltese, Australians, and English – that causes problems.
> There is not much trust in our section between the three different
> shifts. If you think someone has done you a dirty, it is very easy to get
> them back. But you may be only imagining it. We have two operators
> who haven't spoken in the last three years. They don't even
> acknowledge each other. Personality clashes . . . It is pathetic and I
> don't believe it is as bad as some of the operators think it is, but there
> are definite problems.

Within both plants, it was claimed that the majority of staff who were not involved (apart from the nightshift) were recent immigrants that did not understand English that well. As one interviewee commented:

> Sometimes the language barrier is too much of a problem. We can't
> explain everything that is going on that clearly in the meetings. I think
> it is also their culture that they don't bring up trouble. They just do
> their job and then they go home.

There are a number of people employed by Pirelli who are not fluent in the English language. This raises the problem of communication both between employees – who are now expected to work together as a team rather than as individual machine operators – and within the TQM teams themselves. For the most part, there has been a general reluctance for those who speak English as a foreign language to get involved in the TQM groups. Although attempts to integrate these employees into TQM initiatives have been made, there remain a number of problems to full involvement. As one shop floor worker noted:

> The language barrier is a problem. It puts TQM out of its momentum
> if you have to talk really slowly. It embarrasses them too, if they have

> to sit in front of ten guys. We now have English lessons to try and
> better them as operators. This one guy panics, he goes too fast for
> himself. We try to slow him down, but he goes too fast.

Not only is the capacity for TQM to involve non-English speaking
employees severely constrained by language difficulties, but the
attitudinal differences expressed within the dominant Anglo-Australian
culture compared with other ethnic groups also serves to impede
multicultural integration within the workplace. As a shop-floor supervisor
commented:

> When they (the different ethnic groups) first came they stayed
> together a lot of the time. Some of them just didn't speak because they
> have been used to not being able to. Some will always put their eyes
> down and not look at you when they speak, not because they are
> afraid, but because that is the way they have been brought up. But
> lately I have noticed that the Australian girls have been sitting with
> the others. It is a lot better than it used to be. They seem happy, which
> is good.

In the case of Pirelli Cables Australia, language and ethnicity were
central contextual factors that influenced the capacity for certain groups
of employees to engage with TQM (see also Bloor, 1999: 172). Although
this point may appear obvious, its significance should not be
underestimated given the decision-making authority often invested in
TQM teams. Typically, it is assumed that the option for involvement is
there for any who wish to take it, as one operator commented in
criticizing people who didn't want to be involved in TQM:

> Well, they still have to change as they go. If they don't like the
> changes, bad luck, they are introduced anyway. They have to accept
> the fact that the changes are happening. If they are not involved, then
> they are stuck with the fact they are changing. I don't see why anyone
> wouldn't want to be in on it.

This in turn raises the question of the voluntary nature of TQM (it was
not a compulsory activity within Pirelli Cables Australia). On the one
hand it was argued that people do not have to get involved in TQM, and
on the other hand it was argued that those who do not wish to be involved
must nevertheless accept and live by the decisions of the TQM group. In
this sense, TQM was not compulsory, nor was it freely open to all
employees (in not being able adequately to accommodate non-English
speaking employees), nor was it a non-threatening voluntary activity (in
that decisions made within TQM groups could have significant

consequences for the re-organization of work of those not involved). These contextual and associated cultural factors – from custom and practice, gender and ethnicity, management and employee relations through to the machinery of production, fear of job loss and the organization of work – all serve to influence the speed, direction and shape of workplace change.

Conclusion

This chapter has set out to highlight the importance of context in understanding change. The introduction of TQM into Pirelli Cables Australia provides a good example, as it not only draws attention to a cultural change programme that centres on revising existing organizational attitudes and belief systems, but also tunes into the very different experiences of change within three different local operating contexts within the same broader company context of change. It is argued here that attempts to manage organizational culture towards some questionable common features within multicultural workplaces is at odds with the reality of Australian and British management practice. It should be remembered that Japanese management arose in the context of an extraordinarily homogeneous society, thereby setting the context within which cultural pluralism was deemed unacceptable. In contrast, the continual redefinition of cultural norms within Britain and Australia reflects not only the changing ethnic composition of the workforce but also attempts to accommodate multiculturalism and the diverse range of interest groups with different allegiances, expectations and values. In this sense, there is the added dimension of changing ethnic composition linked with pre-existing cultural pluralism that highlights the importance of contextualizing change initiatives that seek to 'manage' value and belief systems of employees working within organizations.

In the case of Pirelli, employee participation in TQM teams was a voluntary activity. Union representatives did not view TQM as a threat, and supported employee involvement. The main potential benefits for employees centred on removing irritating and sometimes regular problems in their daily work tasks, being able openly to express concerns and frustrations to management, and being able to withdraw from the shop floor for scheduled TQM team meetings. From a company perspective, the potential for improved communication and employee morale, combined with the possibility of improvements in efficiency rates and reductions in scrap, acted as a major financial incentive to continue with the TQM scheme. One of the hidden inequalities of TQM was that while all employees were expected to abide by the decisions made by the TQM teams, employees did not have equal opportunity to participate. The TQM scheme was based on a unitary notion of culture, and was ill-suited to the development of total employee involvement in a multicultural workplace. The case studies demonstrate how English language fluency and ethnic origin were major constraining forces in the proposed move towards TQM. Communication is supposedly at the heart of TQM, and thus an inability to communicate effectively (in cases where English is a second, third or even fourth language) is a significant obstacle to employee involvement in group problem-solving teams. Moreover, the views and beliefs of employees who did not form part of the dominant Anglo-Australian culture were largely down played or ignored in group decision-making activities. As a result, some ethnic minority groups and non-fluent English speaking employees remained outside of TQM, not because of an unwillingness to be involved but because of an inability for these programmes adequately to accommodate these groups and/or individuals.

While TQM may be described as a management strategy for cultural change, ironically it fails to accommodate or account for the possibility of cultural heterogeneity. Within such organizational contexts, TQM can never fully achieve its aim of total employee involvement, and in some cases may even serve to sustain and create ethnic divisions within the workplace. Contextual issues are by their nature complex, dynamic and diverse. As this chapter has shown, they are also central to explanations of the way change processes are shaped and reshaped over time.

4 The politics of change at General Motors

> Our revels now are ended. These our actors,
> As I foretold you, were all spirits and
> Are melted into air, into thin air:
> And, like the baseless fabric of this vision,
> The cloud-capp'd towers, the gorgeous palaces,
> The solemn temples, the great globe itself,
> Yea, all which it inherit, shall dissolve
> And, like this insubstantial pageant faded,
> Leave not a rack behind. We are such stuff
> As dreams are made on, and our little life
> Is rounded with a sleep.
> (Shakespeare, *The Tempest*, Scene I, Act IV)

In Shakespeare's final play, *The Tempest*, Prospero is the Duke of Milan, who acts as a kind of director in orchestrating events through the construction of stories that influence others in seeking his preferred outcomes. The play ends with an epilogue from Prospero in which he seeks the 'indulgence' of the audience to legitimize his position through their applause. This process of orchestration and directorship is an integral part of the political process of change and, it is argued here, an essential dimension of organizational change programmes. This chapter examines the political process of industrial collaboration and change at General Motors' (GM) hardware fabrication plant located at their Elizabeth complex in South Australia. Performance of the plant had been deteriorating over a number of years, and senior management were seriously considering outsourcing small component manufacture to local suppliers. As it turned out, they decided to recruit a new manager, making it clear that the plant would close unless significant improvements were achieved in production, not least of which should involve reductions in the high costs of scrap, re-work and inventory. Under this climate of uncertainty and threat, the newly appointed production manager set about implementing a five-year programme of change involving unions, employees and outside collaborators. The story of this process, and in particular the political aspects of change, are described in this chapter. The intention is not to chart the detail of this transition (which has been outlined elsewhere), but to re-analyse elements of the data in drawing out some of the political processes involved. In so doing, the data has been de-coupled and reconstructed to form a readable historical narrative on the political processes involved in creating the conditions for the introduction of cellular work arrangements in an automotive manufacturing plant.

The story commences with a single player, and unfolds to incorporate a range of different groups and viewpoints. The longitudinal nature of the research enabled data to be collected at a number of critical junctures and resulted not only in the emergence of competing histories of change but also in the re-forming of past events into new organizational stories that served particular political agendas at particular points in time. The contextual temporal dynamics of change are thereby linked with continual historical reformulation to support current decisions rather than to represent any type of 'objective' or 'authentic' account of past events. The difficulties of data analysis in articulating these types of complex issues should not be underestimated, and as such the chapter should be viewed as an attempt to paint some of the political textures around cell design and work restructuring in replaying and expanding on certain facets of 'the story' of plant-level change. The aim is to highlight the importance of politics as a dimension of the processual perspective in understanding and making sense of the way change is shaped and reshaped over time.

In the beginning . . .

The first key figure to emerge in this story of change is the plant manager (PM). The plant was initially built in the late 1950s, and by the early 1980s, operating with old and ill-maintained machinery, a trend of poor performance, heated industrial relations and low employee morale had taken hold. Within this context, PM entered the scene and quickly gained the attention of all employees through highlighting the possibility of plant closure and stressing his commitment to improving the work environment and performance of the plant. Under these contextual conditions (the threat of job loss and unemployment), trade union officials and their representatives were willing to listen to the options open to them in revitalizing the plant and maintaining commercial viability.

In his dealings with union representatives, PM established the importance of ongoing communication and indicated that he would operate an open-door policy. If there was an industrial relations problem, he would like to hear about it immediately and would work with employees and their representatives in trying to find solutions that were acceptable to all parties. Although he encouraged individuals and groups to air their views and grievances, he also ensured that he presented an image of a strong leader who would not suffer fools and who was willing and able to make the hard decisions. Furthermore, he was quick to identify the critical players from the union side and to develop a working relationship based on his policy of open communication.

In manoeuvring to gain greater union support where previous relations had been sour and adversarial, the PM identified a number of areas where fairly minor changes could bring about substantial gains. One of these centred on a programme of cleaning the work environment and repainting battleship grey machines in bright primary colours. Prior to these changes, the plant was a very dark and grey place with strong industrial smells and greasy floors. The high visibility of the extensive cleanup of the plant, in which floors were swept, aisles cleared and machines painted, was important in gaining the general backing from employees and in generating a greater belief in the ability of the local management team to get things done. Employee attitudes towards PM improved, and a climate of hope for the future was nourished and developed by these initial programmes of change. The importance of these changes was also stressed in an interview with two official representatives of the Vehicle Builders Union (VBU), who strongly commended the changes at the plant and contrasted the working conditions with other plants in the GM complex at Elizabeth. Apparently simple changes (painting machinery and tidying the workplace) can have a fundamental impact on employee attitudes and trade union positioning. The significance of the symbolic action of PM is clearly highlighted by this case. For example, in a move to strengthen further the link with the union, PM provided a room for union representatives where employees could meet to discuss burning issues or concerns. This condition contrasted sharply with the vehicle assembly plant, and was an important political move that led to a more open and collaborative arrangement between union representatives and the local management team.

During these early stages, PM repeatedly made it clear to employees and their representatives that they were under scrutiny by senior management and that all jobs were on the line. He quickly built on his early achievements to re-state that some hard decisions would have to be made and that employees would have to make some sacrifices in supporting change. In many ways, PM was building a platform from which a more substantive change programme could be launched. He was also building alliances and gaining the cooperation of key individuals and groups, and displacing others who might serve to impede his objectives and career agenda. Thus, realizing the need to mobilize a network of relations, PM spent considerable time and energy in developing his relationship with other managers within the plant. At this stage, PM was a production manager working in liaison with other managers of equal rank within the plant. In response to this situation, PM was quick to recognize their key position as potential 'blockers' to future strategies of change.

From production manager to plant manager: an untold story

In individual local management accounts on the contextual conditions under which change took place, there is a surprising absence of reference to PM as a production manager. Stories of the five-year change programme typically cast PM as the plant manager and champion of change. Issues of conflict and problems of control are not part of the accepted story. At the time of the study (interviews were conducted from 1989–1997), the reconstituted local management team were working under PM. Moreover, the work cell change initiative was taking place in which PM was viewed as the charismatic leader marshalling the skills and initiatives of a loyal team of senior supervisory and managerial personnel. At this time, commitment and support were viewed as essential requirements for membership into the team. In short, anybody who was not willing to hold the party line was not welcome. A central concern of PM was the image presented of himself and the plant both to significant others within GM and to external agencies. This was to be the last major change programme he would manage prior to retirement, and from a personal viewpoint it was the one that he wanted to be remembered for.

In building a 'committed' group, PM recruited those who would be players on his team. Again, he was quick in identifying those who might block his personal aims to gain promotion and to retire on the back of a successful change programme. As he recounts:

> The first five years were associated with people, getting trust of the shop stewards, tending to weed out the people who were knockers, blockers, just either move those people to one side or get rid of them. And in the majority of the cases we were successful in doing that without any hassles whatsoever. The fact of the matter was, there was an early retirement programme going on and so we allowed some of the people to be pensioned off or retired with dignity.

Interestingly, twelve months into the study and during a third round of interviews, data emerged that questioned earlier accounts. A number of competing histories and revised stories were identified during the course of the research, including a fictitious account that was presented in public and corroborated by a collaborative party. In the case of PM, a further interview was scheduled and the plant manager was asked to clarify his position prior to the cellular change initiative:

I: Is it true that you came as a production manager in 1981?

PM: Yes. Purely and simply in charge of production.

I: So who was in charge of the plant?

PM: The plant was run by a series of managers. There was a manager associated with production control, a manager associated with maintenance, a manager associated with tooling, a manager associated with quality and they were all individual managers. Gradually one by one I took over the responsibilities of each of those functions and over about the last three years I have been operating as the plant manager.

I: So those jobs have been merged into one, whereas before you had the different managers reporting to the main office?

PM: Yes. It was an impossible situation that we had. We had virtually five different managers in the one plant each responsible for a function. The only way we could see that it was going to work was for it to come under one control, so everything could be co-ordinated. In effect what you had up to that period of time was five different people running their particular organization in five different ways and never the two shall meet, or never the five should meet.

I: So that would have implications for the five-year change programme?

PM: Yes it did, because of the philosophy that we were trying to put into place. I had to get approval from each of those other managers, as to how they wanted to organize their organizations and in some cases, it was contrary to the way I wanted to run the plant. So there was some conflict that had to be resolved and fortunately senior management philosophy started to change as well . . . It was accepted that the manner by which we wanted to operate was the way to go.

In other words, while PM has been characterized within many of the popular organizational stories as the single leader of change, in practice change involved a whole range of different change agents and involved processes of negotiation, conflict, displacement and relationship building. These political processes were in turn influenced by contextual conditions and the expectations and support of senior management. In charting the change process a whole series of change roles can be identified, which fluctuate, combine and are often redefined over time. In this case (and as with many other change initiatives), change was not achieved by a single individual but required a network of relationships that consisted of multiple roles, some of which were defined and some of which evolved over time. In this sense, astute political action accommodates contextual conditions and is sensitive to the needs and expectations of significant others in building a network of collaborative relations, in displacing potential blockers and in mobilizing the support of powerful groups (senior management and trade unions).

Bringing the union people on side: inside the rationalized story of the plant manager

Already in this unfolding saga of change, the figure of PM is being explained and cast within a broader network of roles and parties – for example, employees and their union representatives, the local management team, and the relationship of PM to the senior management group. As the story continues we shall see how social networks developed outside of the world of work, attitudes of older workers, early enthusiasts, industrial collaborators and external agencies all come into play in shaping outcomes and influencing decisions. For the moment, however, the story centres on the narrative of the plant manager, who focussed attention on the 'positive' and 'successful' aspects of the change process. In his account of change, other voices were ignored and conflicts were largely down-played. For example, interviews with employees in the initial cells provided favourable accounts about the change. Under these early arrangements, the teams were self-supervising and were able to make daily decisions regarding the way work was organized and tasks allocated. However, as the change programme progressed and widened to involve more areas within the plant, supervision was reintroduced into the cells and consequently some of the autonomy and decision-making responsibilities found in the earlier cell arrangements were absent under later structures. This reimposition of supervisory control generated more negative accounts by employees, and has remained a bone of contention for some. Furthermore, in developing a range of skills within the cells, many employees felt that the work had improved (a small minority did not) and yet they remained unhappy about pay levels and the process through which their new skills were 'officially' recognized by management. The plant manager proved reluctant to get drawn into any discussion on these more sensitive issues, and preferred to talk about past achievements rather than ongoing concerns and potential problems.

After setting up an experimental cell that demonstrated the benefits of cellular manufacture, PM turned his attention to the need to sell this idea to others. As he explained:

> From the union point of view, it wasn't much good talking to the union until we talked to management. After that we talked to our staff and basically informed them of what we were looking at and why we were looking at it. Similarly with the union people, mainly the VBU [Vehicle Builders Union], because the VBU were the people who would be the most effective group. Then we went to the other shop stewards involved as we went further down the track, but they were involved much later. We spoke to them as a team, our management team with the union people. There were times when we had discussions on the shop floor, there were times when I spoke to the union people on my own, especially when we were talking to the union executive further down the track, but there was a general principle that it was a team effort convincing our union people. They would not be disadvantaged by it, the company would be advantaged and that we would be multi-skilling the work force. We had the opportunity we saw to increase the take-home pay of our people and they would share in the improvements that we made.

In approaching the Vehicle Builders Union (VBU), there were some concerns over the implications for jobs. PM claimed that he had to guarantee to the union that there would be no job losses to members. The union also wanted full consultation throughout the change programme, and consequently a lot of time was spent briefing the shop stewards and talking to employees in small groups. In terms of trade union involvement in cell design, this was largely in terms of shop stewards. From the plant manager perspective, all senior shop stewards were involved in discussions with plant management on plant restructuring and the setting up of cells. However, in the view of the VBU there was one particular senior shop steward who got heavily involved with management and made most of the decisions without actually consulting the other shop stewards. A close relationship was formed between PM and this particular shop steward, and a major problem (from the union perspective) was that the information on these decisions was not getting relayed to the union officials. As a result there was a change in leadership, and closer scrutiny was made of the plant by the VBU. As a whole, full-time union officials have tended to leave the process alone and to monitor for any major industrial concerns or problems. As one union official recounted:

> We told shop stewards in the early stages when Paul and myself were servicing the place, just to keep an eye on it and let us know if there's any industrial matters being talked about. Anybody trying to screw the union and so on and none of that ever happened. So it was just mostly concerned about quality and working together and making people happier in the jobs they were doing and so on. So I've never had no problems at all with it and still don't have problems, the only minor problems that came up is the forklift drivers driving into the work cell and making the place dirty. You still got your bloody health and safety problems and your little bloody disputes, but nothing major.

There was also an issue with the forklift drivers over the loss of their jobs and their transfer to positions within the new team-based cellular arrangements. This group was against the changes taking place, and advocated that under the cell system of operation you would still need the same number of drivers. As it turned out, these positions were reduced from fifteen to four over a matter of months, and yet the grievances of this group were not acted upon:

> Some of the old-timers there, especially the production workers and forklift drivers, say: 'shit this is not going to work, how can you go from here to get materials to there and there without forklift drivers'. I think maybe they're talking because they know their future isn't going to be around, because at the moment you have fifteen forklift drivers. So they're kind of looking more at their future jobs than anything else and they're probably thinking about trying to bloody have a negative attitude towards it.

This quotation from a union official illustrates how casualties of change were not only expected but also accepted. An almost utilitarian philosophy predominated, which limited action for the minority in support of better conditions for most. In the context of plant one, relations between employees and management were comparatively good and the narrative of management (in promoting PM as the champion of change), although not endorsed, was not openly disputed. Provided the changes were viewed as being beneficial, then the union's position was to maintain a hands-off approach and yet also to ensure that shop stewards maintained their loyalty to the union and were not absorbed into the more conservative ideology of management and, in particular, the plant manager.

On a number of occasions and throughout a range of interviews, union officials and their representatives pointed out that PM was one of the most conservative managers within the GM complex. For some this raised a contradiction, whereby this more traditional conservative manager was seen to be better at relating to employees than many of the younger 'trendy' managers. Although recognition was given to the organizing, communicative and delegating skills of PM, from the union perspective the notion of PM being the champion of change was seen to overstate his role in the process. There were a lot of stakeholders involved either in actively supporting the process or in not seeking to block what was viewed as a beneficial and important change. The VBU, through evaluating change and speaking to employees on the shop floor, decided not to put any barriers in the way of the process. Their articulated view was that, given the economic threat to the survival of the plant, there would be a lot of support for any change initiative that sought to save jobs and make the plant a commercially viable entity.

In addition to gaining the support of shop stewards and managing a change that was not being disputed or blocked by trade unions, the local management team also set out to recruit a group of external experts to develop a cell design and facilitate the change process. As it turned out, this body of experts also proved central to gaining the financial backing and support of senior management.

Building collaborative relationships: the use of external experts

On the basis of their initial experiments, PM and his local management team were convinced that restructuring the plant under group technology principles could be justified in the pay-off from reduced material handling costs alone (Buchanan and Preston, 1992; Dawson, 2001). However, they required external expert assistance to help them design a workable set of cells. In their search for and assessment of options, they identified an American company that possessed the necessary expertise, but at a cost of over $1 million it was an option that they knew would not be supported by senior management. As it turned out, one of the members of the local management team was friendly with an employee of the newly formed Division of Manufacturing Technology (DMT) within the Commonwealth Scientific and Industrial Research Organization (CSIRO). This group (with operations in Adelaide and Melbourne) was highly qualified but needed to establish itself within the industrial arena within which it intended to work. The hardware fabrication plant at General Motors provided just such an opportunity, and therefore DMT agreed to use the project as a loss-leader, working at only a third of the normal commercial rates. Both parties had a considerable amount to gain from the success of the industrial collaboration, and developed a network of mutual support that lasted beyond the time-scale of the project.

The proposal put forward by DMT, and accepted by GM, advocated that industrial collaboration be undertaken in four phases. The first phase (three months) was to comprise an analysis of current manufacturing operations in order to identify opportunities for cost reduction and to specify (and possibly establish) a demonstration manufacturing cell as a test bed for further development. Three or more CSIRO employees and two full-time GM staff members would work together in the collection and analysis of data, and the installation of the proposed demonstration cell. In the second phase, the lessons learned and the concepts developed over the first few months would be further refined and expanded to formulate a completely revised manufacturing system for the plant. The third and fourth phases were to occur concurrently over twelve months, with the latter involving the design, relocation, procurement and commissioning of all the required hardware for implementing the new methods of work organization.

As it turned out, both the timeframes and the phased approach to industrial collaboration and organizational change were continually redefined through ongoing processes of consultation and negotiation between the two major parties. For example, one of the major changes from the original proposal rested on the need to produce quantifiable results that could be used by the plant manager to justify continuance of the change programme. As a result, a pilot cell was implemented in parallel with the development of cell-build software for full plant layout. Originally DMT had intended to formulate a total design prior to any shop-floor implementation of this new form of work organization. In short, internal politics placed pressure on the plant manager to show real gains for funding purposes, which in turn put pressure on the DMT team to produce workable pieces of the system. The manufacturing cell was scheduled on ten-day runs, and was able to produce 70 individual assemblies. During this time, continual improvements were made in response to problems identified by the operators, and there were regular meetings between plant management and DMT staff to tackle problems as and when they arose.

On the basis of a series of positive results from the demonstration cell, local management submitted a proposal to senior management requesting the necessary financial support for the change programme. This proposal was rejected, with one senior manager suggesting that what was needed was not the rearrangement of old equipment but the purchasing of new machinery. At this stage, the support of DMT proved critical to these negotiations. As a team of qualified experts, DMT was able to substantiate the benefits of change and present a coherently argued case for investment. PM mobilized all the support he could muster and submitted an amended proposal to senior management. He persisted in arguing the case for funding and, through a series of presentations by his local management team, he was eventually able to convince the directors of the feasibility of manufacturing cells. Although the case for support proved difficult and the funding obstacle came close to causing a premature end to the change project, orchestrating others to fight the cause and persisting in the face of rejection were critical political elements to the achievement of desired outcomes.

The political process of cell design in the restructuring of work

In their collaboration with CSIRO, the redesign of the plant into cellular arrangements involved a large number of collaborative group discussions. Problems with the integrity of GM data, the idiosyncrasies of plant equipment, the tacit knowledge of operational processes by employees, the preferences of local management and the values and assumptions of the external change experts all played a part in shaping the process of plant redesign. The iterative process of negotiation and debate on plant design criteria draws attention to the political elements of change in the mutual shaping of the social and the technical. For example, although the material constraints of the press equipment were originally built into the cell design software on the basis of machine specifications, local management did not accept the consequence of this for provisional cell design. They had their own views and position on work cell arrangements, supervision, skill requirements of staff, and the optimum number of operators per cell. In addition, local staff involved in discussions demonstrated their expertise (tacit knowledge/local expertise through experience) by presenting alternative 'technical' assessments of plant and equipment. The technical constraints of particular pieces of machinery became open to debate and discussion. For example, what a machine could and could not do, why it should not be placed in a cell with another specified piece of equipment, why two identical pieces of equipment were quite different in practice, and how the quirks of a particular press required certain operator skills were just a few of a broader range of issues in the mutual shaping of the social and technical change (see also Chapter 5). In terms of power, differing forms of expertise were mobilized from the tacit knowledge of experienced operators to the technical credentials of the CSIRO design team. PM was able to elevate his position during this process by supporting his 'team players' and smoothing over any conflict that might jeopardize progress. Moreover, by involving potential resisters and then rejecting their views in the 'light' of other 'expert advice', PM was able to demoralize and sidetrack pockets of opposition in steering the political process of cell design.

Working within an agreed set of design constraints, the CSIRO presented a first-cut of plant cellularization to local management, and requested their guidance on how the cells should be rearranged to take into account the detailed workings of the shop floor. Plant personnel were then required to examine closely current manufacturing operations in the light of the proposed design. Once they had made amendments to the design it was returned to the CSIRO, which then presented another blueprint. This cycle of events continued for nearly twelve months, and a number of significant changes occurred. For example, this was the period in which a separation was made between the smaller specialized cells (such as handbrake assembly, rocker covers and so forth) and the larger multipurpose cells. The decision to create specialized cells arose from an emerging consensus that high-volume output was required for a small number of parts, requiring a small number of machines.

Under the initial plan formulated by the CSIRO eighteen cells were proposed, but again through a process of prolonged discussion this was reduced to seven multi-assembly cells and seven cells dedicated to single assemblies. As one member of the CSIRO team recounted:

> We spent many, not terribly happy, days in this office here with scrawl all over that board, with me working at some terminal with about 27 windows on it with all the different data files, arguing out how we were going to resolve this problem of not having enough machines. 'This is currently planned on the so-and-so machine: can we shift it to something-or-other else?' 'That will mean re-building the tooling'. 'What does that involve?' 'Oh, that's no problem we can do it' ... I reckon there would have been, out of the final count of 600 parts, there would've been two or three hundred of them that were re-planned in this office. But that, to my mind, was what the collaborative exercise was about, because if I'd sat here as a consultant and said: 'Well it will work if you do that', and they look at it and say: 'You can't do that. No way. Forget it. Goodbye'. But because we worked together on the thing and resolved all these difficulties one at a time over a very, very long period, it worked.

During this process, there was considerable 'room to manoeuvre' in the design and development of cellular work arrangements. The constraint of working with existing plant and equipment was not simply a 'technical' constraint, but also reflected actor interpretations and the tacit knowledge and assumptions held by those involved in these group decision-making processes. The social expectations and the drive for the development of self-supervising multi-skilled teams were also used to close off certain options and direct attention towards certain forms of design. However following implementation, various individuals and groups on the shop floor experienced changes in the organization and control of work in a range of different ways. Although space prevents a detailed analysis of these diverging experiences, as mentioned earlier, changes in supervisory management and the introduction of team-based work are two areas where opposing narratives have been articulated (see also Dawson, 1994: 104–122).

Conclusion

This processual analysis of the longitudinal data has necessarily been selective in focussing on some of the political dimensions of change. It has attempted to show how different groups may recount stories that not only reflect their own interests and perceptions of the change process, but also serve to reshape change to accommodate individual and group interests. The view of the forklift drivers contrasted with the position taken by the Vehicle Builders Union, and the CSIRO were working with a very different agenda to that of the GM senior management team. These different positions and views were not left to float as a type of free market emergent process; rather, there was political engagement in attempts to steer the process in particular directions in order to achieve certain preferred outcomes. For PM, change is a political process that requires the support of other individuals and groups. However, in recounting this process and creating and maintaining a 'story' of change, PM characterizes events in terms of a rational sequence of decisions by a committed team working in collaboration with other key stakeholders. From this perspective there is a tendency to concentrate on the process by which obstacles are overcome, relationships nurtured and potential areas of conflict avoided. From the viewpoint of the VBU, it was deemed inappropriate and a waste of political energy to interfere with a change initiative that was (in their view) generally improving employee conditions of work. The symbolic actions of PM through introducing fairly simple changes to improve the working environment were shown to have a major influence on the views and position of trade unionists. Nevertheless, this group openly recognized the centrality of politics and vested interest in reflecting on union relations with management and on shop-floor change. In the case of the CSIRO collaborators, technology was experienced as a political process in which technical constraints were inseparably linked to subjective constructions and competing actor interpretations. In this sense, there was a mutual shaping between the 'technical' and 'social' during the political process of cell design and workplace change. In the stories presented, the building of relationships between and within employees, unions, management and external agencies are all part of the explanation of the change odyssey, and highlight the political nature of organizational change. Moreover, in re-examining existing data, focus has not been given to the actual period of change to cellular manufacture (see, Dawson, 1994); rather, attention has been given to the complex textures of political activities that form both an historical backcloth and an integral part of processes of organizational change. In this case, the development of a change initiative from within a plant (rather than being imposed by senior management) spotlights the importance of building bridges between groups, developing and sustaining networks of relationships, removing 'blockers' if possible or incorporating them into the change project, and mobilizing significant others in the face of rejection and defeat. All these political facets are part and parcel of the process of change management, yet as with any 'sweet-smelling political rose' there are also likely to be victims who suffer the consequences of the political decisions of others. In many cases these 'victims' may represent the voices of those who are not heard, and the reason for their 'silence' may be due to a composite of different contextual and political elements. The forklift drivers' predicament was not the concern of management or the VBU; their jobs were disappearing in a context where other jobs were being saved and improved. As a small and relatively powerless group, they had little if any political influence over the process of change.

Over time, a common organization story has emerged that represents the view of the dominant narrators. In this case, political behaviours were shown to centre on the power, place and perspective of individuals, and their capacity to develop interpersonal relationships, form and reform groups, orchestrate resources and manage the unfolding and unforeseen processes of change. The arrival of a new production manager, who assumed the role of plant manager, provided an impetus for change that was shaped by various contextual conditions and the cost and availability of options for restructuring. Social networking and the forming of relationships, and the ability to substantiate financial benefits and mobilize an expert body of support, all proved critical to gaining the backing of the senior management team. Taken as a whole, the political process of change involved shifting groups and individuals who took up different positions and roles as the contextual conditions unfolded throughout the life of a project. In constructing a rational story of change, the emergent dominant narrative down-plays conflicts and avoids notions of failure while simultaneously applauding success and emphasizing collaboration. PM is cast as the champion of change, even though in practice there was a whole range of different individuals and groups involved in the change process. These findings support the claim of Buchanan and Storey (1997) that any notion of a singular change agent role is ultimately flawed, as there are both multiple agents of change and multiple players who enter and are drawn into the political arena of change management. Moreover while certain explicit activities can be identified as 'political' these actions may only represent the tip of the political iceberg, for it is the decisions that are not made, the options that never arise and the voices that are never heard, that may remain hidden yet form an integral part of the political process (Bacharach and Baratz,

1962). In the case reported, PM can be viewed as a conductor in orchestrating those around him, and yet he is also playing to the tune of senior management, accommodating the 'reasonable' demands of unions and building relations for external support and expert advice. This dynamic political arena also required the building of collaborative stories and their adjustment to meet the needs of different audiences and to accommodate changing priorities as the change programme evolved. The creation of these stories is itself a political process, and as such characters can be recast and story lines changed to fit current contextual conditions and future strategic objectives. Alternative stories and views, although less prominent, remain within the broader dynamic tapestry of change, and may at any time serve to compete with dominant accounts and/or influence the rewriting of organizational history. Although some of these conflicting views have been presented, it has not been possible within the constraints of space to develop further the consequence of competing histories or the way past events are often reconstructed to form stories that correspond to current political climates (for further discussion see Chapters 8 and 9). The merging and diverging views of DMT and GM is one such area that warrants further attention, particularly as the politics of mutual support have led both agencies to confirm a view in public that they have not held in private. In this sense, the politics of organizational change not only go beyond the organization in question, but also beyond the life of particular change projects.

In recounting the political process of orchestration and the social construction of *post-hoc* rationalizations, it is important not to lose sight of the non-linear and unpredictable nature of change. Unforeseen events and unfolding conditions may necessitate the modification of existing plans, the rethinking of options and the reappraisal of decisions. As the work of Preece (1995) has shown, under conditions of change intergroup conflicts may occur and new groups and alliances may form. Furthermore, such contextual shifts may also necessitate a reconfiguration of the substance of change and a possible reforming of change strategies, and in so doing create a fertile ground for political activity. As already noted, external competitive pressures may serve to enhance commercial sensitivity to the public image of a company and encourage the political re-positioning of groups and individuals in their scanning for opportunities to strengthen group standing and/or further the aims of individual career agendas. Where mutual advantage can be achieved from joint collaboration, then it may appear rational that views and opinions are modified to accommodate a combined cause. However, the question so often posed as to whether this form of political manoeuvring is to be acclaimed or condemned perhaps misses the point, for, as this chapter has shown, political activity is by its nature a part of organizational life and an essential dimension within programmes of organizational change.

5 The substance of change at Shell Expro and Britax Industries

This chapter examines the substance of change and uses data drawn from a study of new teamwork arrangements at Britax Industries in Australia, and the use of video conferencing technology at Shell Expro in Scotland. Attention is given to the timescale of change and the perceived centrality of the change process. The interlocking influence of context and political process is highlighted, and the labels and defining characteristics of the change are discussed. The Shell example is used to unpick issues arising from a change aimed at shifting employee behaviour in the use of video conferencing technology in order to reduce travel costs. It also draws attention to conceptions of technology and the way interpretations are constrained and steered in certain preferred directions. The Britax case is used to spotlight the different assumptions on flexibility and rigidity behind the whole-scale restructuring of plant arrangements. In order to promote the view that change was inevitable and not open to question, management adopted a version of the 'automate or liquidate' argument. This position allowed them to ignore employee concerns and to distance themselves from the need for shop-floor discussion regarding the choice, use and configuration of technology. Both cases illustrate how our interpretations of technology and new forms of work organization influence the way we view and respond to change, and how these social processes have a powerful influence on the way change is shaped and reshaped. In other words, it is not simply technology but actions, and the understanding and interpretation of acts that because they are perceived as real, are real in their consequences in shaping human behaviour. This position echoes some of the work of Child (previously discussed in Chapter 2). His main concern is with the way subjective constructions have objective consequences, and the way these may in turn influence future actions and interpretations. In putting forward what he terms a 'double structuration' process, Child (1997) explains how within organizations actors may seek to influence organizational design and in the process be informed or constrained by the existing structures and routines that they may wish to change. In addition to the cycle of 'inner structuration', Child (1997) also suggests the notion of 'outer structuration', where actors may seek to influence and interact with environmental elements, in which they are 'simultaneously informed of the opportunities for action which environmental conditions present and of the constraints which external circumstances place upon their room for action'.

In adopting a processual perspective on change, the essential position taken here is that there is a mutual shaping between the 'technical' and 'social' during the process of organizational change. It is claimed that political human action may reinforce and redefine certain structural features to service preferred design options. As such, political processes overlap and interlock with the substance of change and may serve to blur or recompose the structural arena in which decisions are made. The shaping and reshaping of structural arrangements or technology is as much a social process as it is a technical issue. The cases that follow thereby seek to demonstrate both the importance of substance to understanding processes of organizational change, and how the technical elements cannot simply be separated, identified and examined as discrete determinants of change. In these examples, the blurring of technology and organization was an essential part of the political process by which the new video conferencing technology and the cellular teamwork arrangements were negotiated and agreed.

The use of video conferencing systems at Shell UK Exploration and Production

In this case illustration, the substance of technology is used to examine the uptake and use of video conferencing systems in an oil company located in Aberdeen. The company, Shell Transport and Trading Company Limited, was created in 1897 as part of the new and expanding oil business. In 1907 the company merged with the Royal Dutch Petroleum Company, and the resultant multinational was structured so that the two companies would continue to operate as separate entities owned by shareholders in Britain and the Netherlands. The Royal Dutch/Shell Group is a major multinational corporation involved in oil and gas exploration and production through to refining, manufacturing and marketing of fuels and other products. Shell UK Exploration and Production (Shell Expro) was established to carry out operations in the North Sea, and following the 1966 discovery of the Leman field the company has grown to be one of the largest operators in the UK. The organization employs around 3,700 people, with approximately 1,000 of these based on offshore platforms. The main operational base is located in Aberdeen.

Video conferencing facilities have been available at all major Shell locations for almost ten years. However, these have remained under-used, with the utilization rate varying between 10 and 45 per cent of the working day. In 1997, a team from Commercial Procurement and the Information Systems (IS) department at Shell Expro was tasked with increasing the use of VCS within Expro. Initially they distributed a business travel questionnaire to determine people's travel routines and views on VCS facilities. One of the main findings of this survey was the need to improve video conferencing facilities by, for example, reducing voice delays, improving document sharing and providing maintenance support. As a result, funding was obtained from the executive leadership team to enhance the existing video conferencing suites to meet these user requirements. At the time of the study, the new equipment was installed in two sites. Equipment included a dual-screen PictureTel Group system with high quality visual and audio equipment to facilitate video conferencing between large groups. Other features of the system included:

- A sound-activated camera that can track the speaker in a room regardless of where he or she is situated.
- A dual screen that pictures the participants at both ends at the same

time. The screen can also be split to show a document or an object, along with the faces of the participants in the meeting.

- A remote controller that can be used to move the camera. The camera can zoom in on a single person, focus on a drawing on the wall, then back off and show the whole group once again.

The technology: understanding the substance of the change

Video-Conferencing Systems (VCS) provide an electronic form of on-line visual communication that enables remotely located individuals and groups to communicate with each other. Meetings can be arranged in which VCS provides the link for audio and visual communication across two or more geographical sites. However, this communication medium does not electronically replicate face-to-face interaction and nor is it fixed in terms of a number of determining characteristics. Different individuals and groups use and interpret the technology in a number of different ways. However this interpretative flexibility was constrained in this case through the use of outside consultants who trained Shell employees in the appropriate use of the technology. This training programme set about delineating a clear set of guidelines and a behavioural etiquette that employees should follow when using the technology. This structured training programme reflected the trainers' own assumptions about the technology and how it should be used 'appropriately' (for further discussion, see Panteli and Dawson, 2001).

In stressing the behavioural side of VCS communication, the spontaneous and creative aspects of group interaction were discouraged and a more highly formalized and structured approach to VCS group meetings was promoted. Through observing the training sessions and interviewing employees on two separate occasions, it is perhaps not surprising that the findings indicated that while this technology may be used to improve the efficiency of structured meetings that are dealing with routine, non-controversial information and well-defined issues, if applied indiscriminately it may blur non-verbal signals and impede unstructured interjections central to the communication dynamics required for more creative discussions of some problems and tasks. The findings from this research demonstrate how the choice of this communication medium depends on the level of interaction required at the different stages in the life cycle of a project. As one interviewee explained:

It's a lot less interactive and you might argue that it is socially not as rewarding, but nevertheless, if it's just to get through an agenda, then it's a lot more structured and to some extent a lot more formal, and the meetings take less time. I've been told that, you know, the meeting that used to take three hours; we're doing them in an hour now because there is none of the chitchat and distraction, and that happens a lot.

There was general agreement that VCS is a useful communication medium that can be used to present and share information across sites and to help maintain geographically distant contacts. On the flip side, concerns were raised about the ability of VCS to enrich conversations, in that the structured use of the medium tended to discourage participants from freely engaging in conversations with either local group members or individuals located at the remote site. For example, despite its audio and visual features (and hence its potential for promoting lively interactive discussions), in a VCS environment local site conversations, as well as sideways eye contact, are not only restricted but are also generally discouraged. Consequently, this formalized approach builds an environment that is more suitable for presentations and one-to-one communication rather than open interactive discussions and group communication. These findings highlight the need to question popular assumptions about VCS technology as well as those promoted by the suppliers of VCS. It certainly questions the appropriateness of VCS for all forms of multi-site meetings. It also demonstrates how the constraints of technology often reflect the assumptions of the powerful, whose voices are heard and accepted by others. In this sense, it is not the introduction of a predefined substance of change (in this case VCS) characterized by certain technical features that determines outcomes; rather it is managing change (changing established practices) and gaining acceptance regarding what technology can and cannot do and how the technology should and should not be used (appropriate employee behaviours) that constitutes the substance of change in the uptake and use of VCS.

Changing established working practices amongst an established body of staff does not occur overnight, but takes considerable time and requires the mobilization of a number of social drivers. Institutionalized practices regarding the running of project groups, the distribution of resources in the support of group meetings and the norms governing behaviour are all open to change through human action. Structural properties that set the context and medium within which change occurs can also be used and interpreted in a number of different ways, such as in setting agendas, justifying decisions, or supporting the views of certain powerful political groups. In the case of VCS, the training programme articulated an etiquette and set of procedures for running a VCS meeting. These rules, which were promoted to guide interaction, became part of the learned knowledge. The procedures governed behaviour in the management of VCS meetings, and in promoting a language and interpretative scheme for making sense of group interaction under such an environment, the dynamic interplay between agency and structure was put into motion. Orlikowski (1992) describes this reciprocal interaction between agency and structure in terms of a 'duality of technology', whereby structural constraints are not fixed but are open to reinterpretation within an ongoing political process. This is particularly noticeable in the case of physical machinery, where technical and engineering constraints may be presented as hard structural features that are not open to change. However, in this case the constraints of restructuring and technology were an integral part of a social process by which a particular view of the change was continually reaffirmed in action, words and training programmes. While there may be limits to choice, structural constraints are themselves open to interpretation and negotiation as part of an ongoing political process. In the company push for the substitution of face-to-face project meetings for VCS meetings, structures of authority (as a senior management initiative) and power (in the control over allocative resources) were drawn upon in limiting travel options (through a reduction in travel budgets) and promoting (through training and publicity) the uptake and use of VCS. Interestingly, although the technology could be used to improve the position of offshore workers (for example, in reducing their sense of isolation), the political agenda of the dominant actors was not supportive of such a use. Although employees could see the sense of using the technology in such a way, there were other elements in the political programme of change that prevented this outcome. In the sections that follow, the promotion of VCS by management and the uptake and use of the technology by employees are discussed. Attention is given to employee experience with using the technology, and their reflections on the social and technical aspects of VCS.

The promotion of VCS by management

Within Shell Expro, the formal project for the promotion of VCS covered a period of eight months from March 1998 until October 1998. During this period, a member of staff was appointed to lead the programme and to tackle the social and people issues behind the uptake and use of VCS. One of the main objectives of the project was to encourage greater employee use of VCS in order to reduce travel costs. (Interestingly, if the frequency of use of VCS increases substantially with confidence in the system, then the experience of Geo-Conference (as a service provider) suggests that VCS might in the longer term actually increase the geographical spread and frequency of meetings.) Within the culture of Shell Expro the opportunity to travel was an accepted practice for many staff, and in some cases company meetings were scheduled to dovetail with other social events. As one interviewee explained:

> You've got to understand that we've got an awful lot of people in this building who are based in the South of England or who are Dutch, and therefore a flight to either London or Schipol is bundled with a couple of days off or certainly a weekend. If you were in the same position you would make a similar decision – may I mention the Australian conference? It does a lot of good for people. It's part of the package in a way. They are happier to live in Aberdeen, which is not a top place to live in many people's perceptions, and that is what we are up against and it will take a lot to change that. But the driving forces are there. There are budgetary forces which I keep on mentioning. There's less and less excuse to exclude video-conferencing because of technical incompetence. There's more of your peers showing enthusiasm for it and there is a bit of a corporate drive.

The processual fieldwork covered the life of the project from the initial training programme through to the transfer of the programme leader to another department. At the outset there was considerable promotion of VCS through emails, leaflets and posters, and through the distribution of personalized invitations. Throughout the training programme, the video conferencing suite was booked and trainees had easy access to the equipment. However, owing to the limited availability of equipment (at the time of the study there was only one suite at one of the main locations, although another was being planned), some employees found it difficult to gain access to the suite to conduct a virtual meeting. In fact, this was one of the most commonly identified deterrents mentioned by those interviewed during the study. Employee use of VCS was also on a voluntary basis, although, with the shifting price of oil and growing constraints on operating budgets, many interviewees anticipated that a more directive stance might emerge in the future. In practice, it is likely to be a combination of social, technical and commercial drivers that influences the uptake and use of VCS by employees. As one interviewee suggested:

> We've got the trained people there. We've got people talking to each other enthusiastically about it. We've got budget cuts. Although the London closure does not affect things, outside of that, *inter alia*, we should see growing use of it by the enthusiasts as well as the people who've been told 'I'm simply not happy you taking that flight for that particular meeting'.

Under the project structure, the IT department maintained responsibility for the technical aspects of VCS while coordination of training with the Fifth Business company and the promotion campaign was managed separately. As one interviewee explained:

> The service responsibility never left the IT department and it will remain there. So there is a manager who is in charge of video-conferencing. However, being an IT department his responsibilities all centred on the technical aspects of the job. One of the reasons we took the campaign out of the IT department's hands – and caused some frustration no doubt – is that we needed to look at people issues and take a broader perspective.

Employee experience of using VCS: first-phase interviews

Employee experience of using VCS varied among the group studied, ranging from those who had limited experience with the technology (up to a dozen or so times) to those who had no previous experience. In this regard, the technology represented a new electronic communication medium for employees to use. Generally, employees viewed VCS as a more impersonal form of communication that had the possible benefit of offering a more structured approach to meetings. For many users, the question of the appropriateness of VCS to different types of meetings was given serious attention. As one interviewee commented:

> If we need to meet somebody who's in another part of the world, how do we assess, how are people going to assess, is it necessary to meet face-to-face or as a video conference? I do feel that if you want to, if you want to get some of this chemistry going or you want to start to develop a rapport with people, I don't think that you are going to get that in a video conference.

In another case recounted by the interviewee, where there was a straightforward presentation with a clear deliverable, VCS was deemed to be highly appropriate as an effective communication medium. The nature of the project, the content of the material for the meeting and the extent to which the conference necessitated the development of new relationships, were all seen to be factors that should influence any assessment of the appropriateness of VCS. For example, if a new project is initiated then the need for face-to-face communication in the building of rapport and the development of social relations may prove central during these early stages. Once relations have become established and the parameters of the project more clearly defined, then VCS may provide a powerful communication medium in allowing quick access to geographically dispersed project team members. Some interviewees also argued that while VCS could not capture the social nuances visible in face-to-face forms of communication, it does add a visual dimension to communication that is not present with audio conference technology or the asynchronous email transmissions:

> Well, you would certainly get some of the body language, I mean we talked before about developing this rapport and maybe that's not the same as face-to-face. But having said that, you can gain a little bit more, certainly there's an extra dimension there in the visual dimension of seeing what the person is actually coming across with when they're making their statements . . . It's easier to talk around a diagram or to doodle on something rather than try and convey all this in words. You can actually do that in a video conference.

The visual dimension in terms of seeing people's reactions and in being able to work around a particular chart or diagram was seen as a major advantage of VCS over others forms of electronic-mediated communication. Unlike an audio conference, with video technology individual contributions can be captured through visual representations (such as changes to charts, the re-sequencing of activities and so forth). This visual feedback to participants may encourage a higher level of interaction and improve the communication flows within a teleconferencing setting. As one employee explained:

> If you get any operational or geological problems, you can get your counterparts (wherever they are) and show them physically what you've got without them having to come over at very short notice. I think that is a very very strong point with the technology.

In the case of Shell Expro, a number of interviewees indicated that there could be greater use of VCS between onshore and offshore activities. It was argued that employees working offshore can feel isolated and would often like more support and input from the onshore base. It was also suggested that with 'globalization' more and more business is being conducted outside of Aberdeen, and that this tendency to do business overseas would increase the opportunities for the uptake and use of VCS technology. In this sense, although reduction in travel budgets was viewed as a major objective behind the promotion of VCS, users of the technology generally viewed VCS as an additional communication tool that is unlikely to bring about a significant reduction in travel even though the actual uptake and use of VCS is likely to increase significantly over the coming years.

> At this stage you need to recognize that it's not a panacea for everything and it's not quite as simple as it may sound . . . For people who are demanded to travel a lot and if that demand is difficult on them, I don't think those people will find any waning off as they'll see it as a serious alternative, that's not an issue. But there's some people who don't travel very often and who will take the opportunity to travel, jump at it and you won't convince them to use video-conferencing instead of getting some air miles or a night away or whatever. What I see as kind of a third area, which is where we use techniques, probably telephone basically or email and the gain of it is not, if you like, some offset in terms of travel gain or other gain, but it is some enhanced value which you got out of having a video conference.

In practice, however, difficulties were encountered in trying to set up video conferencing meetings. First there was the task of getting a geographically dispersed group of people to agree on the time of a meeting, and then, if a video suite was already booked, there was the need to repeat the process a number of times. This was a frustrating and time-consuming task that deterred some interviewees from suggesting VCS as an alternative to a face-to-face meeting.

Employee experience of using VCS: second-phase interviews

Once again, there were a variety of different experiences among the interviewees, ranging from those who had engaged in video conferencing meetings to those who had not had any opportunity to use the technology in which they had been trained. Many of the issues identified in the first phase of interviewing resurfaced during discussions on the uptake and use of VCS in the intervening period. As one interviewee recalled:

> Since we last spoke I have had the opportunity for four video
> conference sessions since then. So not a huge amount, it is not as if it
> has become a new tool with which we are doing business on a day-to-
> day basis. That doesn't mean to say that we are under-utilizing it, but
> there is still some difficulty in being able to use it when you want to
> use it, because you need to book it in, arrange people to get together,
> and I can think of a couple of times when we've resorted to an audio-
> conference.

In the majority of cases where VCS was used, it was for follow-up
meetings within established projects. It was stressed that a decision still
had to be made on whether to hold a video conference meeting or a
traditional face-to-face meeting, and that this often reflected group
decision-making. For example, if a video conferencing meeting was put
forward then it would often depend on how other participants responded
to the suggestion. In other words, there are no clearly articulated criteria
under which a video conferencing meeting is deemed more appropriate
than a face-to-face meeting; rather, these tend to occur in response to the
views and representations of the various participants. Again, the issue of
whether new relationships were being formed or not emerged as an
influencing factor. As one interviewee indicated, after the establishment
of a longer-term project between London, Manchester and Aberdeen, it
was decided that the next meeting should be with the use of video
conferencing technology:

> This week we've got plans to have a meeting which we've had a
> series of every six months. We've had three of them to date: one in
> Manchester, one in London and one in Aberdeen. The next one we're
> having is going to be by video conference, so we've established
> enough of the ground rules to be able to get an update meeting with
> the use of video conference.

In the case above, there were two people located in each of the locations
and the intention was to provide a general update on how things were
progressing, with a response from the other participants. It was
anticipated that the use of VCS might stimulate further usage during the
life of the project.

In setting out the facility for a video conference, one interviewee
recounted an experience where not every member was visible on the
screen. In this case those sitting on the side of the table could not be
identified, and it was argued that this impaired the process of
communication and dialogue within the meeting. This experience would
suggest that an important element of video conferencing is the

visualization of all the participants. If users are unable to see other participants, then it may severely limit the effective use of the technology. It was argued that if you were not familiar with the position and role of the various participants then it could be very difficult, if not impossible, to contextualize the contributions made by these individuals during the meeting. The structure and formality that accompanied a video conference meeting was seen to highlight the need for pre-established relationships:

> It creates an air of formality. There is always a degree of 'check before we start the meeting' . . . Certainly the video-conference, and a recognition that you're on the air now, does create a very business-like atmosphere. Maybe we waste too much time over the social interlude, maybe there's a place for both. That's what underlies why we say you establish the rapport and so on, and then you're happier and you're being equally efficient in being purely business-like and stick to the topic and map your way through it and that only.

Questions regarding the social use of the technology, to facilitate greater communication between offshore and onshore staff and to enable employees located offshore to have greater access to technology that improves communication with their families, were seen to be outside of the scope of the VCS programme. In concluding, one interviewee summarized the project as follows:

> The project completed the training by mid-June, with 120-odd individuals taking up training and attending half-hour sessions arranged by Fifth Business. That represented about 15 per cent take-up, which is a record for voluntary training. We did get a very strong response from people who do a lot of travelling and we evoked genuine interest from people who had a dormant interest – it became active. We probably on anecdotal evidence were not very successful in stimulating interest in people to whom video conferencing was a no-no. With a voluntary campaign you cannot reach that level of penetration with your market really, that would have been extremely difficult. Since then, we've run out of video-conferencing space and we have 500 people further to train, if we can get another video conferencing suite installed here. I understand that this is on the schedule, but then whether the training budget will still be available is another issue.

Epilogue: the future of VCS at Shell Expro

Although the immediate development of VCS is unlikely, the use of this technology as a tool for communication is likely to increase significantly over the coming years. With the decline in oil prices and the closure of Shell Expro's main London operations with the transfer of over 200 staff to Aberdeen, there may be less travelling between London and Aberdeen but there is also likely to be more communication on a global scale. There will be greater reliance on advice from Holland and from contacts in other parts of the world. As a core base, Aberdeen may seek to upgrade its communication systems to facilitate networked projects with other operations scattered around the world. With the concentration of exploration and production staff in Aberdeen, the costs and timescale involved in travelling longer distances may question the viability of face-to-face meetings and stimulate the further uptake and use of VCS.

Technical reconfiguration of work: the case of Britax Rainsfords South Australia

Britax Rainsfords is located in Lonsdale, South Australia, and is part of the Britax Automotive Components Division, a global manufacturing operation (with locations in America, UK, France and India) that manufactures fuel filler caps, lighting equipment, electrical components and rear vision systems for the automotive market. It produces over thirteen million exterior mirrors annually, and services a range of customers (including Ford, General Motors, Toyota, Mitsubishi, Renault and Volkswagen), capturing approximately 13 per cent of the world market.

Britax Rainsfords designs and tests rear-view mirrors, and approved products are then manufactured and supplied to customers. It is the single supplier in the Australian automotive market (100 per cent of the market, which accounts for over 300,000 domestic exterior vehicle sets per annum). In addition, it exports over 850,000 exterior mirror sets per annum and in 1998 supplied 2,429,000 passenger mirrors to the world market. The manufacturing plant covers an area of 13,800 square metres, and in 1998 employed nearly 600 people (331 direct personnel and 264 indirect personnel). The plant comprises injection moulding equipment (there are forty-four injection moulding machines), a fully automated robotic paint facility with a computerized inspection and recording system, a motor mechanism section with a potential capacity of one million mechanisms per month; and mirror assembly. Motor mechanism operates three transfer assembly lines and four work cells, while mirror assembly operates, four transfer assembly lines and four work cells.

The introduction of cellular work arrangements

In response to customer demands for more complex products (in the range of glass and type of glass, colour spectrum, and the need to service left-hand and right-hand drive vehicles), existing arrangements suitable for the manufacture of a single high-volume product were no longer deemed appropriate. Cellular work arrangements had been shown to be commercially viable by their sister company in the UK, and hence it was decided that local management should examine the possibility of adopting the cell concept in their Australian operations. Over a nine-month period during 1996, engineers were sent over to the UK and an initial experiment in the setting up of cell manufacture was introduced into the plant in South Australia. The change was viewed as successful from the outset. From the viewpoint of the plant manager, the main benefits were savings on people; it became more efficient as a process (more value-added per person), the plant was able to cut-down on stock, and yet it was still getting the same volume out. One major advantage was that the cell could be run with only four people whereas the line required between six and eight. Furthermore, if volume increased it was possible to add one or two extra employees to the cell and by so doing raise output to meet increasing customer demands. The new cell form of work organization proved to be a far more flexible system for meeting the changing requirements of the automotive market. As described by one interviewee:

> The UK had been doing it for a while. We could see the benefits, the way they could do fairly rapid changeovers, minimal stock. In fact, what they are building today went into our warehouse and was effectively gone that same day. It was shipped to Toyota effectively the same day. So you are really making today what Toyota are using tomorrow. It was that close. It was so very tight that obviously you had no stock within the system and the benefits cost-wise were there. So we sent a couple of engineers over to work with the UK group. There was a specialist in the UK who had developed this system and grown with the Toyota people and he became their plant expert. So we sent engineers over to work with him for a couple of weeks to

> understand the principles of what you did, why you did it, how you
> did it. Then we brought that back and decided that we would try the
> process on a line that was already running, which was a Suzuki line.

In identifying staff to go into the new cell, those picked were ones seen
as being the 'best multi-skilled' employees (those cross-trained in all
operations) who were also willing to be flexible in moving between cell
tasks as required. During the early period of change, there were some
problems with a supervisor, but this person was simply replaced with
someone who was seen to be more open and not tied to any traditional
operating culture. Local managers were aware of the political
significance of ensuring that the system was 'successful'. It had worked
in the UK, and there was a perceived need to show that the system could
operate efficiently in the Australian context, and that it could be modified
and adapted in a way that improved the system as a whole. In particular,
the Project Manager knew that it was important for his own career
agenda to succeed in this change initiative and to be able to demonstrate
and report this achievement to the Manufacturing Director and the
Managing Director of the company. On this count it was noted that:

> We don't just copy we try to improve on what we see. The UK system
> used a slightly different system to what we use and because it was a
> UK system we Australianized it . . . The next project that we decided
> to address cells with was the Holden and Toyota contract, which are
> the most complicated products that we have, not only in the way it is
> assembled but also by the fact of its diversity.

In progressing with the use of multi-skilled teams within cellular work
arrangements, the company shifted from a more traditional form of
work organization with a fairly simple product to a more complex
operating situation. In this example, the cell had to be very flexible in
being able to accommodate frequent rapid changeover, not only from
product to product (in having two customers) but also in being able to
deal with all the variations associated with each product. In 1997, a lot
of time and effort was put into developing the equipment and planning
a fairly simple cell layout. The cell equipment was designed and
developed in-house, and was then either manufactured internally or
contracted out to other firms. All the programming was done internally so
that there was no dependence on external expertise (it was viewed as
essential to have access to this knowledge within the company in case of
problems or breakdowns). The new cell arrangements were implemented
in 1998, and the change programme has been ongoing for a number of
years.

In the search for improvements in cell design, the Australian team reduced the size of cells and are now looking at the possibility of having two U-shaped cells facing each other with one line-leader in overall charge of cell operations. Between the line-leaders and the local manager there are a number of roving supervisors, who wander throughout the facility dealing with unforeseen events (whether of a technical or human nature) and checking that the system is operating efficiently. Their main role is as problem-solvers and system checkers in ensuring the smooth running of the manufacturing facility. In reflecting on the change in supervision, it was argued that there is now a need for a broader understanding of the operating system. Today, there are fewer supervisors with a wider area of control responsibility:

> In the old traditional days you had supervisors who were effectively on the line and in the line. I guess moving to the next level it allows supervisors to cover a wider area. You know, just checking all of the systems and knocking roadblocks down, if there are any roadblocks. And doing a lot of the non-valued activities but not directly affecting the lines. Effectively, I guess, she (referring to a supervisor) is the bee to the flower. Then all the line people have to worry about is their patch.

It was argued that in the past leading hands were very focussed on their particular area of responsibility, whereas today line-leaders have a broader range of skills and understanding that goes beyond the cells and includes an understanding of how their operations link with the broader system. They are also aware of how the company and corporation is doing and show a greater interest in commercial aspects outside of their own domain. Prior to the change to cellular layout, there was a line-leader within each unit. Currently, there are two line-leaders who are in charge of more than one cell. The intention is to get the U-shaped cells facing each other so that there is one line-leader per two cells. Essentially, line-leaders are direct operators responsible for allocating work within the cells, working out the runs for the day, recording production data and keeping track of how the cells are operating (such as efficiency levels, scrap and absenteeism). Although performance information is available in the cells, the local manager also runs communication sessions where he informs employees how things are going.

Social resistance to technical constraints: the human dimension to substance

In support of the findings on change elsewhere, there are a number of outstanding and emerging human resource issues that remain central to the change process. For example, it has been found that some individuals are not well suited to team working and are finding the new work arrangements difficult to accept. Linked to this has been the 'challenge' of getting employees to accept the concept of cells. As one interviewee commented:

> A lot of the people come off the Bosch line and they still can't see the concept, they say 'why are we in a cell when we used to make more per hour on a Bosch line?'. But they don't see the advantages of flexibility when production numbers vary. They are starting to see why that is. But with the line the flexibility wasn't there. Before we used to make as much as we could to fill the store up.

Another change required by the cell system is the need to take greater responsibility over the pace and pattern of work. Under the line-conveyor system the machinery of production dictates the progress of work, but under cellular work arrangements individuals are part of a team in securing performance targets within broader time-frames. Teams are aware of the work that should be done and they also know that their performance will be monitored and evaluated in terms of the group rather than the individual. Under these conditions, the pressures to perform come from within the group and are not pre-determined by the technology of the line. However, this pressure to conform to group norms and meet expected performance targets also raises a number of internal tensions. As a production engineer pointed out:

> People in the cell know that there is a certain amount that they have to produce in a half-an-hour space of time. If you got two people who want to do it and there's a third person that doesn't want to do it, you can guarantee these two people are going to drive that person to get him up to that level.

The general view from those interviewed was that there is a lot more peer pressure under cellular work arrangements. Working within a team is not necessarily a good environment for all employees. It was claimed that just as some people are more interested in team sports and others in individual sports, so it is with the new teamwork arrangements. Under these changed circumstances there are therefore casualties; employees who find the new working conditions uncomfortable and difficult.

Nevertheless, it was noted that there are always tasks within the sector that are less team-based:

> There is a lot more peer pressure. Some people don't fit and you have to make the hard decision. And they can admit that they don't fit with this process. And so you find other work for them where it is not so group-dependent.

With between 20 and 25 per cent contract labour, permanent jobs are viewed locally as premium employment and hence employees in these jobs are reluctant to admit to difficulties that they perceive may threaten their position within the company. Economic fluctuations in the level of activity within the automotive industry do create a less stable environment in which contract staff are keen to show commitment, and over time they would expect such loyalty to be rewarded with the offer of a more permanent position. In terms of trade unions, there have been no major industrial disputes at the company for a number of years. The trade unions have been kept informed about change, the reason for change and the expected outcomes. From the perspective of management, the way ahead is clear; there is no choice, they must adapt or else jobs are on the line. The aim is to develop the cells further and to use pre-production builds to get employees involved in the design of work operations. The suggestions made by employees are tried and tested (often through the use of cardboard engineering), where temporary changes are implemented and problems identified. The quick response to employee suggestions is seen as critical to gaining employee commitment to the change initiative and taking ownership over the new forms of work organization. Although as one manager commented, they would probably achieve the necessary changes by stealth:

> They now know that all new lines and product groups are going to be produced on these cells. There it is. It's there in front of you. Particularly when the old Bosch lines die, there is no choice. You choose to adapt or you choose not to. There are only so many sub-assembly processes which can absorb some of these people. I'm not saying that all the people in sub-assembly are resisters by any means. But it is going to get to a stage where you as an individual either go with the flow or you've got to get off. You know, it's a fact of life. You either adapt to change or you fall by the wayside.

Substance and change at Britax Rainsfords

Unlike the team-based initiatives of the 1970s, there is now greater strategic importance placed on the use of work teams in organizations (Buchanan, 1994; Proctor and Mueller, 2000) and in particular on the use of team-based cellular manufacturing (Badham *et al.*, 1997; Venugopal *et al.*, 2001). Under these new team arrangements, greater responsibilities for operational decisions are devolved to teams, supervision is redefined, and job tasks are allocated and often rotated within the new team structures. However, as Baldry *et al.* (1998) have also argued, some employees may find team-based structures no less coercive than the individual-based work regimes that they replace. In this case, the uptake of cellular work arrangements was decided by management and involved little consultation with and participation by shop-floor employees. From the outset, the programme of change was viewed as a technical solution to the increased demand for more customized and complex products that would also further the strategic competitive position of the company in the manufacture and supply of automotive mirrors. Engineers were sent overseas to gain the necessary knowledge to implement cell-based production, and on setting up cellular work arrangements, employees were handpicked by management. Any employees who did not fit in were replaced (there was no consideration of their concerns or views), as 'success' was viewed by the Project Manager as critical to his own future career within the company. The increased peer pressure of teamwork, and employee preference for more individual forms of work organization, was not accommodated within the new shop-floor production design. Although there is still some work in spare-part production, many employees who shifted into these positions felt sidelined and marginalized. Management adopted an 'automate or liquidate' approach (see McLoughlin and Clark, 1988: 2), arguing that in order to remain commercially successful technical reconfiguration of production was essential. To use a social construction of a technology term, there was 'closure' on the new design with room for only minor modifications in response to the cardboard engineering exercise. In other words, the design constraints were not determined by the technology but by a political process in which the views and assumptions of management predominated shop-floor redesign. In this case, the local management team conveyed a fairly rigid and predetermined position on technology in order to influence employee views through limiting their interpretations of possible choices and options. Ironically, this projected rigidity was legitimized through the need for greater production flexibility to meet changing customer demands for more sophisticated and customized products. Consequently, this case also demonstrates how the substance of change was purposefully managed through a political process that sought certain preferred outcomes over others.

Conclusion

This chapter has set out to illustrate both the importance of substance in understanding the change process and the way that the rigidity and flexibility of interpretations are less a reflection of technical determinants and more a consequence of social action and political process. For example, the Shell case provides a useful demonstration of how the shaping and reshaping of the substance of change (in this instance VCS technology) involves interaction between conceptions of technology, the structural features of an organization and political processes as part of an ongoing social dynamic. While human action is enabled and constrained by structures, these rules and resources are the consequence of previous actions. Action is situated, in this case, in our oil company, and employees using VCS are able to reflect on what they are doing while they are doing it, and articulate their experiences to others. However, there can also be unintended consequences of action and problems in articulating the more unconscious elements involved. Some aspects of the process, while not articulated (for example, tacit knowledge), might nevertheless through action create and sustain practices that eventually become institutionalized and in so doing become part of the structural property of organizations. In this sense there is a duality of mutual interaction between agency and structure that is ongoing, and although at times structural elements may appear solid and unyielding, this appearance is a consequence of the reciprocal interaction that ultimately highlights the social nature of this process.

In the case of Rainsfords, the rigidity of interpretation was a process managed by management to ensure acceptance by employees of the new workplace arrangements. This position was further supported by a stance that stressed the commercial necessity of change in order to sustain competitive advantage. In this sense, there was an attempt to raise the perceived centrality of the change by stressing the criticality of the new work arrangements to the future survival of the company. Unlike the GM case in Chapter 4, employees did not endorse this view and were sceptical about such claims given their dominance within the Australian market place. The Project Manager was nevertheless highly motivated to ensure that the change programme was 'successful', and he was aware of the consequences of 'failure' for future career opportunities. Those employees who resisted change or questioned the new work arrangements found that they were sidelined and/or displaced. In this example, competing and alternative interpretations of technology were constrained as part of the political process of shop-floor change.

In both examples, the substance of change was used to shape the process and outcomes of change. It acted as a powerful vehicle for promoting preferred options in a 'neutral' fashion, even though the process was politically charged and shaped by a range of competing views and assumptions. In the case of Rainsfords, management provided little opportunity for employees to participate in discussions over the redesign of work arrangements. They defined the change as a technical and engineering programme that was not open to interpretative debate. In Shell, the relationship between the differing vested interest groups was less clear. Management were concerned with reducing the high costs of travel, the training consultants had a particular view regarding the way the technology should be used (captured in the VCS etiquette), and the experiences of the different users of the system reflected contextual and social issues as much as the technical considerations associated with using VCS. In these, as in other case examples in this book, even when the substance of change may appear fixed and determined, this lack of interpretative flexibility is not structurally determined but is part of the political process of change. As with the other main elements of a processual perspective, the substance of change overlaps and interacts with political process and context in the shaping and reshaping of organizational change.

6 Conceptualizing processual research: methodological orientation and the design of longitudinal studies

- The growing popularity of processual research
- Processual research: in search of knowledge
- Putting in the time: the design and practice of longitudinal research
- Conclusion

In the next three chapters we turn our attention to the theory and practice of doing processual research and the nature of data analysis in the presentation and publication of case study data. No attempt is made to provide an inclusive definitive account of how research should be conducted and data analysed; rather, the chapters provide a reflection – from over 20 years of studying change in four different countries – on the practice of doing processual research in organizations. A number of practical issues that can influence research design and fieldwork schedules are discussed, ranging from problems of access and constraints on researcher time through to funding issues and geographical logistics. In this chapter, the main focus is on the methodological orientation of processual research and, in particular, its contribution to knowledge. In Chapter 7, the need to gain fieldwork experience, methods of data collection and the task of data analysis are all discussed. Chapter 8 examines the future development of the processual perspective in an evaluation of the way data are used in case study publications, and provides a critique of some of the more recent attempts to combine a processual approach with more quantitative studies. A call is made to maintain the integrity of the qualitative longitudinal case study in capturing the multiple narratives and competing histories of change.

The growing popularity of processual research

In Europe and, to a lesser extent, in North America, Canada, Australia and New Zealand, there are growing numbers of academics who are embracing the value of processual research for understanding management and organizations (Pettigrew *et al.*, 1992; Van de Ven and Poole, 1995; Harrison and Samson, 1997; Ropo *et al.*, 1997a; Collins, 1998a; Langley, 1999; Preece *et al.*, 1999). In the case of organizational change, the process of transition is generally studied over time and within an historical and organizational context (Pettigrew, 1987a). The approach is often multi-disciplinary (Clark *et al.*, 1988), drawing on a range of perspectives and methods such as those applied by the business historian, the corporate strategist and organization theorist (Whipp *et al.*, 1987), and centres on the collection of longitudinal data over periods of real and retrospective time (Pettigrew, 1985).

With the growth in academic interest in processual research and the publication of associated case studies, the value of processual approaches to understanding the dynamics of organizational change is gaining increasing recognition (Van de Ven and Huber, 1990; Hinings, 1997; Ropo *et al.*, 1997a). They highlight the importance of context in examining unfolding processes of change, yet, unlike contingency models, they are not drawn towards unidirectional episodic theories of change (Dawson, 1996: 21–29). Detailed examinations are made of one or a small number of organizations, and considerable time and attention is spent on the processual analysis of what are largely qualitative data (Pettigrew, 1985; Clark *et al.*, 1988; Dawson, 1994, 2003; Preece *et al.*, 1999). Concepts and ideas are formulated from the literature and from data-driven induction. There is no attempt to build grand theory, nor is there a removal of preconceptualization, as suggested by some elements of grounded theory (see Parry, 1996: 23–25). Under the processual approach, there is a continuous interplay between academic preconceptualization (based on a comprehensive knowledge of the area under study) and detailed empirical descriptions of emerging themes and topics, out of which new concepts are refined and interpretations developed.

As 'real-world' examples of company experience, processual case studies are able to tell their own story of the way change unfolds in practice, and how the substance, context and politics of change all interconnect and overlap in shaping the dynamic odyssey of workplace change. As such, processual research offers the possibility for widening our interpretations through enabling the presentation of complex change data. Although to predict the process and outcomes of large-scale change accurately is to foresee the future (something that is beyond the scope of processual analysis), this type of research can question many of the taken-for-granted assumptions about change and allow us to see issues that have previously remained hidden.

This chapter opens by contrasting the theoretical and methodological orientation of processual research with more quantitative scientific approaches to the study of organizations. The meaning of the term 'processual research' is explained, and the use of the concept 'processual' is compared across theoretical developments in organization studies and archaeology. By then turning attention to the practice of conducting processual research, some of the key elements that need to be considered in the design of longitudinal field research are discussed (see Chapter 7 for an exposition of data collection techniques and processual analysis). In an examination of longitudinal designs, my own experiences are drawn upon to illustrate points raised and to clarify the 'realities' of carrying out this type of processual research. It is hoped that the material presented provides some rich description and useful insights into the practice of conducting longitudinal case studies on organizational change.

Processual research: in search of knowledge

At the outset, it is worth clarifying the place of processual research within the broader epistemological debates on knowledge acquisition. For example, is knowledge something that should be verifiable through applying the scientific method of observing and measuring phenomena that are separate and independent of our subjective ideas? Or are subjective ideas the way in which individuals make sense of, and experience, the world? If we believe that the way of knowing (epistemology) is through questions that objectify concepts (a positivist approach), then we will adopt a scientific research design to our studies. However, if we believe that knowledge of people's experiences of change can only be achieved through questions that examine the meanings and interpretations of people in their social context and over time (a processual approach), then we will be more interested in a non-scientific qualitative approach to our research. In considering these issues, there are three key questions that we need to address:

1 What do we understand by the term processual research?
2 How does it compare and contrast with a scientific approach to the study of organizations?
3 Is the processual concept commonly used across disciplines, or does it have different meanings in different areas of study?

The empirical-based chapters should already have provided the reader with illustrations of the rich data that can be generated from processual research. The case studies of Pirelli, Shell, Britax and General Motors all highlight the value of qualitative data for understanding the dynamic and murky processes of change. These studies are interested in the beliefs and attitudes of people in organizations in order to capture their experiences and views of the world. As such, processual research rejects the scientific focus on objectivity and the search for universal laws. Rather, the processual researcher maintains a close engagement with data during fieldwork activities and is never entirely absent from the process of data analysis. This dynamic inductive–deductive interplay highlights how, unlike in a positivist view of science, there is never a clear division between data and theory. As Pettigrew (1997: 344) reflects:

> It is in this constantly iterating cycle of deduction and induction that the real creative process of the research takes place. My experience of doing this in many studies, and observing many colleagues and doctoral students engaging in the process, is that the creative challenges very quickly expose big differences in conceptual ability, capacity to inductively recognise patterns in data and, of course, skill and perspective in the process of data collection itself. On top of these critical factors, writing skill also becomes crucial in representing patterns identified in the research process.

Through attempts to make sense of the data and reflect the meanings and experience of others, the processual researcher must inevitably engage in a form of empathetic thinking. In trying to see the world through the eyes of certain individuals and groups the researcher is not passive but active in the construction of post-analytical descriptions of complex meanings and positions (for a further discussion, see Chapters 7 and 8). A difficulty with this type of research is how to convey dynamic complexity and contextual movements in a way that remains accessible and understandable to the reader and yet still conveys the processual character of the study. The essential aim is to examine the whole picture over time as a dynamic tapestry, with competing histories, future trajectories and ongoing multiple narratives of change.

In attempting to interpret and assign meanings to people's experiences, the main methodological focus of processual research is on in-depth qualitative research rather than any reliance on quantitative data techniques. According to Felstead (1979), the quantitative approach uses a fundamentally different framework to qualitative research for evaluating acceptable knowledge. Quantitative data are often associated with 'science', and are seen to be systematically rigorous and reliable. They adopt an epistemological stance that true knowledge can only be obtained in the pursuit of science, and hence automatically discredit and devalue research that actively engages in the subjective and non-scientific world of the actors' interpretation.

In their book *Understanding Management Research*, Johnson and Duberly (2000: 1) stress the importance of these epistemological differences and state that:

> How we come to ask particular questions, how we assess the relevance and value of different research methodologies so that we can investigate those questions, how we can evaluate the outputs of research, all express and vary according to our underlying epistemological commitments.

On this count, one of the most common distinctions between philosophies of research is that between positivism and interpretive research (Easterby-Smith *et al.*, 2001). Essentially, a positivist approach would 'assume that the research method of the natural sciences ... can be applied unproblematically to the study of social phenomena' (Riley *et al.*, 2000: 10). In contrast, interpretive or 'phenomenological' research is interested in the way in which individuals and groups interpret and shape social processes in the ongoing construction of shared meanings and individual experience. As such, they adopt a more qualitative methodological approach in the study of social processes. From the qualitative camp, the main criticism levelled against a quantitative approach to the study of society is that the research methods produce superficial data and may result in the complete physical separation of the researcher from the field they are studying (Whyte, 1984: 267; Bryman, 1988a: 104). While quantitative analyses of existing survey data can be used to uncover changing relationships and stimulate healthy academic debate (see, for example, De Vaus, 2001; Creswell, 2002), this method can also be used as a way of achieving the 'fastthesis', with little concern for the origination of the data or the research process. For example, with developments in communication and information technologies, Whyte notes that the quantitative approach to original research is being discredited through increasing academic awareness of the popular modern method for doing doctoral theses, which is to get hold of some existing (computer-readable) data, to devise some hypotheses, to test these with the use of some sophisticated statistical techniques, and then to write up the findings as a thesis (Whyte, 1984: 267). In this example, the intention is not to devalue quantitative methodologies but to illustrate how the application of the scientific model does not by itself increase our stock of knowledge, and that it can be used as a means for masking poor research. It is not therefore a question of which approach is adopted, but of how it is used in practice.

For strong advocates of the scientific approach, qualitative research has been described as having limited generality, being subjective, unscientific, and 'soft'. Whilst qualitative researchers have not proven to be so vocal in their criticisms of quantitative methods, Whyte suggests that this may largely be a reflection of the powerful influence of physics as *the* model for social scientists to follow (Whyte, 1984: 266). He describes his early research years as being a period of guilt for violating scientific rules, and pleasure for learning about social processes through transgression.

Although in the twenty-first century these epistemological differences remain, what is different is that an increasing number of researchers are more interested in using the appropriate 'tools' to tackle a research problem, rather than maintenance of a preconceived set of assumptions about how the world operates. In this sense, there is a considerable amount of exploratory and innovative research being carried out that is more concerned with overcoming technical problems than winning epistemological points. For example, Bryman (1988b: 17) notes that:

> By and large, the broader epistemological issues of positivism versus phenomenology in the social sciences, which have underpinned many renditions of the debate about quantitative and qualitative research, are absent in spite of various attempts to inject them into the study of organizations.

Similarly, Silverman argues that it is not a choice between polar opposites, but rather a decision about balance in intellectual breadth and rigour (Silverman, 1985: 17). Thus, the agenda appears set for greater communication and understanding of the value of quantitative and qualitative approaches to social research (see also Creswell, 2002). Although the empirical data presented in this book are based on qualitative longitudinal research, they reject neither the use of quantitative methodologies (for example, a quantitative approach may be required for the purpose of identifying the diffusion of robotic technology in the automotive industry compared with other areas of manufacturing), nor the value and significance of qualitative methodologies for understanding the complex processes associated with change. Moreover, what is published in journals and what takes place in the field are often worlds apart, making it difficult for the new researcher to learn from published material. For the quantitative researcher the world is more clearly defined and the methods well documented, the biggest problem being whether the issue lends itself to 'scientific' inquiry. For the processual researcher, everything is grey, ambiguous, and at times 'spiritual', with the biggest problem being how to make sense of the data and find a suitable outlet for publication. There is, however, a very simple lesson to be learnt from each perspective, namely, that there is nothing intrinsically wrong with quantification or with phenomena that cannot be explained quantitatively. As Bryman (1988a: 170) has suggested, 'the two research traditions can be viewed as contributing to the understanding of different aspects of the phenomenon in question'. He uses the example of social mobility to substantiate his claim, arguing that quantitative studies contribute to our understanding of rates and patterns of social mobility, whereas in-depth qualitative research of particular institutions (for example, schools) would be needed to identify the processes associated with the perpetuation of the class system (Bryman, 1988a: 170). We can therefore see the complementarity of quantitative and qualitative approaches and how they can be applied to various other areas of research, such as unemployment, where we may be concerned with both the rates and patterns of change (quantitative dimension) and what unemployment means for the unemployed and other household members (qualitative dimension). Moreover, some topics (such as the changing structure of employment) lend themselves to a quantitative classificatory methodology; others, such as documenting the complex and dynamic processes associated with major organizational change programmes, require a more qualitative approach.

In addressing our final question on whether processual research means the same across disciplines, it is interesting to note how similar developments and labels have been used very differently in the field of archaeology (Johnson, 1999). For example, within archaeological theory the processual perspective developed in the 1960s as a scientific approach that sought to deal with multiple changing variables. Unlike the processual perspective discussed in this book, processual archaeologists adopted a systems theory that is more appropriately linked to a positivist epistemology in the use of statistics to control for biases. Following the work of Ian Hodder (1982, 1986) and the birth of post-processualism, this search for the 'truth' is no longer so fashionable in archaeology. Post-processualists generally take the view that data are always theory-laden and reject the scientific (hypothetico–deductive–nomological) model of hypothesis testing. In his book *Fragmentation in Archaeology*, Chapman (2000) uses a post-processual approach in drawing out the social aspects of culture, arguing for the need to accept alternative non-western explanations from different times and cultures. Similarly, our processual perspective on organizational change calls for a recognition that:

1 Individual experience may be reshaped within a group context.
2 Different groups may generate different stories on change.
3 There are consequently multiple voices and different experiences of change.
4 Change stories are often rewritten and revised over time.

In both approaches, it is this dimension of temporality that needs to be understood in terms of interpretations of the past that are part of our political present. For the post-processual archaeologist, the focus is more on the way people interpret and actively manipulate material culture. In the case of the processual researcher, there is a concern with events that have already occurred, with studying change as it happens, and with the influence of future expectations on current interpretations. The different disciplinary use of the term processual (crudely, functional–processual versus interpretative–processual) highlights the importance of not assuming the characteristics of an approach (or change initiative) on the basis of the label attached (as argued in Chapter 2).

Following this conceptual clarification of the place and methodological orientation of processual research, attention needs to be given to the practice of longitudinal fieldwork studies on change. Before researchers can go into the field, they must first plan and design a feasible research programme. In designing a processual study on workplace change, one critical element centres on building a longitudinal element into the research design. In addressing this aspect, the next section summarizes the slightly different designs of a number of research projects that were all aimed at collecting longitudinal qualitative data. The objective is to illustrate the intentions and practice of this type of case study research regarding organizational change, which does not occur in a vacuum but must take into account various contextual opportunities and constraints. These include the willingness of companies to participate in the study, the time limits to the research, the geographical location of the researcher, and the size and availability of travel funds.

Putting in the time: the design and practice of longitudinal research

In a special issue of *Organization Science* on longitudinal field research methods for studying processes of organizational change, Van de Ven and Huber (1990: 213–219) argue that research questions that seek to examine organizational change over time require a framework that can explain the unfolding temporal processes of change. They note that: 'process studies are fundamental to gaining an appreciation of dynamic organizational life, and to developing and testing theories of organizational adoption, change, innovation, and redesign' (Van de Ven and Huber, 1990: 213).

In practice, longitudinal research can refer to a number of quite different types of study. For example, longitudinal designs are often proposed for quantitative studies that seek to identify the temporal relationship between two causally related variables. Alternatively, cohort studies may be carried out over a number of years in order to take a number of time-spaced sequential snapshots from which more general trends and explanations can be derived. However, this static snapshot view of social life runs contrary to the primary characteristic of processual research, which seeks to explain the interconnected and dynamic processes inherent in everyday life. Through a concern with holistic and detailed descriptions of social settings and a commitment to reporting actors' interpretations of events, the final product is commonly a narrative temporal account of interaction and change. As Jon Clark (1995: xi–xii) explains in his detailed case study of workplace innovation at Pirelli's Aberdare plant in Wales:

> This is not a conventional academic book. The main body of the text has no references, footnotes or other academic conventions. It is written largely in a narrative style. The main characters are real people . . . At first sight it might appear that this is simply a story about managers . . . As the book progresses, the reader will find that the workforce figures ever more prominently. By the end they emerge, together with a small group of 'leaders', as the central characters in the story.

In working towards processual accounts, participant observation over a number of months or years has been the classic approach to studying a 'time-sequence of interpersonal events' (Whyte, 1955: 358). Whyte's *Street Corner Society*, which involved observational work over three years, is an exemplar of this type of research. The incorporation of long periods of continuous observation into study designs require observers to be largely free from other obligations and, as a consequence, it is rarely an option for full-time members of university staff (Barley, 1990: 244). For the majority of researchers in the late twentieth century, time constraints and other influential pressures (such as funding arrangements and pressures to publish) all impinge on the practice of carrying out processual research.

In dealing with some of these constraints as well as contextual opportunities, attention should be given to the practicalities of engaging in longitudinal research during the design stage. Questions such as company access, teaching commitments, resource availability and the like, all need to be accommodated in the design of a research programme that may not be as intensive or sustained as the researcher might wish for in a 'perfect' world. Few of us (apart from some full-time PhD students) have the freedom to spend even twelve months in a company as a participant observer, let alone three years. In response to these constraints there has been an increase in the use of other methods, such as taped interviews, and the development of research designs that collect this type of data over a number of specified periods during the life of a project (see Pettigrew and Whipp, 1991; Clark, 1995).

Although Bryman claims that studies that use semi-structured interviewing as their primary method of data collection are generally characterized by an absence of a sense of process compared to participant observer studies (Bryman, 1988a: 115), this method is widely employed by those adopting a processual perspective in organization studies. Moreover, whilst much of the qualitative research in which I have been involved has relied heavily on taped interview data, a longitudinal element was built into the research design at the outset and the method of observation was also a key data collection technique. For example, in the work of the New Technology Research Group at Southampton University, three longitudinal case studies were conducted by an interdisciplinary research group that sought to examine the introduction of new electronic and computer technologies at the level of the individual workplace. The first of these case studies was concerned with exchange modernization in British Telecom (Clark *et al.*, 1988), the second with the introduction of a computerized system of freight information control in British Rail (Dawson, 1986), and the third with the introduction of Electronic News Gathering (ENG) in Southern Television (Jacobs, 1983). The longitudinal case study method was chosen for the purpose of achieving the group's principal objective of examining the processes associated with technological change at the workplace.

In each of the case studies a variety of methods were used, centring on the use of documentary data, observations and interviews over periods of up to two-and-a-half years. However, because of the timescales involved in major change programmes, only parts of the change process could be covered 'as it happened' in British Rail and British Telecom. In the latter case, some of the fieldwork involved observing the switchover from electro-mechanical Strowger exchanges to a semi-electronic telephone exchange system known as 'TXE4' (see Clark et al., 1988). In the former case, the study comprised a retrospective analysis of management strategy and industrial relations issues regarding the process of change, and an examination of workplace activities under routine operation (see Dawson, 1987: 47–60, 1994: 48–69).

Another variation on longitudinal research design is illustrated by a study into the process of change from job shop layout to cellular manufacture of the hardware fabrication plant at General Motors–Holden's Automotive Limited (GMHAL) manufacturing complex in South Australia. Although in this case the time span of the research was slightly longer, the time constraints were no less pressing as a consequence of other projects and teaching commitments. The main period of data collection occurred between October 1989 and July 1992 (although some interviewing occurred in 1995 and 1997), and consisted of ongoing observation and a planned interview programme. The collection of taped interview data comprised three main elements: a two-phase shop-floor interview programme; a key player interview programme, and a one-off series of operational work cell interviews. The two-phase shop-floor interview programme consisted of pre-change and post-change interviews with plant employees. The first-phase interviewing was completed in 1989 and the repeat interviews were concluded in March 1991. The major objective was to get descriptions of current work practices prior to change and an in-depth discussion of their primary concerns about change, and to then compare these with their actual experience and concerns under routine operation.

The supporting programme of observation involved regular visits to the plant in order to observe changes and to crosscheck data collected during the semi-structured interviews. The main point of contact at the plant was the project implementation manager, who, as a part of management, worked on the morning shift (shop-floor employees rotate between the morning and afternoon shifts). The focus on the morning shift was necessary because most of the collaborative decisions on work reorganization were made during this period (it was also the shift in which most of the changes occurred), although I also spent time on the afternoon and night shift, observing and informally discussing work with plant operators.

In a programme into the effects of Total Quality Management (TQM) on employment relations in a number of Australian and New Zealand organizations, an attempt was made to incorporate a longitudinal element into the research, which commenced in 1989 and concluded in 1992. On a practical note, we realized that it would not be possible to chart the movement of a range of companies from the conception of a need for a quality initiative through implementation to operation and ongoing change. Therefore, we decided to identify organizations that were just thinking about the possibility of a quality programme, were currently engaged in implementing TQM, or were embarked on a range of quality initiatives and saw themselves as operating with a TQM programme. In so doing, we hoped to be able to capture and comment upon a number of different workplace issues and employment themes from conception to operation of TQM, as well as presenting new empirical case study data on company change.

As it turned out, the geographical size of Australia posed a major problem to sustaining a presence in some organizations over a prolonged period of time. Close collaboration with two research teams, one located in Brisbane and one in Adelaide, allowed collection of some longitudinal data from companies located in South Australia and Queensland. However, as we aimed to draw examples from New South Wales, Victoria and Western Australia, geographical constraints (reflected in terms of time, funding and accessibility) limited the nature of some of the case studies undertaken. Consequently, with regard to the longitudinal character of the study there was some disparity in the amount of processual data collected between the various case sites.

Another element that further complicated data analysis and case presentation was that the one company identified as only beginning to think about the need for a TQM initiative had very little to say on the subject (as there had been no discussions of TQM at the workplace, there was a general lack of empirical data). Nevertheless, although there was significant variation in the amount of data collected across the eight case studies, we decided to give each study equal treatment in the published book (see Dawson and Palmer, 1995: 59–148).

In a study of Video-Conferencing Systems (VCS) with Niki Panteli, an opportunity arose to engage in a far shorter (in terms of overall time-scale) yet comprehensive longitudinal study of VCS as a medium of business communication. Not only were we able to observe critical moments of the implementation process; we were also able to study the use of the medium in a follow-up study. This highlights not only how there is not one ideal type of longitudinal study but also the importance of adapting and accommodating to opportunities in the design of a processual research strategy and methodology. In this case, the fieldwork for the project involved the collection of new empirical data through a study of the development, training and use of VCS on two sites of a large multinational oil and gas corporation located in the Grampian Region of Scotland (see Panteli and Dawson, 2001). The company, Shell UK Exploration and Production (known locally as Shell Expro), allowed us access to observe a series of staff training sessions on VCS, interview employees and project leaders and analyse a small number of internal documents. The supplier training organization, the Fifth Business, also accommodated our research needs and allowed open access to company personnel and facilitated our observation (and as it turned out participation) in the video conferencing training sessions. The study commenced in May 1998 and the last set of interviews was conducted in October 1998. The study consisted of three phases, and different data collection techniques were developed for each phase. During the first phase (March–April 1998) we aimed to gain a better understanding of VCS as a business communication medium. Documentation was collected and analysed and interviews took place. Interviews were held with the VCS project leader, the trainers and their managers. These aimed to gain insights into the reasons for implementing the VCS project and the nature of the training programme. Before commencing the second phase of the project, documentation about Shell Expro and its VCS were gathered, including the summary findings of a business travel questionnaire carried out in January 1998. The VCS training programme in Shell Expro began in May for a period of two months, and this marked the beginning of the second and main phase of our project. There were around seventy Shell Expro employees who received training during this period. During this phase, data were collected through the use of participant observation studies, individual and group discussions and in-depth interviews.

Observation was one of the main methods of data collection by which Niki Panteli and I attempted to gather first-hand information on VCS training. Both researchers participated at different training sessions. Essentially, we participated in the training programmes, made observation notes, and engaged in informal discussions with the other participants both before and after each training session. There were up to a maximum of four trainees at each session. During the programme we observed participants in the video conferencing suites, monitored interactions between trainer(s) and other participants, and made notes on the level of confidence in using the video conferencing equipment, any questions and comments made during the training session, and any immediate verbal and/or non-verbal responses to the video conferencing training environment. When time and location permitted, informal interviews were also conducted after and/or before the session. Typically the training sessions were run at two sites with a trainer and two trainees (plus a researcher at one site, or one researcher at both sites), thereby allowing the training to be presented through the use of the video conferencing equipment. In the case where trainees were at a site distant from the researcher, it was not possible to organize interviews or informal discussions immediately after the training sessions. This observational work was also complemented by the findings of a short survey questionnaire distributed to all training participants at the end of their training session. In-depth interviews were also carried out with a number of employees (across the hierarchy) who underwent VCS training. The third phase comprised a follow-up to the second phase, with the aim of collecting data on the subsequent use of VCS after the training sessions. This phase took place between September and October 1998, three months after the completion of the training programme. Finally, a follow-up telephone survey was made to supplement the data collected through observation and the two-phase interview programme.

A common element linking these research programmes is that a longitudinal dimension was incorporated during the design phase of the research; at the same time, however, they all tackled the longitudinal aspect in a rather different way. The British Rail case study opted for a retrospective analysis of the process of implementing a computerized system of freight information control combined with an eighteen-month study of the ongoing effects of change under routine operation. In contrast, the study at General Motors sought to examine the process of change as it unfolded over time. This involved interviewing staff before and after the setting up of team-based cell manufacture and collecting data during the process of organizational change. In the TQM study, data were collected over a specified period of time (determined by Australian Research Council funding) within companies that were identified as being at the conceptual, implementing or operating stage in their use and application of TQM principles. Finally, the Shell study was carried out over a far shorter period (eight months in all) and involved three different phases of data collection comprising a range of different techniques. Although in this case observation was one of the main methods, documentary analysis, questionnaire and telephone surveys, and in-depth repeat interviewing were all important to data collection. All of these studies were designed in different ways, and yet they had the common aim of studying processes of organizational change. They also combined a range of different data collection techniques in order to gather data for processual analysis (see Chapter 7).

Conclusion

This chapter has been concerned with the subjective interpretations and meanings that people give to their experience of work. It has emphasized the importance of processual research to knowledge acquisition in the collection and analysis of data that further our understanding of people's lived experience. It is not concerned with, nor does it attempt to justify, data in terms of verification, falsification, generalization or quantification. Under the processual approach, *one* is significant. Following the more abstract discussion of knowledge creation and acquisition (epistemology), attention was turned to options in the design of qualitative longitudinal studies of change. In drawing on fieldwork experience, it was stressed how time was consistently an important element both in terms of observing change over a prescribed period (rather than engaging in a one-off snapshot) and in terms of being visible ('putting in the time') in the work environment. To put it another way, processual research sets a timeframe of reference for explaining change and, by so doing, requires the collection of data over periods of real and retrospective time. As such, incorporating a longitudinal element into fieldwork design is a critical part of the research process. It was also argued that during this design phase, researchers require a degree of honesty and realism if they are to develop feasible programmes that can accommodate contextual constraints and opportunities.

Drawing on my own practical experience, it was argued that the commitment of a researcher is reinforced by a prolonged physical presence in the workplace setting being studied. Increasing acquaintance with the work process and familiarity with interviewees enhances prospects of access and lessens workplace concerns. As a consequence, the researcher is likely to find greater opportunities to observe and informally discuss workplace practices and opinions. Such an engagement in the research process also illustrates how there can never be a clear distinction between data and theory. In the chapter that follows, decisions regarding the choice of data collection techniques and the difficult task of processual analysis are examined in the light of my own research experience and the views of other leading researchers in the field.

7 Doing processual research:
tacit knowledge, data collection and data analysis

- Tacit knowledge: there is no substitute for dirty hands
- Doing it: processual research and the task of data collection
- Processual analysis: the long vigil
- Conclusion

In this chapter we turn our attention to the practice of doing processual research, the role of the researcher, the different types of data collection techniques, and the nature of processual analysis. In examining the practice of conducting processual research, the importance of tacit knowledge through 'hands-on' fieldwork is raised and discussed. The process is briefly illustrated through recounting an early unforeseen incident during my night-time observational work of a British Rail marshalling yard. The chapter provides an overview of the key elements that need to be considered in the choice of data collection techniques and during the complex task of data analysis. There are three central concerns of this chapter: first, the question of tacit knowledge and the importance of learning from the field; second, the value of combining a range of data collection techniques and the need to accommodate multiple perspectives from one or a number of different data sources; and third, data analysis and the need to ensure that sufficient time is allocated to this difficult task. Processual analysis is an activity that requires a lot of time and patience, and yet it is often the element in the research process that is most likely to be shortened or curtailed because of other pressing demands. Processual data may have taken many months or years to collect, and the detail or the amount of qualitative material can soon accumulate and make the thought of data analysis an extremely daunting task, even to the most experienced researcher. Analysis is an absorbing and often lonely task, which can be difficult to share with others. Interestingly, processual researchers rarely attempt to reflect on their experiences through the written word, and the sections on research strategy and methods found in scholarly journal articles often shed little light on the actual practice of data collection and processual analysis (for an example of some reflections, see Pettigrew, 1990; Ropo *et al.*, 1997a).

In this chapter, the intention is not to provide an all encompassing account of data collection and processual analysis (which would include options of using critical incident techniques and the use of computer software to aid analyses), but to outline general practice through illustrative examples drawn from my own fieldwork experience (for a useful discussion of computers in qualitative research, see Flick, 2002). While reference is made to the work of Van de Ven and Huber (1990) and Pettigrew (1990, 1997), who discuss a number of pertinent issues that arise from longitudinal studies and process analysis (see also Langley, 1999), the sections that follow use fieldwork examples to illustrate the 'realities' of carrying out processual research. This experience is not sanitized into a kind of textbook script, but instead tries to capture some of the 'flavour' (warts and all) of doing this type of longitudinal research.

Tacit knowledge: there is no substitute for dirty hands

The concept of tacit knowledge, developed by Polanyi (1962, 1983), refers to the ability to use knowledge acquired from experience in carrying out tasks and activities in the pursuit of particular objectives. This tacit knowledge has been described as a form of 'inarticulate intelligence', where individuals are often unable to explain the 'theoretical basis for their action' (Gray and Pratt, 1991: 164). In exploring the concept of tacit knowledge, Wagner and Sternberg (1986: 51) argue that a considerable amount of knowledge and skill is accrued in the process of carrying out everyday activities and in the absence of formal instruction. Moreover, this knowledge is generally difficult to extract and make explicit to others (Kantrow, 1987: 163), as the following anecdote by Turner (1988: 108) illustrates:

> There is a story about a farmer's wife who won a national strudel-making competition in Austria. Asked by a journalist to say how she made strudels, the farmer's wife looked puzzled. Eventually she said, 'Well, I put on my apron, wash my hands, roll up my sleeves and then I go into the kitchen and make strudels.' I feel a little of her puzzlement when I am asked to talk about how I study organizations: I find an organization, get into it, and then I study it. Research, like strudel making, has elements of craft about it, so that some of the knowledge acquired by those who do it is tacit knowledge, embedded in the skills of the craft, and it is sometimes difficult to be explicit about these skills, which are easier to transmit by example and by apprenticeship.

Barry Turner's comparative description of the bewildered farmer's wife and the tacit knowledge associated with studying organizations usefully captures some of the longstanding dilemmas that surround qualitative processual research. Even before questions of external validity and generalizability are raised, there is the seemingly straightforward question, how do you do processual research in organizations? The glib answer is with great difficulty, a lot of patience and plenty of time. For many researchers in the field, their knowledge largely derives from 'going in at the deep end' and gaining experience in the companies they are studying. Although there are an increasing number of 'inside' accounts of social research in organizations (Bryman, 1988b) and the publication of *The Discovery of Grounded Theory* by Glaser and Strauss (1967) and *Basics of Qualitative Research* by Strauss and Corbin (1998) provide potential resource guides (see also Dey, 1993; Flick, 2002), many researchers enter the field with a grasp of the literature but not of the practice of carrying out processual research.

Although qualitative researchers often recount their feelings of 'drowning' in data, 'floundering in the deep end' often begins with their first step into the field to collect primary data. For example, in 1981 I vividly recall being in a large British Rail marshalling yard armed with a tape recorder, some questions and prompts, and a notebook. The stress of the first few days of making contacts, developing a rapport and getting to know the layout of the yard remains an intense memory. Most of the freight work was carried out at night, and there were a number of critical rules governing the safe working of the various yards. In my enthusiasm to collect data I decided to take photographs of shunting activities, but following the first flash (green and red hand-held lantern lights were used to aid the night-time marshalling of freight wagons), the alarm and concern of yard staff immediately made the foolishness of my action transparent. Greatly embarrassed and a little shaken by the response, I remembered the need to manage internal emotions and continue in the task of data collection. It was only over time, through growing familiarity and acceptance, that I was able to build a lasting rapport with shunting gangs and supervisors at the marshalling yard.

Three weeks later, in being offered a drink at the local pub and being invited to social events outside of work, I knew that I was becoming accepted into the world I was studying. One older supervisor, by the name of Percy, took me under his wing and went to great lengths to ensure that I was getting all the material I needed to satisfy the requirements of Southampton University. Although he found it difficult to understand the purpose of my research, he had taken on the role of guide and teacher of freight yard regulations and marshalling operations. In my experience, it was not long before employees in the freight yards were learning as much about my history as I was about theirs. At this stage and under these conditions, researchers are well placed to develop both their known and their unknown research skills.

As my experience and the time spent collecting data and observing the work of yard staff increased, I started to build up a knowledge and understanding not only of the workplace I was studying but also of the practice of engaging in processual research. However, not unlike the farmer's wife, I tended to concentrate on *doing* the research rather than documenting the nature of the skills acquired during fieldwork. Immediate concerns with the day-to-day practicalities of the study (especially with early morning starts, twelve-hour days, maintaining observational notes and records of research, and arranging interviews and additional trips) place numerous demands on the researcher during these rather intense periods of empirical study. Fieldworkers immersed in data collection are rarely able to reflect on their own personal development as a researcher, or to consider the methodological consequences of missing a connecting train and being late for a scheduled interview. The focus is often on dealing with research contingencies in developing and maintaining good interpersonal relations and collecting a vast barrage of material, which all seem so critical to the research questions being posed by the study.

To those not experienced in this type of research, what might appear to be relatively minor issues, like the general outlook and dress of the researcher, can all influence the process of carrying out this type of study. Examples include the ability to understand and listen to people with different views and perspectives without taking sides, dressing and acting appropriately to the environment in which the study is being carried out, being familiar with the workplace and demonstrating your seriousness by spending significant periods of time at the place of study, and maintaining a bright and cheerful outlook even when frustrated and/or tired at the end of the day. All these are part of the tacit knowledge – a sense of what is appropriate in the context of fieldwork – and form an integral part of the process of engaging in 'hands-on' processual research.

An interesting illustration of this issue was raised when a research colleague and I carried out a longitudinal study of the financial strategies of low-income families in London. Although we were from different backgrounds, we both had previous experience with qualitative research and there was a common unstated understanding, particularly with regard to the practicalities of carrying out the research. However, in working within a larger national group of researchers who were not familiar with techniques of qualitative data collection, we found ourselves spending considerable time justifying and explaining the rationale of our proposed study. Apart from the more clearly delineated methodological issues, there arose a concern about our decision to wear casual clothing (jeans and sneakers) to a deprived London housing estate. To our mutual astonishment, some of our colleagues sincerely felt that we should dress smartly (jacket and tie) in order to ensure a level of objectivity and to maintain a 'professional manner' as 'representatives' of the research team.

This may seem a minor issue, but persuading our bewildered colleagues was not easy – and yet dress codes can significantly influence the development of research rapport in the field. Essentially, our argument was that attention should be given to the environment in which the study takes place (for example, a study of decision-making at the shop floor or among senior executives might suggest that different forms of dress would be appropriate), in order to build up ongoing interpersonal relations over a sustained period of time. We also stressed the need for researchers to be honest and truthful about their own background and the nature and purpose of the programme of study.

Researchers engaged in this type of study must also be willing to take advantage of unanticipated opportunities (serendipity) in the collection of data. An example of this arose in a study of change and trade unions carried out between 1997 and 2001 (with the main fieldwork being conducted between 1998 and 2000) in which I found myself at an informal gathering of trade union officials at a local pub. Trade unionists from all over Australia were present, as they were attending their Annual Convention, and the hotel provided a fertile environment for discussing issues that had already been raised in a number of previous union interviews. When talking to one official on an outside upper level balcony overlooking the parklands, I asked whether he would mind if I recorded our conversation as my memory was unlikely to be very reliable the next day. Laughing knowingly he agreed, and the tape recorder remained running for the rest of the evening. On a sunny Adelaidian evening leaning up against a balcony with a beer in one hand and a tape recorder in the other, I did begin to wonder how this would be viewed in one of those often rather dry methodology textbooks. In my defence, I would contend that beer drinking was important to build on relationships that had already been formed. It also enabled me to gain wider general acceptance through interactions in a fairly relaxed and friendly atmosphere in which the researcher was not viewed as an 'outsider'. Although there was clearly a lot of 'political' activity going on in this setting, and too much for the researcher to accommodate overall, it was a productive ground for conversation and observation. Several beers later and after a long evening, I took a taxi back to Henley Beach (where I was staying) armed with three hours of taped discussion. I was to find that this method of data collection was well suited to my study of the Australian Services Union, and proved particularly informative at the annual end of year union barbecue. It was also very interesting and enjoyable to listen to the material the following morning. As it turned out, this method of data collection, combined with the more typical one-on-one and group interviews that were conducted in the office/home environment, provided a far richer source of material than I would have anticipated and was not part of my initial research design.

In reflecting on some of the tacit knowledge gained from practical experience, there is a wide range of elements (many of which may appear trivial) that researchers start to accommodate automatically in carrying out processual research. The activity of building up knowledge about the practice of conducting this type of case study research typically occurs unknowingly over a number of years, and can often be difficult to express or convey to new researchers prior to their initial fieldwork immersion. What reflection tells us is that it is important for new researchers to 'get their hands dirty' and to experience and discover new skills and understanding by engaging in the practice of data collection and drawing close to the subject of their study. As Peter Frost and Ralph Stablein (1992: 278) conclude in their edited collection on doing exemplary research:

> Teaching students to do exemplary research goes well beyond formal courses. It is a craft that must be learned through doing. It is an apprenticeship, and those who teach the craft play a vital role in the system . . . Only with the experience of 'doing it' will the lessons of the classroom truly make sense.

Doing it: processual research and the task of data collection

In carrying out processual case study research, two main methods of data collection are generally used in tandem; namely in-depth interviewing and observation. Each of these techniques is discussed below, and the main benefits of combining observation with in-depth interviewing are outlined. The section concludes with a brief overview of a number of supplementary methods that may aid processual research.

Observational methods

Observational techniques can be divided into participant and non-participant observation. Participant observation refers to the situation where researchers actually participate in the work in which they are investigating. This may be done overtly (through agreement with a company to work as a temporary member of the workforce over a specified period of time), or covertly (through becoming an employee of an organization without letting the employer know). Typically, observation has been used by researchers as a method for getting close to the lives and activities of others in order both to observe behaviours and to share in their felt experiences (Gill and Johnson, 1991: 109). Howard Becker (1973) provides an interesting example of this type of 'immersion' in his studies into the sociology of deviance as a participant observer. As a professional piano player working in Chicago, Becker relied heavily on participant observation in capturing a musician's view of the world (Becker, 1973: 83–85). As he describes:

> Most of the people I observed did not know that I was making a study
> of musicians. I seldom did any formal interviewing, but concentrated
> rather on listening to and recording the ordinary kinds of conversation
> that occurred among musicians. Most of my observation was carried
> out on the job, and even on the stand as we played.

Similarly, in his study of organizations Dalton (1959) maintained that it is important for researchers to immerse themselves in the cultures under investigation in order to understand and explain differences between official expectations (revealed in formal interviews) and unofficial ways of doing things (evident through participant observation). Notebooks were used to reconstruct contextual data, such as sequence of actions, behaviours, and non-verbal expressions, as soon as possible after the event. One advantage of these types of covert observational studies is that they minimize the effects of the researcher upon the data. However, the element of deception associated with covert research does raise a number of ethical issues, particularly with regard to the development of trust, confidentiality, and the potential threat of putting an informant's job in jeopardy (see Gill and Johnson, 1991: 119–120).

In taking an overt approach to observational research, William Foote Whyte also recognized the importance of 'seeing through the eyes' of those being studied. In his famous sociological study *Street Corner Society* (1955), which was published in 1943, Whyte gained access to the Norton Street Gang (located in a slum district in Boston) through a social worker who introduced him to Doc (a main character in his study). In order to gain ongoing proximity to the members of the gang, he decided to live in Cornerville and learn Italian. As an observer participating in the life of Cornerville he was able to establish his sincerity, and his attempt to learn the language was symbolically important in gaining acceptance and allowing him to get closer to those he was studying.

In his later work, Whyte used a combination of participant observation and semi-structured interviewing in his studies of Chicago restaurants, factories in New York State, worker cooperatives in Spain, and oil companies in Oklahoma and Venezuela (Whyte, 1984). The processual research of Pettigrew (1985), and more recently my own (Dawson, 1994, 2003), is also characterized by the use of multiple methods, which have included the use of in-depth interviews, an analysis of documentary and archive data, and the collection of observational and ethnographic material. This multiple method approach makes it possible to cross-check different types of data in constructing a narrative on the process of change. For example, in Pettigrew's early work on the politics of organizational decision-making he spent four days a week over a ten-month period participating as observer in Michaels between July 1967 and April 1968; a less frequent programme of ongoing visits followed (see Pettigrew, 1973: 52–75). During this research Pettigrew was aided by Enid Mumford (who liaised with the directors of the company), and concluded that: 'having two researchers operating at different points in the system is a major advantage in a decision-making study where the key participants work at different levels in the organizational hierarchy' (Pettigrew, 1973: 60).

The use of multiple observers is also evident in Whyte's (1944–1945) intensive one-year study of twelve Chicago restaurants (less detailed studies were also made of thirteen other restaurants), where Whyte and his three research assistants spent between one and six months performing and observing various restaurant jobs. As Whyte (1948: 361) states:

> In addition to interviewing and participating, we spent a good deal of time in observing the interaction of the various people who make up the restaurant organization. For example, we observed waitresses getting their food from service pantry girls and picking up drinks from bartenders, and we stood with the checker while she checked the waiters' orders as they left one kitchen we were studying.

Whyte (1984) notes that whilst access through employment may be relatively straightforward, the nature of the job may limit observational and interviewing opportunities. On the other hand, negotiating access into organizations can prove difficult in gaining permission from 'official gatekeepers' without unduly limiting the scope of the intended study. From reflecting on my experience in British Rail, relationships developed from initial observational work within the Western Region enabled the study to be extended to a number of additional marshalling yards in other regions across the national rail network. Furthermore, in examining routine operation over a period of eighteen months, observational work and repeat interviews became critical methods of establishing the process of change under so-called 'stable' conditions. Voluminous research notes were taken during months of observation of the work of yard staff in British Rail marshalling yards. Typically, I would arrive at a marshalling yard just prior to a shift changeover and then leave just after the next shift changeover. All shifts were observed in each yard studied. Ironically, the timetabling of British Rail passenger services to these large marshalling yards sometimes meant that I was left stranded at the yard for periods of twelve hours or more, trying to fight off fatigue and to remain personable and interested in the work, issues and problems of shunting staff.

In practice, the time spent at the yards proved instrumental in establishing good relationships, building up rapport and eventually being seen as an acceptable participant within the organization. By the end of the study I had been invited to a number of outside social events, I was attending informal group discussions in the local pub, and, in the absence of a passenger service, would be accommodated by an outbound freight train to return to my lodging accommodation. This proximity to the people being studied, and familiarization with their work routines, produced very rich and detailed data. Thus, the value of observational data in understanding processes of change should not be underestimated.

As Whyte (1984: 63) concludes in evaluating this type of intense long-term observational research:

> Full-time participant observation over an extended period of time tends to be an age-graded phenomenon. Such studies are most likely to be done by young people, in our student years. When we are established professionals, with teaching or other professional responsibilities, we are unlikely to have the time and the motivation to make such a full commitment.

Attempts to develop research designs to accommodate the demands of other commitments and yet maintain the processual character of the research are noticeable in the work of a number of academics. For example, Jon Clark's (1995) single researcher study of Pirelli's Aberdare factory in South Wales used a compendium of methods (mirroring some of the earlier work carried out within the New Technology Research Group), yet in this case emphasis was placed on the use of interviews and documentary material. Whilst a series of structured observations were made (lasting between 90 minutes and two hours during a total of 27 visits to the Aberdare plant between June 1990 and April 1994), these were primarily for the purpose of gaining a clearer understanding of the cable-making process (Clark, 1995: 245–248). In terms of analysis, the bulk of the data rested upon 272 Aberdare staff interviews, which consisted of 137 interviews of 146 employees in 1990 and 135 interviews of 135 employees in 1992 (Clark, 1995: 246).

Similarly, in examining the research strategy developed at the Centre for Corporate Strategy and Change at the University of Warwick, the influence of Pettigrew's early experiences are evident. Although the time allocated to case study research is reduced, Pettigrew describes three-person project teams as the norm, with fieldwork tending to comprise two or three days over a five-month period supplemented with further intermittent contact (Pettigrew, 1990: 278). In the work carried out between 1985 and 1989, over 350 recorded interviews were conducted in two automobile (Jaguar and Peugot Talbot), two merchant banking (Kleinwort Benson and Hill Samuel) and two book publishing (Longman and ABP) companies, and one financial service company (Prudential). Sadly, in reporting on the later work less emphasis has been placed on observation, with greater attention being given to the use of documentary material and the use of semi-structured tape recorded interviews (Pettigrew and Whipp, 1991: 26).

The use of interviews

Regarding the use of interviews, Burgess claims that they provide 'the opportunity for the researcher to probe deeply to uncover new clues, open up new dimensions of a problem and to secure vivid, accurate inclusive accounts that are based on personal experience' (Burgess, 1982: 107). In practice, however, it may be that certain types of people are drawn towards certain types of research, and that in-depth interviewing is not a task that can be accomplished by just anyone. On this count, Buchanan *et al.* (1988) claim that the success of informant interviews may be determined not simply by technique but also by the personality of the interviewer. Whether or not this is true, in the case of processual research the interview remains a major method of collecting data. Moreover, the process of carrying out this form of qualitative research can be very time-consuming and taxing. For example, Turner indicates in his 'inside' view of the research process how considerable time needs to be given to both the analysis and the collection of qualitative data. In discussing initial fieldwork, Turner (1988: 110) notes that:

> At an elementary level, the researcher embarking on a qualitative study of an organization needs to be warned that this is a time-consuming exercise. It takes time to gain access, to meet people, to let them tell their stories and to make sure that their telling has included all that you want to know. It takes a long time to transcribe or write up field notes and tape recordings: as a rule of thumb, a one-hour taped interview takes two to three hours to transcribe. But even then, the analysis of non-standardised, non-survey data is in itself a lengthy process. For each study an appropriate approach needs to be devised and implemented, and these tasks cannot be accomplished in a couple of hours.

In collecting interview data, the researcher is able to cross-check the statements of interviewees with his/her observation notes and documented accounts (an example of interview schedules is provided in Appendix I). Discrepancy between these various sources of data was usefully highlighted in a study of cultural change at Laubman and Pank in Adelaide (an optometry company introducing a services excellence programme, see Appendix II). Under a quality management initiative, the optometrists were expected to give up their 'white coats' and to refer to members of the public as 'clients' rather than 'patients'. Although there was formal agreement that this change had taken place (in company documents and the public image projected), the word patient was frequently used not only by optometrists but also by the branch level retail staff, who criticized optometrists for using the word 'patient' (Dawson, 1996: 116–117).

As an interviewer, it is also important to distinguish between respondents' descriptive evaluations of the way things ought to be, their perception of the way things actually are, and the way they feel others interpret their situation. For example, in the case of Percy (a British Rail freight-yard supervisor) there was a formal job description of what supervisors should do; then there was the supervisor's view of what ought to be done and what the job actually entailed (he had his own views on how others, such as managers, other supervisors and yard workers, perceived his role); then there were the articulated and often different opinions of line management, senior management, and shop-floor employees.

Discrepancy between the views of employees occupying different hierarchical positions is not uncommon, and nor would it seem unusual. However, in collecting data throughout a company, from the Chief Executive Officer (CEO) to shop-floor employees, there can be surprising ignorance among senior management of the views held by employees. For example, in a study of one Australian automotive supplier (who was receiving good media publicity through winning a North American contract), there was a marked mismatch between the opinions expressed at different levels within the organization. Three of these are printed below to provide a flavour of some of these differences:

Management interviews:

> We're very much a work-together team . . . We're heading towards being a world-class operation, and our people will be world class too.

Supervisory interviews:

> They should tell the workers what is going on in the company and keep them informed about decisions. Information should go to all employees, and not just supervisors and leading hands.

Employee interviews:

> It's not like what you read in the chapters. The managers get the limelight at the expense of the workers, and they don't give them sufficient recognition.

In the context of change, clarifying the status of these various statements is often a central analytical task in making sense of interview data. Discrepancy between the views of different groups is not problematic, but is part of the rich data accessible through processual research. Unlike studies that seek to construct a single account of change, the coexistence of competing histories and views can be accommodated under processual research. In the same automotive component company, another senior management member later recast the charismatic champion of change as a dishonest and underhand management fiend, after his replacement. Thus the longitudinal data were able to capture this movement from hero to villain, and make sense of the political motives of rewriting company history to fit current commercial objectives and the required public performance of the senior management group.

Combining observation with in-depth interviewing

The combination of observation with in-depth interviewing enables both the cross-validation of data and the integration of contextual and temporal observations with the more perceptional and attitudinal data gathered from interviews. The importance of being able to cross-validate data was highlighted in a longitudinal study of change at an automotive hardware fabrication plant in South Australia (see also Chapter 4). In this instance, interview data had indicated that supervisors were using a computer-based shop-floor scheduler in the planning and re-scheduling of daily work operations. This information that had been obtained through management interviews (and through discussion outside of the plant with some of the external industrial collaborators) presented a version of 'the ways things should be done' rather than of 'the way things were being done' (see also Dalton, 1959). In other words, the interview data depicted an account of change in which the scheduler was identified as a new central tool to shop-floor operations. This version of change was also presented to outsiders by both management and their industrial collaborators. In practice, however, this (the public face) did not align with the daily practice of shop-floor operations that were observed (the computer-based scheduler was only used in the initial set-up of the cells and not for daily scheduling purposes). This inconsistency between interview and observation data highlights one of the benefits of combining the two methods of data collection.

This discrepancy between the day-to-day practice of cellular manufacture and the formal intentions and aspirations as to how the system would ideally work in practice emerged from the observational work carried out in the plant. On the basis of these disconfirming data, further questions were then formulated and asked in later interviews. Thus, a major benefit of carrying out research over time and that utilizes a range of different methods is that it allows for the cross-validation of data and enables the modification of research strategies in the collection of further data. In this case repeat interviews allowed the researcher to return to some of these issues, which, as it turned out, raised interesting questions not only about official expectations and actual work processes but also about the creation and revision of group histories to accord with particular vested interests.

The example used above illustrates some of the limitations of simply using interview data. Similarly, in the case of observational work data collection problems may arise in the course of a research programme that prevent a full understanding of the area being studied. For example, in studying the job of the Area Freight Assistant (AFA), considerable time was spent observing their work (interactions with others, time spent on the telephone and so forth). However, in contrast to the yard supervisors, where observational notes provided rich contextual data on local yard culture, daily shunting activities and supervision (see Dawson, 1987), the job of the AFA would have remained undisclosed and hidden if sole reliance had been given to this technique. The AFA spend most of their time using a telephone and computer, so it was observed that computer use, and the activity of liaising and communicating with operating staff over the telephone, took up the greatest proportion of the AFA's time. Consequently, observing AFAs at work did not by itself generate material that explained the content and patterns of communication.

In tackling this issue, a questionnaire was developed and personally administered to AFAs (see Appendix I). This modification in research strategy enabled the collection of data on communication patterns (although, as it turned out, the second largest category was 'others', indicating that certain key individuals had not been accounted for during the design of the questionnaire). Further attempts to clarify their job centred on a series of interviews with AFAs, attendance at supervisory training courses, and ongoing discussions with AFAs as they carried out their daily job tasks. On gaining a greater understanding of job content (and of who the AFA liaised with over the telephone), the observation method then proved useful in providing data on the way decisions were made in practice. For example, although AFAs were formally required to alter, cancel or arrange inter-area services in liaison with divisional controllers, data collected during periods of observation and discussion with AFAs made it clear that these decisions were often made without

phases of the research, and are part of the ongoing processual analysis that occurs throughout longitudinal studies of change. Observation also enables the researcher to contextualize some of the data collected during the semi-structured interviews, and to compare, contrast and cross-check material collected through other data collection techniques. Although the more detailed and systematic analysis of observation notes generally occurs after data collection is complete, data collected during periods of observation do help shape the questions and avenues of study addressed during the research.

In discussing longitudinal field research on change, Pettigrew (1990) refers to the work carried out by the Centre for Corporate Strategy and Change (CCSC) at Warwick Business School in examining strategic change in a number of private and public sector organizations. In their health service work (Pettigrew *et al.*, 1992), they used documentary and archive data, observation notes and the transcripts from key informant interviews. In this research, the CCSC team averaged about fifty key informant interviews per case 'selected because of their lead position in the organization or in the change process under analysis; those affected by the changes as well as the initiators of change; different elites and interests groups internal and external to the focal organization' (Pettigrew, 1990: 277). Thus, there has been a tendency within this body of comparative research (see Pettigrew *et al.*, 1992; Pettigrew and McNulty, 1995; Ferlie *et al.*, 1996) to minimalize the interviews conducted with employees at lower levels of the organization hierarchy and to focus on the 'movers' and 'shakers' of change, and in particular on senior management and change agents. While there is a commitment to listen to all sides of the drama (Pettigrew, 1990: 278), the focus on strategy has resulted in workplace voices of the less powerful being rather too silent in the published case studies. To be fair to Pettigrew (1990: 227), he does emphasize that their central aims are to:

> Collect data which is *processual* (an emphasis on action as well as structure over time); *comparative* (a range of studies in various sectors); *pluralist* (describe and analyse the often competing versions of reality seen by actors in change processes); *historical* (take into account the historical evolution of ideas and action for change as well as the constraints within which decision makers operate); and *contextual* (examine the reciprocal relations between process and contexts at different levels of anlaysis). This means producing case studies and not just case histories – going beyond chronology to develop analytic themes.

In an article on processual analysis, Pettigrew (1997) goes on to identify five essential needs.

1 The need to study changes in their context, or what is referred to as 'embeddedness' (Pettigrew, 1997: 340).
2 The need to study change over time and to identify the timing and sequencing of events.
3 The need to recognize that context and action are always tangled together, or, in Pettigrew's (1997: 341) words, 'context is not just a stimulus environment but a nested arrangement of structures and processes where the subjective interpretations of actors perceiving, learning, and remembering help shape process'.
4 The need to identify patterns and interrelated links among a range of features.
5 The need to examine outcomes in comparative case settings in order to explore how context and process explain divergence in outcome.

These five assumptions of: embeddedness, temporal interconnectedness, intertwining of context and action, holistic explanation, and the use of outcomes as a focus for processual analysis – are seen to guide the researcher towards the case write-up as an 'analytical chronology' in which patterns in the data are identified and clarified (Pettigrew, 1997: 346). Emphasis is placed on comparative analysis, with the goal of achieving broader thematic writing through 'meta level analysis and presentation'. The central aim is to weave an argument that constantly moves from the general to the particular in 'linking the theoretical and empirical findings across the case to wider bodies of literature' (Pettigrew, 1997: 346).

The research conducted by Pettigrew and the CCSC group at Warwick has undoubtedly made a major contribution to organization theory and processual research. Nevertheless, while there are a number of elements that resonate with the processual perspective advocated here, there are also a number of significant differences. For example, it is argued here that Pettigrew's tendency to move towards higher levels of academic abstraction is not always reconciled with the data of processual research. More often, these broader comparative generalizations or abstractions become increasingly divorced from the rich contextual nature of the processual data and draw the reader away from the more useful insights and explanations that could be on offer. In particular, the different perspectives and views of individuals and groups in their experience of change may consequently be down-played in the search for broader patterns on which to generalize. For example, in a large piece of collaborative research on *the innovating organization* (Pettigrew and Fenton, 2000a), we get no sense of the effects of change on the lives and experience of workplace employees. In fact, although the published research details eight intensive case studies there is very little in the way of qualitative data presented in the book. The key informant interviews are largely centred on senior and local management (see, for example, Quintanilla and Sanchez-Runde, 2000: 213–214), there are hardly any quotations from the interview transcripts within the main body of text, and the few that are used relate to directors, chairmen (Pettigrew and Fenton, 2000b: 57–61), heads of section (Ruigrok *et al.*, 2000: 204), and top management (Quintanilla and Sanchez-Runde, 2000: 272). Although the book concludes by claiming that the research has achieved the best of both worlds in identifying macro-patterns (through the quantitative survey) and micro-patterns (through the detailed case studies), in practice it has largely distilled out the qualitative data and left in its place a far more hard-going and turgid series of case studies. In other words, caution should be given to studies that, in trying to combine quantitative surveys with in-depth processual case studies, end up hiding the rich processual data from the reader in the production of a rather more bland, yet some would argue more 'scientific', case study. Moreover, in this focus on management we do not get the multiple voices, the different interpretations and views of change, and as such the orientation of these studies contrasts significantly with the type of processual case study being advocated here.

An essential argument of this book is that it is important to examine change from different viewpoints. There is a need to listen to the views and experiences of different groups and individuals working under conditions of change (see, for example, Dawson, 2003). Although time-consuming, such data should form an integral part of processual analysis and not just be acknowledged in discussions of methodology. Thus it is argued here that a single longitudinal case study can make a major contribution to knowledge (as witnessed by the early work of Pettigrew), and that multiple narratives and competing histories should not be treated as a type of 'deviant noise' or 'disruption' to dominant patterns, but should be analysed as an integral part of processual research. Such rich data often provide insight into the use of, for example, power in organizations and is also the material from which we can critically reflect on a range of issues and concepts (such as conflict, resistance and political process) and question some taken-for-granted assumptions (for example, the commonly held view that strategies of participation are more humane than others, and that 'resistance' is an 'obstacle' for management 'legitimately' to overcome) that tend to dominate the change management literature. In short, the later work of Pettigrew has tended to move away from the strength of processual analysis with an emphasis on academic abstraction through the identification of more general patterns within a wider range of comparative data. As already indicated, this movement away from multiple narratives and experiential stories is misplaced, for these are the very data that shed greater light and understanding on social processes within organizations. Consequently, the next chapter focusses on the place of narratives and the use of stories in processual research on organizational change.

Conclusion

In drawing on over twenty years of fieldwork experience, this chapter has reflected on the practice of carrying out processual case studies and the importance of 'putting in the time' in the collection of data. It has been noted that although prolonged periods within a work environment can be demanding and at times stressful, the visibility of the researcher over entire working days may go some way to signalling his or her commitment to the study, and act as a significant factor in the development of interpersonal relations and the building of rapport and trust. In this sense, 'putting in the time' is important to the research design in the collection of processual data, and in becoming an accepted part of the workplace under study. Essentially, it is argued that there can be no substitute for researchers 'getting their hands dirty' in doing research. This 'hands-on' need is reinforced by the importance of tacit fieldwork knowledge, which is often difficult to express and document in a form that makes it accessible and meaningful to students. This chapter has further illustrated how many of these unexplained elements of carrying out research (which at first glance may appear superficial and trivial) can be crucial ingredients to the successful completion of processual fieldwork. For example, knowledge gained from experience enables the researcher to make judgements about the timing and appropriateness of questions, and on the practicality of a compendium of methods within the context of the research setting. The way researchers present themselves, their ability to develop and maintain good interpersonal relations, and their capacity to remain open to competing data and not to restrict their research gaze, all form part of the tacit skills of the experienced researcher. For the novice seeking guidance, research skill acquisition is a process where the taught techniques and knowledge of research methodology should be added to and influenced by stories and anecdotes of experienced researchers, who can convey some of the less tangible dimensions associated with processual research. However, while there is an important place for the taught research course, handling data in context and learning from the experience of fieldwork is an essential element in training new researchers wishing to develop their practical skills in carrying out processual studies on workplace change.

A range of different data collection techniques have been described, and it is suggested that these should be used in combination for the purpose of longitudinal studies of change. For example, observational techniques can be used in conjunction with other methods in order to contextualize, contrast and cross-check interview data. Whenever possible, a compendium of different methods can be used in studies that seek to collect longitudinal processual data on workplace change. It is also argued that the time required for processual analysis of this qualitative data should not be underestimated, nor the need for blocks of uninterrupted periods when researchers can immerse themselves in the body of data they have collected.

On reflection, conducting processual research on organizational change may require a lot of patience and plenty of time, but it also offers the researcher the chance to study unfolding issues and events as they occur. The 'deviant' or 'outsider' no longer has to be viewed as problematic in final data presentation, as fine-grained contextual accounts can easily accommodate diversity. As will be highlighted in the next chapter, the focus is not on working the data to strengthen the generalizability of the findings, but rather to provide narrative accounts of the complex dynamics of change from an analysis of documents, contextual observations, and in-depth interviews of people's experience. Although general trends can be identified and typical responses recounted, under the processual framework, *one* is significant.

In practice, the longitudinal design of the research, the use of a compendium of data collection techniques and the time allocated to data analysis and case study write-up will be influenced by various 'opportunities' and 'constraints', such as funding, period of grant, staffing of the project, and the geographic location of the principal investigators. For example, although the benefits of working within a research group and the use of multiple observers were briefly discussed, in my experience (from participating in a number of research group and single researcher studies) there are also advantages in working outside a bigger group. These include the strong identification and ownership of a project, the capacity to innovate and be creative throughout the study without the need for continual discussion and debate, and the high levels of self-motivation in wanting to see the conception of 'your' research idea developed into a study that is eventually published. What these individual and group-based processual studies have in common is their use of multiple methods and their longitudinal research designs. As a result, a major benefit of this type of strategy is that it enables the development of processual theories that are able to unmask some of the common myths about organizational change, such as the linearity myth that change goes through a logical sequence of stages, the improvement myth that change is marked by a line of continual improvement, and the leadership myth that there is one leader of large-scale change rather than a number of leaders with a range of roles that may emerge, evolve and decline at different times during the process of change. Thus the capacity of this type of research to provide new insights, question many taken-for-granted assumptions, and widen our knowledge of the topic under study marks the journey as being not only academically worthwhile but also satisfying on a more personal level.

Apart from the benefits of processual research, one area of possible concern in the context of increasing international pressure to 'publish or perish' is that the more time-consuming processual study may be increasingly replaced by the shorter case study. These more concentrated cases are planned to minimize time commitments whilst maximizing potential publication output. On this count, it could be argued that a weakness with some of the more recent interview-intensive studies has been their tendency to down-play the contribution of observational work to processual research. Therefore, it is important to stress the value of observation as a method for generating rich contextual data for processual analysis. For example, observation notes can be used to provide: a chronology of events, an account of routine and unforeseen activities and tasks, an awareness of the informal organization of work, contextual stories, decision-making activities, and textures of the non-linearity of processes of change. Unlike the snapshot study or the broader questionnaire approach, processual case study research on organizational change uses a compendium of different methods over time in order to chart the complex and muddied waters of organizational life. In collecting rich empirical data and getting behind the seductive appeal of consultant techniques and quick-fix solutions to company ills, the researcher must learn to 'swim in the deep end' through surviving sustained periods of 'hands-on time digging in the field'. Through the wide collection of detailed data (in the use of company documents, interview transcripts and observation notes), the researcher is able to engage in a more critical processual analysis and, by so doing, unravel and break open many of the popularized myths about management and organizations.

8 Disseminating processual research: the written case study

- Stories and storytelling
- The written case study
- Conclusion

The chapter commences with a discussion of 'stories' and how they can be used to shed light on processes of organizational change. It is argued that change consultants and popular management writers, in identifying simple recipes of success, often use executive anecdotal stories. These stories are powerful tools for capturing the imagination of management audiences and for transferring knowledge on change management. However, when the basis of this knowledge is the *post-hoc* rationalized accounts of senior management – which are often used in the popular management literature to identify various success factors – then the contribution of these stories to our knowledge of change processes becomes extremely doubtful. In fact, a more critical analysis of this material provides an explanation of why the majority of large-scale organizational change initiatives fail to achieve their objectives, despite a rapid growth in the literature on change management (see also Dawson, 2003).

In disseminating knowledge from processual studies of change, the researcher has to consider venues for presentation and outlets for publication. For example, once the demands of fieldwork activities have diminished, a research group may target a number of academic conferences in order to present preliminary findings and discuss potential conceptual developments. Unlike the popularized accounts, more attention is given to research strategy and methodology, and the potential for the study to contribute to the growing body of academic literature on organizational change. As papers are developed, presented and circulated for comment and discussion, then the researcher may consider chapter publication, journal articles, or a research monograph through securing a book contract with an academic publisher. Wider management audiences rarely access these publications, which form an integral part of establishing an academic career, and it is usually only the high-profile and successful international figures that make a significant and broader impact. Interestingly, these high profile figures are often professorial academics located in highly prestigious management institutions such as the Harvard Business School or the London School of Economics (see, for example, the work of Kanter, 1990; Hamel and Prahalad, 1994; Kotter, 1997; Hamel, 2000; Handy, 2001). During their early work, they may have followed the traditional route described above (see Kanter, 1983; Handy, 1986). However, in the development of later work and in their presentations to management executives, stories emerge as a common and central feature. Although these stories are often drawn from experience and research, the emphasis is not on relaying the details of the data or outlining the methodology of the study; rather, the story progresses with plots, characters and memorable events, and is often marked by a liberal use of humour. Embedded within the story is an important point or message about change management that is generally reinforced in a concluding statement or punchline. In providing accessible and memorable stories that combine practical application with an intellectual focus and legitimacy, these celebrity professors are successful modern-day storytellers (see Huczynski, 1993). As the popularity of these 'guru professors' extends, so does their ability to disseminate their ideas and research to a wider practitioner audience. Although there has been some academic criticism and analysis of guru works (see Huczynski, 1993; Collins, 2000; Jackson, 2001), academics have tended to be silently scornful and have largely ignored the wider influence of these developments. As Jackson (2001: 178–179) notes:

> We have lamentably few good analyses of what roles management gurus actually play for practicing managers, let alone how they affect them. These studies together with anecdotal evidence suggest that, on an individual level at least, managers tend to be quite ambivalent in their attitudes toward management gurus, yet substantial book sales and widespread and far reaching organizational change efforts suggest otherwise.

For the processual researcher, this may question whether the time and effort spent on longitudinal research can be justified, especially if the findings that we wish to disseminate are only heard by a few and have little influence on people in organizations. This, of course, raises a dilemma. As academic researchers we seek recognition by our peer group, and the refereed journal article has become a key indicator of academic research ability. However, if our intention in carrying out research is to further our understanding and knowledge of organizations, then we may also want the output from our research to reach as wide an audience as possible. Thus in preparing our findings for presentation and publication, account needs to be taken of the audience and outlet we are targeting. Consequently, the content and form of the material is likely to vary as we shape our outputs to align with audience expectations. These considerations inevitably raise more questions than they answer, for example:

1 What are the different authoring and audiencing roles, and how are they likely to influence the way we present and publish our research findings?
2 If stories are powerful tools for transferring knowledge and making sense of the world, what are the implications for research design, data collection and analysis, and the presentation and publication of case study findings?
3 Does the continuing popularity of linear sequential stage models of change reflect the demand and prevalence of stories of company success that provide a chronology of events from which a key lesson is derived?
4 As academic researchers, should we be disseminating our findings to as wide an audience as possible or should our attentions be focussed within an academic community?

In exploring the notion of change stories, the position of the processual researcher as analyst and storyteller is considered and the influence of the audience on data analysis and written output is examined. The chapter forwards a typology of the written case study, and briefly examines form and content issues in a discussion of the use of interview transcripts in publishable documents. The chapter concludes by endorsing the heterogeneity and richness of processual research and by suggesting that there is considerable room for further development of the processual perspective.

Stories and storytelling

For over 40,000 years, the Aboriginal people have used storytelling as a vehicle for relaying their culture and knowledge of the land from one generation to the next. Dreamtime stories tell how evil came into the world and explain how life began and the world came into being with its vegetation and animal life forms. These and other stories are often imaginative and colourful, working on the emotions of the audience and carrying various social messages. Today, these tales are regularly used as bedtime stories for Australian children. The short extract from the story of Gidja the Moon provides an example (Trezise and Roughsey, 1991):

> Far off in Dreamtime when the world was still being made, Gidja the Moon lived by the Yangool River, in Cape York Peninsula, with the rest of the Bullanji people. Gidja was unhappy as people made fun of him because he had a round fat face, fat body and thin legs and arms.

These stories are often highly expressive and capture the fears and aspirations of the Aboriginal people and, unlike the myths and legends of Greece, have remained largely unaltered for thousands of years. In New Zealand, the myths of the Maori similarly predate those found in western civilization and the creation story is argued to be the oldest surviving myth in the world (Campbell, 1976). The power of stories has never been lost in human society, and their purpose in and influence on processes of organizational change become evident not only in the analyses of qualitative longitudinal data, but also in the way that anecdotal stories of company success are used within the popular management literature to sanitize the process and offer data for change experts to formulate neat linear prescriptions on how best to manage change. In the short section that follows, the way that anecdotes have been inappropriately used to generate recipes for 'success' is briefly examined prior to a discussion of storytelling in organizations.

The anecdotal story as a recipe for success

Anecdotal stories about organizational change are not uncommon in the popular management literature. Kotter (1996), for example, uses the story of a pharmaceutical company to illustrate problems of complacency, and in his interactive CD he draws on discussions with leading executives to make a distinction between management and leadership (Kotter, 1997). Similarly, Kanter uses stories in her famous public presentations to senior executives on how to be a master rather than a victim of change (Kanter, 1990). These stories are not only drawn from innovative high technology companies and the more established corporations such as General Motors, but also from other familiar places such as the Bible and the popular media. These stories are used to illustrate and support general claims about how best to manage change. They also entertain and engage the audience with the speaker, and provide a useful vehicle for transferring knowledge and ideas. The narrator often provides an orientation to the story, selecting pertinent issues or noticeable events (often using humour and depicting action events with heroes, villains, fools and victims) and then concluding with a message, an evaluation or a moral/lesson to the story. There is often a linear historical structure of temporal stages (this happened, then this happened, causing this to occur and so forth) in which we are introduced to key characters and events. In the presentation of these public stories, academic consultants such as John Kotter and Rosabeth Moss Kanter are able to capture the imagination of their audience. It could be suggested that much of their high-profile success rests on their abilities as good narrators and storytellers, rather than as leading academic thinkers. Some academics may be scornful of their popularist approach and question the academic substance of the material presented; for others, their 'success' in getting their ideas widely listened to signals the poignancy of storytelling as a method for transmitting knowledge on change management. In short, stories provide well-bounded and structured accounts that are able to convey complex issues in a simple format. But what are the implications of this for studying and understanding company change processes?

Storytelling in organizations

Within organization studies, the place and purpose of storytelling has only more recently become an area of growing debate and discussion (Gabriel, 2000), and yet, as Boje and Dennehy (1993: 18) state:

> Stories make experience meaningful, stories connect us with one another; stories make the characters come alive; stories provide an opportunity for a renewed sense of organizational community.

In a study of an office supply firm, Boje (1991) used interview transcripts to uncover the character of stories and the way individuals and groups rewrite the past to make sense of the present. These stories are partial and open to change; they do not reflect the stories found in novels with plots and characters, but are socially constructed narratives that seek to make sense of the world in which people live. On this count, Gabriel (2000) cautions the use of the term and suggests that it should not be applied to all forms of narrative. For Gabriel, the narrative craft of storytelling is about creating and sustaining meaning as well as providing a vehicle to discredit other worldviews. Storytelling is not simply about description, but also about emotional engagement with an audience, it is about entertainment (Gabriel, 2000: 6–28):

> Stories interpret events, infusing them with meaning through distortions, omissions, embellishments, and other devices, without, however, obliterating the facts . . . Entertainment distinguishes stories from other narratives . . . I believe that it is necessary to distinguish between description, which deals with facts-as-information, and stories, which represent facts-as-experience for both tellers and listeners . . . In fact, the narrative test for a story is relatively straightforward: would a listener respond by challenging the factual accuracy of the text?

Gabriel argues for the distinction between narratives that blatantly embellish and restructure story lines to engage the audience and narratives that provide a chronology of events (attempt to be factual even if they are not). This leads him to focus on organizational folklore and stories that have clear characters and plots and are used variously to reassure, justify and explain, advise and warn, or to provide a form of moral education. These stories entertain (they are recreational), and in the telling of the story the storyteller seeks to stimulate the imagination of the audience. However, this focus draws attention away from the process by which individuals and groups construct stories to influence decision-making and processes of change. It is not appropriate to reject the importance of stories that are politically motivated, or to ignore the experience of particular individuals or groups. These stories will be partisan and partial, open to flux and change, and may well attempt to get their version of events publicly accepted as the organizational ('authentic') story of change.

In this type of processual analysis, researchers also need to reflect on their role as storyteller, chronicler and analyst. For Pettigrew, the process analyst goes beyond the storyteller in building up a chronology for identifying comparable patterns and their shaping over time. It is a narrative that combines 'facts-as-information' (a chronology) with 'facts-as-experience' to provide an analytical case study (Pettigrew, 1997: 339):

> Historians are often stereotyped as storytellers; mere describers of events; pervaders of chronologies. Meanwhile the superior social scientist rises above and beyond mere events and describes and conceptualises, models, analyses, measures and explains. For the process analyst events and chronologies are crucial building blocks, but only building blocks. The aim in a processual analyst is not to produce a case history but a case study. The case study goes beyond the case history in attempting a range of analytical purposes. Firstly

there is a search for patterns in the process and presumably some attempt to compare the shape, character and incidence of this pattern in case A compared with case B. Secondly, there is a quest to find the underlying mechanisms which shape any patterning in the observed processes . . . The third analytical factor which may turn a case history into a case study reminds us that inductive pattern recognition has also to go hand in hand with deduction.

These different characterizations of stories and storytellers by Gabriel (2000) and Pettigrew (1997) restrict processual analysis of political processes of change by either placing the story and storyteller in the category of poetic interpretation, or emphasizing comparative patterns that ignore deviant stories and outlier interpretations. However, it is argued here that stories, the audience and storytellers are central both to understanding processes of change (data and processual analysis), and to the writing of case studies for particular outlets (the author and audience). The assumption that the analytical interpretation of stories – 'unlocking the inner meaning of a story' – is largely in the province of the researcher (Gabriel, 2000: 43), and that the case study is the ultimate analytical piece identifying patterns and their shaping through a focus on the temporal routes to comparative outcomes (Pettigrew, 1997), down-plays the politics of organizational stories and storytelling. It is the organizational stories of the less powerful that also need to be explained, for they often remain unheard or absent in studies of organizational change. This is perhaps understandable in comparative studies that search for broader generalizations in addressing such managerial themes as *Managing Change for Competitive Success* (Pettigrew and Whipp, 1991). However, for the processual researcher it is important to remember that case studies are written in a particular context and time by one or a number of researchers (who may themselves be constrained by time and pressure to publish) who are generally aware of the audience they are trying to reach in the use of material for case study purposes. For example, one of the downsides of working within a research group can be the pressure to produce case studies to a prescribed structure within a certain timeframe. The push for closure in moving on to other programmes and/or grant applications can significantly curtail the time allowed for data analysis. Such time constraints will often inhibit the researcher from spending too long reflecting on data interpretation, from which the possibility for different case study write-ups may arise. The researcher may experience peer-group pressure to work 'efficiently' towards a single case write-up on which the research team can generally agree.

These debates question whether we should place the analyst above the storyteller and chronicler in our processual analysis and case study write-up of organizational change. But what do we mean by the terms chronicler and storyteller? According to *The Shorter Oxford English Dictionary* (Onions, 1973: 333), a chronicle is 'a detailed and continuous register of events in order of time'. As a narrative that captures a sequence of events of 'this happened, then this happened, then this happened', the chronicle brings to mind causal links in the analysis and arrangement of past events. Although the chronicler is not concerned with multiple interpretations or moral messages, such records do remain open to historical reinterpretation. In contrast, storytellers may modify and adjust their stories to accommodate their audience. As Gabriel (2000) explains, they may steer their audience towards a certain understanding and interpretation of events that influences their worldview.

In the case of organizational change stories, narratives may be composed and presented as an accurate chronological account, they may reflect competing stories of conflict and dispute, or accounts may be appropriately modified to fit different audiences. Although there are always going to be different views, perspectives and stories on change that will coexist within organizations, the poignancy of stories in being able to influence the views and attitudes of others makes them powerful political tools in the orchestration and management of change processes. As a consequence, dominant narrators may actively construct and sustain a particular narrative within the context of other competing voices and views. These competing narratives on change reflect the power relationships between certain individuals and groups, and the political process by which certain 'voices' get heard and others remain hidden and/or are silenced. In many cases, it is possible to identify a dominant company narrative about the change programme being studied; the processual researcher can then monitor and evaluate the way that this dominant story is maintained, modified, redefined or replaced as other competing accounts emerge. Past events may be rewritten in the construction of a narrative that seeks to influence current decision-making. This narrative may also be informed by future expectations and, as a consequence, is open to further modification and revision over time. The coexistence of these multiple stories provides rich material on processes of change and is only deemed problematic in studies that seek to discover the one authentic timeless account, or by researchers who seek to act as the ultimate arbiter in being the expert process analyst. Any search for such an account is misplaced, as is any attempt to insist that a written case study can capture all elements of change. This is clearly an area that warrants further processual research. It also has implications for the way we present and publish data on change.

The written case study

The written case study presents a particular narrative of change. It is an interpretation of the data (post-analytical case narrative) that is necessarily selective. The author is not outside the analysis but is part of the process, and on revisiting data at some later date may reanalyse the data and identify new themes and patterns. Not only is the case write-up by a researcher today likely to differ from what would be written by the same researcher using the same data in ten years' time, but other researchers analysing the data may also draw out different issues, themes and interlocking patterns. This possibility for multiple interpretations does not devalue the research, but draws attention to the way others interpret and make sense of the world. It also highlights the benefits of presenting data in the case study write-up in order to allow for some interpretative flexibility. By so doing, readers need not only follow the author's line of argument, but they may also interpret the data in different ways, drawing out dissimilar issues and unusual conclusions that may further question some base assumptions. As Riley *et al.* (2000: 17–18) point out:

> Interpretive researchers can never be absolutely sure that they have acquired the 'world view' of the people they study, nor that they give the meanings they encounter the correct or only valid interpretation. Indeed, a major popular objection to much sociological commentary of the last two decades is that in seeking to interpret people's behaviour, social scientists read into that behaviour too much meaning, or even meanings that are 'not there'. There is probably some justice in this view. The dividing line between interpreting meaning and imputing it indiscriminately to people's behaviour, speech or whatever is a very fine one and reflects the inherent and unavoidable tensions and dangers that arise because of the commitment of interpretive research strategies to the inseparability of the researcher from the researched because of the former's own position as a member of society.

Unlike oral stories, which may be more rapidly adjusted to meet the changing needs of audiences, the written case study is often more tightly constrained. Pettigrew (1990: 280) identifies four levels of output. First, the analytical chronology clarifies sequences of events through analysis of the inner and outer context of change over a period of time. Second, the diagnostic case is essentially an analytical chronology with some strategic recommendations thrown in for presentation and discussion with management. Third, the interpretative theoretical case is an attempt 'to link emerging conceptual and theoretical ideas inductively derived from the case both to stronger analytical themes within the case and wider theoretical debates in the literature' (Pettigrew, 1990: 280). Fourth, the comparative analysis across case studies draws out patterns that are more generalizable. This meta-level analysis across cases is seen as the highest level of output. Once again, however, there is a tendency to elevate analysis that could be viewed as more 'scientific' in drawing on a larger body of comparative case material to strengthen the generalizability of the data and thereby downgrade the contribution of processual analysis from the single case. The view that meta-level analysis across cases is the highest level of output sadly undermines some of the very foundations of processual research, although Pettigrew is right to suggest that different outlets may expect a certain style, language and structure that will constrain the way in which data may be 'legitimately' used and presented. It is important not to try to standardize processual research and publications, or to suggest that there is a particular higher form of output to which all processual researchers should aspire. The richness and heterogeneity of processual studies and the different crafting skills, abilities and interests of the processual researcher are to be encouraged.

Within larger research groups, there may be pressure placed on researchers to formalize and codify their approach. As Hinings (1997: 496) notes: 'Multiple researchers and multiple cases raise continuing issues of internal validity and the reliability of data. Ensuring that all those involved in the research are following agreed procedures of interviewing, observation, coding and so on, is a basic way of dealing with the issue.' He goes on to suggest that a more pressing yet negative need for codification is because publication in prestigious US academic journals requires clarity on these issues. Reviewers' concern and scepticism regarding the write-up of qualitative processual research may largely stem from the papers not meeting reviewer expectations that have been forged by the dominance of nomothetic standards in North America (Hinings, 1997). This push for standardization and codification is evident in Pettigrew's move from individual scholar (Pettigrew, 1985) to being a member of an international multidisciplinary team of researchers (Pettigrew and Fenton, 2000a). While this shift in emphasis may be understandable, it is not necessarily a desirable development. The different positions taken on this issue are captured by Hinings (1997: 497), who advocates the benefits of this move to codification:

> It is through such codification that more and more people can be reached and the practices can be somewhat more easily transmitted to new generations of process researchers. However, Dawson provides us with timely reminders that processual research will always involve tacit knowledge and sustained fieldwork activity. But again, as Pettigrew points out, it is incumbent on processual researchers to specify research objectives and research questions, to explain and justify data sources and to state how the data were analyzed.

Thus another dilemma facing the processual researcher centres on the publication and output of the research. If the more prestigious US refereed academic journal is the target, then there are likely to be far more constraints on the form and content of the written case study. However, within the European arena there are far more potential outlets for the publication of qualitative research on change. It is argued here that the contribution of the single longitudinal qualitative case study should not be lost or undermined by a call for larger multidisciplinary research programmes that promote standardization and are more readily accepted as 'legitimate' because of their stronger 'scientific' base. Under a processual perspective, *one* is significant. Consequently, while Pettigrew's four-fold characterization of output is useful, it is also misleading in its hierarchical representation of 'lower' and 'higher' forms.

In an attempt to counterbalance this notion of 'higher level' outputs, Figure 8.1 provides a characterization of four different types of case study that are written with a particular audience or outlet in mind. The written case study can take various forms, ranging from the summary accounts of key events through to long and detailed post-analytical explanations of change. More broadly defined, a case study can be used to refer to the experience of an individual subject, an event, a piece of legislation or a future scenario (see Riley *et al.*, 2000: 100–102), or it may aim to 'provide experience and practice in managing skills through "hands-on" sets of exercises to enhance an awareness of "how to do it" issues' (Clegg *et al.*, 1999). In this latter case study collection, each chapter is well structured with clear objectives and a session outline is

provided for teaching purposes. Among these many different types of
case study, those concerned with capturing processes of change in
organizations often range from the short compressed summary to the
larger research-based monograph. These are represented in Figure 8.1,
which is intended to be a guide (rather than a definitive typology) to
processual case studies on organizational change.

As well as listing case study types, Figure 8.1 also draws attention to the
importance of the audience in shaping the presentation of the data and the
write-up of the case study. The structure and content of the case material
is generally shaped to meet the expectations and requirements of the
intended audience. In being aware of the audience (or intended outlet),
the researcher may focus more on the details of events and their sequence
(chronicler), the contextual flavour of processes of change and key

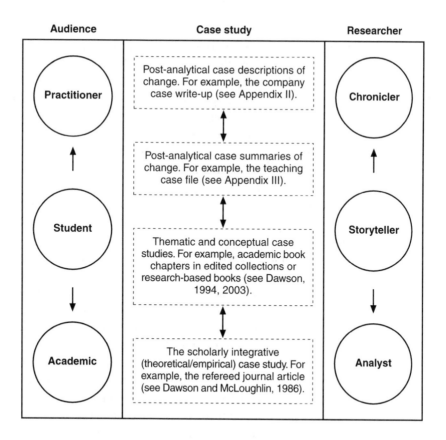

Figure 8.1 *Written case studies on change: an illustration of four common types*

characters or groups (storyteller), or the contribution of the empirical study to theoretical developments and conceptual debates (academic analyst). Typically, a more systematic and formal approach is used in a company case write-up or in the submission of an academically rigorous article for journal publication. There is always a sense in which the writer acts as a scholarly analyst in seeking to unravel and explain change. However, in what might appear as a less analytical and more descriptive approach to the case study write-up (in the composition of teaching case files) the author may act more as chronicler-cum-storyteller in the construction of a case narrative. In practice, this distinction between the analytical and descriptive is a false one. As already discussed, any search for an authentic scholarly account is misplaced, as there will always be competing histories and multiple narratives on change. Furthermore, in this type of processual research even the most basic case study write-up involves data analysis and is better described as a post-analytical case narrative.

Figure 8.1 categorizes four types of written case study, namely the company case write-up, the teaching case file, the academic book chapter, and the refereed journal article. There are of course other types of case study that could be added, such as the research monograph and the skills-based case scenario, but no attempt is made here to provide an exhaustive list. The main aim is to discuss some of the more common forms of the written case study and to provide some practical illustrations (see Appendix II and III). In our first example, the company case write-up, the researcher may opt to submit a compact executive case history (see Dawson, 1996: 156–159), or a rather longer and more detailed chronicler description (see Appendix II). In both cases, the written submission is normally checked for factual accuracy by the participating organization. It also provides the company with an opportunity to identify any issues or comments that they may feel are commercially sensitive and should not be published. One advantage with more weighty submissions is that once the company has cleared the data, the researcher then has a larger body of material that can be used for a range of different purposes. At this stage in the process, there is generally little attempt to integrate academic themes and theoretical debates into the case study write-up. The main intention is to gain company agreement that the material can be used for the purpose of academic publication (the currency of many academic careers). Once the material has been checked and released by the participating organization, the researcher is able to use this body of material for a series of publications.

The example of the tutorial teaching case file refers to a type of summary case history that is able to capture the basic chronology of change in a readable way and is able to raise a number of key discussion points or 'problems' for student debate. These readable case descriptions can be used in tutorials or as part of a management development programme. In being condensed the teaching case files can be used unseen (without the need for prior student preparation), in contrast to book chapters, which normally need to be read and analysed prior to tutorial group discussions. An example of this shorter case history is provided in Appendix III (the original case write-up was over 250 pages long). As a lecturer using this type of case material at the undergraduate and postgraduate level, I have also found it useful to provide a student guide on how to approach the analysis of the case study material (an example of such a guide, developed with Liz Kummerow at the University of Adelaide, is reproduced in Appendix III).

The academic book chapter can take a number of different forms. There is normally some integration of certain concepts with data analysis in addressing academic debates or in comparing findings with other comparable studies. One common structure is where the chapter opens with an overview of the appropriate literature, prior to case analysis, conceptual development and academic discussion. Although written for an academic and student audience, these case studies sometimes provide richer descriptions (post-analytical narratives) than those written for submission to a refereed academic journal (Dawson, 1994, 2003). In writing the case for a respected academic journal, concepts may be revised and developed, and data analysis is typically integrated with the literature in order to illustrate and debate scholarly issues (Dawson and McLoughlin, 1986). The illustrative use of data is often sparse in journal articles when compared to book chapters, although there are certainly instances where this would not be the case. While there are many different forms that the written case study can take, they are often developed and shaped to meet the expectations of their intended audience or to meet the requirements of the proposed outlet for publication. The researcher and author may also seek to influence the expectations of their audience. This is often an important and necessary strategy for processual researchers, who should, in managing their relationship with those being studied, always consider preparing the case organization for what is likely to be contained in their case study submission. It is also a useful point to stress for new researchers and students who are about to embark on case study research, for it is in those instances, where the two are at odds, that research problems usually arise.

Content and style of the case material

During the task of processual analysis and case study write-up, the researcher also needs to consider the extent to which certain types of primary data may be included or excluded from the case narrative. This is most in evidence with regard to taped interview transcripts, and is an issue that is often raised by students and new researchers in this area. In practice, some authors minimize the amount of qualitative data in their final case write-up (see, for example, Pettigrew and Fenton, 2000a), while others may draw heavily on interview transcripts to illustrate points and themes raised in the text (see, for example, Dawson, 2003). A benefit of data inclusion is that it allows readers access to the data (however limited), enabling them to form judgements on how the data is being used in analysis, and encouraging them to reflect on the content of the case material in considering alternative possible interpretations.

As analysts and authors, we decide on the space that should be made available for data within our text. If primary data are absent or are spread thinly in the text, then the reader is less able to engage with the words and views of respondents and must rely on the written narrative. However, if we allow more space within the main body of the text for transcribed data, then the author will have less control over the interpretations of the reader and may find that his or her analysis is challenged or questioned. Clearly, if the researcher provides too much data then the reader may get lost in the detail; too little, and the data are no longer able to speak for themselves. While gaining the right balance is not an easy task (and is one that is likely to reflect the style and preferences of the researcher), there is considerable value in allowing readers access to chunks of data to support and illustrate arguments made in the case study text. In my view, studies that fail to use primary data in their case narratives tend to offer rather dry accounts that do not capture the rich texture, emotionality and subjectivity that is part of people's lived experience of change. The rich tapestries of these contextual stories lie at the heart of processual research, and, as previously argued, such accounts are not strengthened by the importation of quantitative survey data. The detailed quotations from taped transcripts enable readers (students and practitioners) to gain access to data that helps them to identify with people's experiences of work, and in so doing also assists them in making sense of issues or problems being discussed. Written in such a way, these case stories make change processes and employee responses more understandable, allowing readers to empathize with the behaviour of individuals and groups towards programmes of change. In short, a good case story is highly readable, with plenty of clear data illustrations that makes the research accessible and yet provides space for further interpretation and discussion.

In the writing of case studies, authors should make the focus of their study clear to readers and highlight the type of data collected and used. For example, in some studies the focus of the research may be on a particular group, such as senior managers, supervisors or older employees; while in others processes of change may be examined from a range of perspectives, such as those of shop-floor employees, unions, change consultants, senior management, supervisors and local management. If done well, the processual case study can provide access to the multiple stories, anecdotes and histories of change, as well as to versions of events captured in observation notes and documentary material. There remains considerable room to develop the processual perspective, and one area that is picked up and developed slightly further in the concluding chapter relates to our use of stories and storytelling in making sense of organizational change.

Conclusion

The four questions posed at the start of the chapter remain open to further discussion and debate. It is evident that there is a range of different authoring and audiencing roles, and that these will influence the way we present and publish our research findings. As storytellers and analysts, we may seek to influence our audience in preparing the ground for written submissions on company change. As academic authors, we may adhere to the expectations and requirements of certain journals through using previous published material to inform the writing of our own text. As a processual researcher, there is also a story about the research process (Orton, 1997) as well as the multiple storylines that are present within the rich contextual data on change. In addition, storytelling is an important tool for high-profile 'celebrity' professors in providing a powerful medium for relaying simple lessons on company change.

However, such stories may also mask the complexity of change processes in promoting a linear sequential view (for example, this happened, then this happened, causing this to happen). As processual researchers, we must face the challenge not only of providing a critique of these simplistic yet popular models of change, but also of how we can best disseminate our findings more broadly. This raises a further interesting question about stories, for while they may be used to promote practical advice that requires academic critique, they also offer an avenue for the more widespread dissemination of our ideas. As a character in a David Lodge (2001: 83) novel reflects:

> Of course one can argue that there's a basic human need for narrative: it's one of our fundamental tools for making sense of experience – has been, back as far as you can go in history . . . you could relate the old familiar tales over and over, the matter of Troy, the matter of Rome, the matter of Britain . . . giving them a new spin as times and manners change . . . When you think of the billions of real people who have lived on this earth, each with their unique personal histories, that we shall never have time to know.

This chapter has set out to provide some insight into the practice of processual analysis and case study write-up. Illustrations and examples have been drawn from my own research, and a number of methodological issues and concerns have been discussed. The contribution of processual research to organizational studies has been stressed, and it has been argued that there are still a number of further developments needed in order to fully realize the potential of the processual perspective for understanding change. Any attempt to make such an approach more 'scientific' or the findings more generalizable through multiple comparative case studies is, in my opinion, misguided. The strength of processual research and analysis lies in its ability to accommodate diversity, to deal with complexity, and to examine the experience of individuals and groups over time. There is no search for an illusory authentic story; nor is there a need to elevate the views of one group over another, or to seek 'scientific' approval. Although there are clear strengths in comparative processual research, caution is needed in ensuring that fieldwork and analysis are not increasingly compressed in order to increase the total number of case studies in the false belief that this will in turn increase the 'validity' of the data. It may also lead the researcher to focus on identifying replications of certain patterns rather than on the variations between data, deviant accounts and the unheard stories of the less powerful, as well as recurring patterns. Essentially, it is the quality of the research and the research practice that counts, and this requires that, among other things, sufficient time be scheduled for processual analysis and the write-up of the case study. There are no shortcuts to this type of research, but neither is there a need to feel under pressure to engage in a 'respectable' number of case studies.

9 Conclusion: the process of organizational change

In a way we are at a crossroad where it is the variety of processual publications that captures the eye on the one hand, and the pressure to systematize and standardize the way processual research is carried out on the other hand. Individual researchers may easily find themselves in the muddy waters of different lines of argumentation, and varying expectations in terms of research design, data collection, analysis, and reporting the results. Agreement on the rules of the game clears the water, but when pushed too far such agreement may lead to a straitjacket with little room for true experimentation and learning. One might ask, whether we wish to develop process research practices toward generic, standardized patterns, or whether we would rather leave more space for personal orientations, individual voices and self-reflections that is inherent in social theory development?

(Ropo *et al.*, 1997b: 332)

In this short and final chapter, it is worth reflecting on our understanding of a processual perspective for making sense of change. As the opening extract suggests, we may be at a crossroad where a decision has to be made about the future direction and development of processual research. There are clearly many alternatives and options available in reshaping and refocussing the theoretical, methodological and practical applications of the processual perspective. Some of the main objectives of this book, and some possible areas for future development, are discussed in the sections that follow. However, first let us consider the choice between the track where the processual researcher develops his or her own tacit skills, as an innovative and creative analyst, and the path along which the researcher adopts a more generic model in applying standardized procedures. Whichever direction is chosen the choice should not be made lightly, as it is a critical decision both for the researcher and for the future development of processual research. At this critical juncture, Hinings

(1997) would stress the need for standardization and codification; Pettigrew (1990) would advocate the benefits of comparative case studies that can be carried out within the larger multidisciplinary research group (with future possible links to more quantitative survey data; see Pettigrew and Fenton, 2000a; Starkey and Pettigrew, 2002: 24–25); while this book has argued that the full, multifaceted, in-depth textured inquiry of the longitudinal case study should be the mainstay of processual research. Also, that critical self-reflection, experimentation and innovation are what are required in the further refinement and development of a processual perspective for understanding processes of organizational change.

A brief review of the processual perspective

Before reflecting on some areas for possible further development, it is worth summarizing some of the main topics, issues and questions that have been addressed in our examination of the processual perspective. These have included:

- An overview of the origins and development of a processual perspective in organizational studies.
- The use of empirical case study material to illustrate the three key dimensions of the politics, substance and context of change.
- A critical discussion of the methodological orientation of processual research.
- Identification of key issues in the design of longitudinal fieldwork and the recounting of practical experiences of doing processual research.
- An examination of processual analysis and forms of publication in the dissemination of research findings.
- Defining areas for further development through such concepts as multiple narratives, stories and competing histories.
- The ardent encouragement for processual researchers to maintain a commitment to the smaller intensive qualitative longitudinal case study.
- A critique of attempts to codify and standardize the approach (and also attempts to link processual research with more quantitative measures of change).
- A demonstration of the need to look at processes of organizational change from multiple perspectives (all employees, and not just management).

- The explanation of a processual framework for understanding processes of organizational change.

In examining these issues, it has consistently been argued that change is a process and not an event. It can be described as an odyssey that individuals and groups attempt to steer, and yet they must also be aware of the need to reshape and reappraise in the light of the unexpected and unforeseen. While planning is often an integral part of major change programmes, it is not, nor should it be seen to be, a solution to the management of change. In putting the plan into practice, outcomes rarely if ever match detailed prescriptions on how the future should be. Change does not occur in a neat linear fashion, but is messy, murky and complicated. It involves twists and loops, turns and returns, omissions and revisions, the foreseen and unforeseen, and is marked by the achievement of planned targets, failures, resistance, celebration, ambivalence, fatigue, conflict and political manoeuvring. To understand these complex non-linear dynamics it is important to examine change temporally, as it happens, rather than to take a single snapshot of events. As such, the ongoing reshaping processes of change are best viewed through the lens of a processual perspective that is able to capture these realities in flight.

The substance, context and politics of change, as well as multiple narratives and competing histories, form an integral part of the processual approach developed in this book. The conceptual framework outlined in Chapter 2 argues that people's interpretations and perceptions of change, their stories of past events, as well as their expectations of future outcomes and possibilities, all serve to influence the dynamic ways in which these various elements (the substance, context and politics of change) overlap and interlock over time. These processes were illustrated in the case study chapters that examine new ways of organizing at Britax, the training and use of video conferencing technology at Shell, the implementation of a total quality management programme at Pirelli, and the uptake of cellular work arrangements at General Motors. These studies were followed by three chapters examining the theory and practice of doing processual research, which also discussed options in the presentation and publication of research findings. It was shown how the post-analytical processual case study is a narrative that has been written by a researcher (the author) with a particular outlet in mind (the audience). Such accounts are by their nature partial, incomplete and a reflection of the context in which they are written, the author, and the intended audience.

Taken as a whole, this book has set out to demonstrate the value of a processual perspective in making sense of organizational change. It has questioned the label of 'emergent' and argued that the processual perspective is also interested in critical junctures and planned programmes of change. It has been critical of studies that focus too heavily on management and do not give equal treatment to all employee perspectives. It has also signalled grave reservations over more recent attempts to 'push the numbers' through ever larger multidisciplinary research programmes that attempt to integrate survey data with the more intensive case study. Within these broader studies, tacit skills and the creative process of qualitative longitudinal research and data analysis can be lost or remain hidden, especially in final outputs and publications. Such programmes also impose greater pressure on the researcher to consent to the codification and standardization of group research procedures. This of course leads us back to the epistemological debates raised in Chapter 6, where we questioned whether the larger, more objective and scientific study should be seen as producing research findings of a higher academic order. Unless we are critical of such views, then one distressing consequence is the possibility that researchers in smaller groups, or working alone on a single processual case study, may find their work devalued. It is argued here that longitudinal in-depth studies of change should be publicly supported and developed, and that processual researchers should not accede to the North American model of 'scientific' research. There is a growing cadre of researchers in Australia, Canada and New Zealand, as well as the USA and UK, who are doing this type of processual research, and it is hoped that this trend will continue.

Processual developments: multiple narratives and competing histories

While there is nothing like a radical change to stimulate political manoeuvring at the top of an organization (Starkey and Pettigrew, 2002: 22), a central argument of this book has been that political processes occur at *all* levels within an organization and should be central to any explanation of change. To put it another way, it is a mistake only to focus on the powerful in examining politics, for it is also the less powerful and those voices that may remain unheard or are silenced that are critical to understanding the political process of organizational change. It is therefore important that the processual researcher accommodates the different views and perspectives of various individuals and groups.

Documentary evidence, workplace observations and multiple interviews with employees in different sections and holding different hierarchical positions inevitably draw attention to the diversity of people's lived experience. These experiences are captured in the stories of individuals and groups who often compete to get their particular version of reality heard. It is not surprising, therefore, that stories are powerful tools and are much in evidence in change programmes, where multiple and competing narratives often coexist and yet popular case histories typically talk of a single story of change. These single stories of change tend to down-play outlier data or stories of the less powerful in drawing out case study lessons on the 'successful' management of change. The focus on 'successful' stories of change has promoted the development of rational models that ignore notions of competing histories and multiple change narratives. However, this book has shown how organizational narratives and past experiences of change combine with future expectations and projections to influence individual and group interpretations of change. Within this contextual tapestry lie a number of storylines and competing narratives that seek both to explain change (such as the reason and purpose of change) and to provide an ordering of events in making sense of the (complex) change experience. As such, these rational models of change also aim to provide *the* story and in so doing they impose their own linear rational world on what is a far more dynamic non-linear process (which may account for the high level of failure associated with such approaches).

In engaging in this type of longitudinal research, processual researchers are chroniclers, storytellers and analysts. They are chroniclers in recording the time sequence of events and activities through the use of documents and observations, and in linking interview transcripts to a particular time and context. Researchers are also storytellers in their use of observational commentaries to narrate stories from fieldwork experience, and in the composition of stories that are built upon different interpretations of change. Finally, in identifying patterns, unlocking meanings, and accommodating deviant and outlier data, researchers are also analysts in that they develop post-analytical explanations of change. The skills of the storyteller, chronicler and analyst are each important and intertwine during the process of data collection, data analysis, and case study write-up. At the same time as being aware of the particularism of individual and group narratives, researchers are also concerned with constructing a case study narrative that describes change processes in a broader sense. Although one or a number of case studies may be used to widen theorization from the particular to the general, there remains a tension between individual subjective narratives and broader sociological explanations. As such the concept of 'multiple narratives' is useful, as it accommodates diversity whilst recognizing that during the political process of change a dominant narrative is likely to emerge as the 'authentic' story.

The longitudinal study of plant-level change at General Motors (Chapter 4) usefully illustrates how change narratives can compete and the way in which *the* company story of change was managed and sustained. The study demonstrates how different individuals may recount and reconstruct stories that reflect their own interests, and how the maintenance of common organizational stories often reflects the influence and political action of certain powerful actors and groups. In the General Motors case, the plant manager set about orchestrating a rational narrative in the process of implementing plant-level change. This involved creating a stakeholder coalition comprising internal managerial and supervisory staff, trade unionists, and a body of outside experts to advise on plant redesign. Fascinatingly, although the trade union officials recognized that the narrative constructed by the plant manager was a rather biased account of events, they did not seek to undermine this account. Their main concern centred on the employment and working conditions of staff and on ensuring that the plant was not closed by senior management. Consequently, in managing their own political agenda they decided to monitor events closely from a distance. The union was prepared to intervene if the situation warranted such action, but officials readily accepted that *the* story of change presented by management was never going to reflect accurately the lived experience of their members.

Interestingly, this case also highlights how 'stories' of change can be modified over time. Two brief examples are: first, during the third interview with the plant manager (some twelve months into a longitudinal study of shop-floor change), a number of competing histories and revised versions of change emerged. In part, these revisions reflected recognition of a greater understanding of the change process by the researcher. In other words, the plant manager recognized that his audience (in this case the researcher) was becoming more sophisticated and knowledgeable about events at the plant. It was no longer feasible for the plant manager to avoid discussion of some of the more 'negative' aspects of change. A second example arose when the researcher witnessed the plant manager providing an account of change on the shop floor that did not reflect actual operations. Although the plant manager was aware that the researcher knew that this was not the case, he maintained his story (perhaps knowing that the researcher needed continual access to the plant to complete the study). The public story of change recounted to a manager from another manufacturing company was not revised in this external context (for example, to accommodate the researcher). In this example, we have someone who was identified as a key change agent who refined and modified *the* story of change according to his assessment of his audience. In this sense, not only are there likely to be multiple change narratives associated with different individuals and groups, but also individuals may change their narrative to accommodate a different audience. Thus this processual study was useful both in highlighting competing histories between groups and in demonstrating how individuals revise their accounts over time and according to their audience.

In examining mutually negotiated narratives, it is important to consider the storytellers, the actors and the audience (which include the various individuals and groups who attempt to make sense of change, as well as trade unionists, managers, change agents, external collaborators and so forth). In practice, different change stories are likely to be promoted at different levels within an organization, as well as within particular groups (for example, local management) and areas of operation (for example, the machine shop). The process of scripting *the* story and on agreeing how organizational change has occurred and is occurring is part of a process in which management (more than any other group) often reinforce positive elements of their own involvement, and down-play, suppress or ignore those elements that are seen to represent 'minor disruptions' to an otherwise 'successful' programme. From a local management perspective, it is often easier to agree and support a positive story of success than one that might question the decision-making of senior management. The narrative, once agreed, is continually replayed (often with minor modifications) in an attempt to sustain the narrative as the 'authentic' story of change. Paradoxically, these managed accounts can be drawn on later as a body of practical knowledge to inform future change initiatives. In this sense, the authoring of the change script and the process by which key players agree (in creating and sustaining a dominant narrative) is a central element to understanding change, and is an area in need of further critical research.

The recognition of the importance of multiple narratives and their modification for different audiences also has methodological implications. It is fairly common in conducting a case study analysis of company change to use interview accounts as one data source that is broken down and recombined with other accounts in constructing a case story on the process of change. However, if each account is used to present a 'story' on change, then it raises the question of how these 'stories' can be presented in a way that provides greater insight and understanding of change processes. In utilizing such an approach we would need to move away from an examination of emerging patterns, common themes and deviant outliers, to an analysis of plots, chronologies and major and minor characters. We may turn our attention to the assumptions that lie behind the construction of a chronological narrative of causality. This would signal the need for us to continue our multi-level analyses of data, but in so doing also consider the implications of competing narratives both for an understanding of the place of organizational stories in the context of work, and for the further development of conceptual frames for understanding organizational change. Our research strategy and methods might usefully be revised in order to tap into the rich tapestry of organizational stories, not only as they exist at any point of time, but also as they emerge, shift and are redefined over time by different individuals and groups. Such a shift in focus also raises issues about the relationship of group stories to the way individuals narrate their own characters in their individual storytelling of processes and events. This area is also in need of further processual research and analysis.

In the writing of case studies, the researcher also becomes an author in presenting a case script on change. Although the use of the narrative approach does allow the writer to capture some of the complexity and ambiguity of change, the researcher has nevertheless sifted, selected and interpreted data in a way that is likely to reflect his or her interests. Another researcher carrying out a similar study is likely to produce very different results. In part, this is because researchers are not in a position to take themselves outside of this type of research, which requires significant periods of time to be spent with respondents, both interviewing and observing activities in their place of work. In this sense, the researcher is an author of a narrative he or she has shaped. From a processual perspective, the intention is to present a case narrative that invites the reader to question, challenge and reinterpret the case material, rather than passively to accept any singular account of change.

One final issue that may be worthy of further consideration centres on the theoretical and practical implications of narratives of organizational change. As already discussed, Yannis Gabriel (2000) focusses on the development of a theory of organizational storytelling. This perspective draws attention to the 'entertaining' aspects of storytelling and how they are used as a means of escaping the rigours of our daily work lives. As Gabriel (2000: 239) states: 'Stories are narratives with plots and characters, generating emotion in both the narrator and the audience through a poetic elaboration of symbolic material'. Processual studies engage with the experience of others in their retelling of characters and events, and in the replaying of emotions and actions in response to change initiatives. These stories are in abundance in longitudinal studies on change and take many forms; for example, individuals and groups use stories to make sense of their everyday lived experience, as well as to paint a particular picture of change programmes (which may in turn be modified for different audiences). Although we can examine the way a particular narrative emerges as a dominant story and is maintained, refined or perhaps replaced over time, stories are not *per se* the domain of the powerful. They provide platforms of resistance for the less powerful, and are a useful way of blending so called organizational 'facts' with the fictions of management in questioning assumptions imposed on the workplace by more 'powerful' others. Moreover, if there are multiple authors of change who present competing narratives that further influence change stories, then it is important to understand how narratives are further influenced by competing histories, and the shifting positions associated with authoring and audiencing roles. The interplay between audiencing and authoring may also combine with certain narrative expectations about the way 'clear' stories should present a chronology of events whilst the less acceptable narratives are 'muddled and confused'. Again, the story seeks to make sense out of what is a complex non-linear process by providing an easily accessible story of change. Explanations and casual links may also be embedded within change narratives and a series of underlying assumptions may in turn influence the construction of such stories that are used to inform change management practice. In this we come full circle, and see the need for further processual research to develop the potential of a processual perspective for understanding organizational change.

Appendix I: example of interview schedules and supervisor's questionnaire

This appendix provides an illustration of two interview schedules used in a study of freight yard operations in the early 1980s, and a supervisor's questionnaire. At the outset, it was anticipated that the British Rail research would form part of a larger number of studies on workplace change. Professor John Smith of the University of Southampton, through a letter to Arnold Kentridge who was then Director of Strategic Studies on the British Railways Board, initiated the study. As the letter states: 'We estimate that the study will require a period of 2–3 weeks in at least two Marshalling Yards: the methods to be used would be observation of Yard operators and interviews with Area Freight Assistants, Yard Supervisors, Chargemen, Area Managers and Operations Assistants' (Dawson, 1986: 224). However, as the author became established within British Rail the interviewees provided further links and recommendations that resulted in eighteen months of intensive research (between 1981 and 1983), in which the use of observation became a key research method. Interviews were conducted with 80 British Rail employees (plus repeat interviews) at national and regional headquarters, two British Rail training centres (where the author underwent supervisory training) and a number of British Rail marshalling yards. Considerable time was also spent with 'shunting gangs' on the day and night shifts and at various social activities. Consequently, while the questionnaire was initially intended to be a major vehicle for data collection, by the end of the study observation notes, taped interviews and documents were central to processual analysis. Also, the time given to this longitudinal study did not allow for further case studies to be conducted on change.

Interviews were held with senior management, local management, supervisory staff (including the chargeman and leading hands) and shunting yard staff. The interview schedules were used as an *aide memoire* rather than a fixed structure. Essentially, the author soon became very familiar with the areas to be covered and used the schedule as a check that questions had been asked. It should also be noted that the interviews would generally involve other questions arising from observations and the time spent at the various marshalling yards. For example, if there was an issue or concern then the interview would be used as an opportunity to explore the interviewees' views and position. There were also opportunities to leave the tape running during group discussions in the yard huts. Thus these illustrative schedules (the two examples shown below relate to supervisors and yard staff) did not prevent a more conversational flow during the interview, as they were not used to structure it.

Supervisor's interview schedule

A. *Career*
Why did you decide to join British Rail?

Were there any other jobs that you considered?

What made you seek promotion to your present position?

Do you intend going for promotion in the future?

Could you give a brief summary of your career in British Rail?

- Position, location, dates

B. *Job tasks and work organization*
As a supervisor, do you feel that you have too much, about right, or too little:

- Freedom of action?
- Responsibility?
- Authority?

Could you describe your basic duties and responsibilities as a supervisor?

Could you briefly describe the work involved in a typical day/week?

What do you feel is the most important job task that you perform?

- How much time does this involve?

Looking at your job overall, can you estimate what percentage of your time in an average week is spent:

- Supervising staff?
- Dealing with contingencies?
- Other?

What are the main reasons for having contact with yard staff?

Do you feel that the job of the supervisor has changed with the introduction of the TOPS computer system?

- What was it like before?
- What changes have occurred?
- Has it made the supervisor's job easier/harder? In what way?

C. *Training*
What type of training did you receive when you first took up your present position?

- Length and type of training
- Whether: local, self-instruction, or formal course

Have you ever had any general supervisory training?

- When was that?
- How useful was it?
- Evaluation: need more/less

Have you been trained in the use of the TOPS computer system?

- When?
- Type of course, length of training
- Adequacy of training

Do you feel that you have received: too much, about right, or not enough training in the use of the computer system?

- Why is that (e.g. training programme too short/long, course too complex/simple)?

D. *Job satisfaction*
What do you like/dislike about your work?

- Pay
- Job security
- Opportunity for exercising autonomy/management control
- Variety of job tasks
- Dealing with variations and unforeseen events
- Making decisions
- Working with other supervisors, yard staff, managers

In your opinion, what are the key areas in which improvements could be made?

Could you briefly discuss any aspects about your job that you feel should be carried out by someone else?

- Type of task(s)
- Why, by whom?

Do you feel that there is anything that the supervisor should be doing that at present he doesn't do?

Do you feel that the introduction of computer technology has made your job more satisfying, less satisfying, or has it remained about the same?

E. *Computerization and industrial relations*
Are you in a union?

- (If no) why, nature of reason/objection
- Date joined union
- Reasons for joining

How do you feel about the way the national implementation of the computer system was handled by management?

- Local level

How do you feel about the way the national implementation of the computer system was handled by the trade unions?

- Local level

What are your own personal views on modernization and the railways?

F. *Personal details*

- Age
- Position
- Grade
- Place of birth
- Marital status
- Occupation of father/mother/spouse
- Previous employment

Yard staff interview schedule

A. *Career*
Why did you decide to join British Rail?

Were there any other jobs that you considered?

What made you seek promotion to your present position?

Do you intend going for promotion in the future?

Could you give a brief summary of your career in British Rail?

- Position, location, dates

B. *Job tasks and work organization*
As a head shunter/shunter, do you feel that you have too much, about right, or too little:

- Freedom of action?

- Responsibility?
- Authority?

Could you briefly describe the work involved in a typical day/week?

What do you feel is the most important job task that you perform?

- How much time does this involve?

Looking at your job overall, can you estimate what percentage of your time in an average week is spent planning and supervising the work of others?

Do you feel that the job of the head shunter/shunter has changed with the introduction of the TOPS computer system?

- Freedom of action
- Responsibility
- Has it made the job easier/harder, in what way?

C. *Supervision*
How much contact do you have with your supervisor?

How much say does he have over your work?

Do you feel that supervisors have an important role to play in the running of the yard?

Do you feel that the job of the supervisor has changed with the introduction of the TOPS computer system?

What do you feel are the qualities needed to make a good supervisor?

What kind of relationship do you have with your supervisor?

- How important is it to have a good relationship?
- Are supervisors generally a help or hindrance?

D. *Training*
What type of training did you receive when you first took up your present position?

- Length and type of training
- Whether local, self-instruction, or formal course

E. *Job satisfaction*
What do you like/dislike about your work?

- Pay
- Job security
- Variety of job tasks
- Making decisions
- Working with other yard staff, supervisors

In your opinion, what are the key areas in which improvements could be made?

Could you briefly discuss any aspects about your job that you feel should be carried out by someone else?

- Type of task(s)
- Why, by whom?

Do you feel that there is anything that the head shunter/shunter should be doing that at present he doesn't do?

Do you feel that the introduction of computer technology has made your job more satisfying, less satisfying, or has it remained about the same?

F. *Computerization and industrial relations*
Are you in a union?

- (If no) why, nature of reason/objection
- When did you join the union?
- Why did you join the union?

How do you feel about the way the national implementation of the computer system was handled by management?

- Local level

How do you feel about the way the implementation of the computer system was handled by the trade unions?

- National level

What are your own personal views on modernization and the railways?

G. *Personal details*

- Age
- Position
- Grade
- Place of birth
- Marital status
- Occupation of father/mother/spouse
- Previous employment

Supervisor's questionnaire

The questionnaire outlined below was designed solely for use with supervisory graded staff and was intended either to provide data that could not otherwise be obtained, or to act as a supplement to interviews conducted with supervisors. As it turned out, data elicited by the questionnaire were largely used to supplement other methods of data collection.

A. *Personal details*

1 Present job title:
2 Present grade:
3 Age:

B. *Career*

1 Jobs held in BR (please give grades, location and approximate dates where possible)?

2 Could you please indicate which of the following factors did or did not influence you in seeking promotion to your present post:
   (a) Better basic pay
   (b) Better earnings
   (c) Increased responsibility
   (d) Greater freedom within the job
   (e) A sense of achievement
   (f) Better working hours
   (g) The need for a change
   (h) Other factors (please specify)

C. *Training*

1 Have you attended any of the NEBBS course? (If yes indicate the *date*, *stage* and *location* of the various courses attended)

2 As a supervisor, do you feel that the NEBBS course(s) have been:
   (a) Very useful
   (b) Useful
   (c) Of minimal use
   (d) Of no use at all?

3 Have you had any formal TOPS training? (If yes indicate the *date*, *title* and *location* of the course)

4 As a supervisor, do you feel that TOPS training has been:
   (a) Very useful
   (b) Useful
   (c) Of minimal use
   (d) Of no use at all?

Additional comments?

5 Have you received any other training in relation to TOPS? (If yes, explain and give dates)

6 Please list any other training courses attended during you employment with BR

7 Could you please list in the space provided any other formal qualifications (e.g. G.C.S.E.s, 'O' levels, City and Guilds, et cetera)?

D. *Work organization and the job of the supervisor*

1 As a supervisor, how many people are you responsible for?

2   What is the job title and grade of *your* direct superior?

3   What is the job title and grade of *your* immediate subordinate?

4   What are the average weekly hours that you work?

5.1 Who decides when you work?
5.2 Who decides the number of hours that you work?

6   *Area Freight Assistants answer this question*: looking at your job
    overall, can you estimate what percentage of your time in an average
    week is spent dealing with the following people?
    6.1 Your Area Manager
    6.2 Your immediate superior (as in question 2)
    6.3 Other AFAs
    6.4 Yard supervisors
    6.5 Your immediate subordinate (as in question 3)
    6.6 Your shift leader
    6.7 Other TOPS clerks
    6.8 Other yard staff

7   *Yard Supervisors answer this question*: looking at your job overall, can
    you estimate what percentage of your time in an average week is spent
    dealing with the following people?
    7.1 Your Area Manager
    7.2 Your immediate superior (as in question 2)
    7.3 Your AFA
    7.4 Other yard supervisors
    7.5 Your immediate subordinate (as in question 3)
    7.6 Head shunters
    7.7 Other yard staff
    7.8 TOPS clerks

8   Looking at your job overall, can you estimate what percentage of your
    time in an average week is taken up by the following?
    8.1 Allocating work
    8.2 Doing paper work
    8.3 Communicating over the phone
    8.4 Face-to-face communication
    8.5 Directly supervising your staff
    8.6 Appraising your staff
    8.7 Arranging unscheduled services
    8.8 Free time
    8.9 Other

9.1 What would you say are the most common types of unforeseen
    events/emergencies that you have to deal with in your present job?
    (Could you also please indicate approximately how often they occur,
    e.g. daily, weekly, et cetera).
9.2 Which of the above is the most difficult to deal with?

10 As a supervisor, do you see yourself as being part of: (a) management,

(b) the operating workforce, (c) somewhere in between, or (d) not in any of these?

11 Do you feel that your immediate supervisor consults you (a) too often, (b) about right, or (c) too little?

12 In general, do you think that managers in BR consult supervisors (a) too often, (b) about right, or (c) too little?

13 Do you feel that you have (a) too much, (b) about right, or (c) too little of the following in respect to your job?
   13.1 Freedom of action
   13.2 Responsibility
   13.3 Authority

14 Do you feel able safely to delegate responsibility to your immediate subordinate? (If answer *no*, please go to question 16)

15 How useful is it for you to know that you have a subordinate to whom you can safely delegate responsibility?
   (a) Very useful
   (b) Useful
   (c) Of minimal use
   (d) Of no use at all

Additional comments?

16.1 Could you please indicate the typical types of supervisory duties that would be carried out by your subordinate in an average week?
16.2 Could you please estimate what percentage of your immediate subordinate's time in an average week is spent doing supervisory duties?

17 Which of the following groups of people is it most important for you to have a good relationship with?
   (a) Your area manager
   (b) Your immediate superior
   (c) Your/other AFA(s)
   (d) Your/other yard supervisor(s)
   (e) Your immediate subordinate
   (f) Your other staff

18 Which of the above groups of people is it least important for you to have a good relationship with?

Additional comments?

E. *Computer technology and marshalling yard supervision*

1 When TOPS was first introduced, at which yard were you located and what was the approximate date of implementation?

2 What was your job title and grade at this time?

3 As a supervisor, how do you feel TOPS has affected the *freedom of action* within your job? Has it: (a) increased, (b) remained about the same, or (c) decreased?

4 As a supervisor, how do you feel TOPS has affected the *amount of responsibility* within your job? Has it: (a) increased, (b) remained about the same, or (c) decreased?

5 As a supervisor, how do you feel TOPS has affected the *degree of authority* within your job? Has it: (a) increased, (b) remained about the same, or (c) decreased?

6 Which of these improvements due to TOPS do you think is most important for your role as a supervisor?
(a) Increased control over wagons
(b) Increased control over locomotives
(c) Increased control over train crews
(d) Increased control over yard staff
(e) Increased control over freight operations in general

7 Could you please indicate by the appropriate letter – (a) strongly agree, (b) agree, (c) don't know, (d) disagree, or (e) strongly disagree – how far you agree with the following statements about the effect that TOPS has had on your job as a supervisor?
7.1 With TOPS, ground level experience is not of such importance in doing the job of the supervisor
7.2 TOPS enables the supervisor to control freight operations far more effectively
7.3 TOPS enables supervisors to control subordinate staff far more effectively
7.4 TOPS has taken the skill out of being a supervisor
7.5 Management now have far greater control of the supervisor
7.6 The supervisor is now just a servant to the TOPS machine

Additional comments?

8 In general, do you think TOPS has been either (a) a great success, (b) a limited success, or (c) something of a failure?

F. *Unions, modernization and the supervisor*

1 Please could you fill in the following details as appropriate:
1.1 ASLEF (date joined/date left)
1.2 NUR (date joined/date left)
1.3 TSSA (date joined/date left)

2 Is the union of which you are currently a member the union you would prefer to be in? (If *no*, what would be your choice?)

3 Do you feel that supervisors in BR should (a) have a union of their own (b) be part of their subordinates' unions, (c) be part of a management union, or (d) not be in a union at all?

4 Do you feel your union has handled the issue of modernization:
(a) Very well
(b) Reasonably well

(c) Not very well
(d) Badly
(e) Don't know?

G. *Leisure activities and the supervisor*

1 Do you socialize with BR employees away from work? (If yes, please indicate how often this is, e.g. daily, weekly, monthly)

2 What are your main leisure interests?

3 Were or are any members of your immediate family employed on the railway? (If so, please indicate their relationship to you and their occupation, e.g. father, guard)

4 Would you regard the job of a railway supervisor as a good career for a young person?

H. *General section*

1 As a supervisor, what has been the major change in job activity brought about by the introduction of TOPS?

2 Within the yard, which job do you feel has been most affected by TOPS and for what reasons?

3 In general, what are your views on technological change?

4 Have you any comments on the design of this questionnaire?

Appendix II: example of processual case study write-up for company

When fieldwork is ongoing there may be a number of working papers or conference papers that need first to be shown to main company contacts that have provided organizational access for data collection purposes. These can sometimes be anxious periods, and a number of unknown and unexpected responses can occur. During my study of change at General Motors, I remember receiving a call from the plant manager indicating that I needed to see senior management urgently. As it turned out, the concern was over some financial figures that were not pertinent to the academic thrust of the paper and yet were viewed as highly significant and sensitive by the participating organization. Consequently, when the main body of fieldwork is complete it is useful to get agreement on material through the writing and submission of a company write-up. This also facilitates feedback and discussion, as well as allowing the company to rectify any factual errors and to highlight areas that need to be deleted or changed due to commercial sensitivity. One of the major benefits of such a write-up is that once the company has agreed on the material you can then look to use this in a number of different ways (refereed journal articles, book chapters, conference papers, teaching case files) without having to return to the company each time to gain agreement. Below is one such example of a company write-up for Laubman and Bank (for an example of how this compares with a journal publication, see Dawson, 1998). Typically, at the end of these company write-ups there are some recommendations, practical conclusions and/or questions raised for the company to consider. The write-up replicated below formed part of a series of longitudinal studies on TQM in Australian organizations, and is solely for illustrative purposes (the original appendices and references cited in the document are not reproduced here).

The company write-up: total quality management at Laubman and Pank

> I sit back and look at other organizations and think, 'They're miles behind us'. It's one of those situations where there's no right or wrong answer. You can't say – you know, you've got to be here in two years and you've got to be there in three; otherwise, it fails. Every organization's going to move at its own pace. But no, there's no down side. In the vision that I have, that's the way to go. It doesn't matter where I turn, when I see excellent companies, the things they're doing are exactly the same as us.
>
> (Senior Management Interviews, 1991)

Introduction

This paper reports on data collected from Laubman and Pank Pty Ltd in South Australia. Between August 1991 and January 1992, interviews were conducted with senior management, middle management and other employee groups. The paper sets out to provide an overview of the change programme, management rationale and the key issues surrounding the introduction of a Total Quality Management (TQM) programme. Section two commences with an outline of the research strategy and methods used in the study. A section that provides some background information on the Laubman and Pank Group of companies follows this. In the fourth section the context in which TQM was established is examined and the process of implementation is described. Section five then identifies a range of unforeseen 'problems' and analyses senior management evaluations on the 'success' of TQM. In section six, the management and organization of Tecsol Pty Ltd is briefly outlined and the effects of service excellence on the work of laboratory staff are examined. Section seven then discusses the consequence of TQM for the optometry and retail arm of Laubman and Pank. Finally, the paper concludes with a summary of the eight major lessons on managing the introduction of TQM in the Laubman and Pank Group.

Research strategy and methods

The study formed part of a national programme of case study research on the introduction and effects of TQM on Australian organizations. The project was undertaken by two research teams: one was located at the Key Centre in Strategic Management at Queensland University of Technology under the direction of Professor Gill Palmer, with research support from Cameron Allan; the other was based at the University of Adelaide under the direction of Dr Patrick Dawson, with research support from Verna Blewett. Additional case studies were commissioned in Western Australia and New Zealand, and data collection was completed in June 1992. In all, a total of eight organizations were studied, comprising Pirelli Cables Australia Limited, State Bank of South Australia, Metway Bank, Accom Industries, Laubman and Pank, Alcoa, Tecpak Industries, and Hendersons Automotive Limited.

The main methods used in the study were:

1 In-depth interviewing of key personnel
2 Management, union, and shop-floor interviews
3 Participant observation
4 Non-participant observation
5 Documentary analysis

The case studies are largely based on qualitative data that were collected between 1989 and 1992. A longitudinal element was built into the research strategy, and where practicable repeat interviews have been carried out at a number of different stages during the process of organizational transformation (for further details of the research strategy and methods used in the study, see Dawson and Palmer, forthcoming).

In the case of Laubman and Pank, discussions with the manager of the Adelaide Branch began in 1989 and a final agreement on the nature and the scale of the case was reached in December 1990. Data collection was completed by 1992, and mainly consisted of semi-structured interviewing with some observational notes on work activities.

Laubman and Pank

The history of the Laubman and Pank Group can be traced back to the establishment of a partnership between Laubman and Pank in 1908. Founded in Adelaide, the group has expanded considerably in recent years and now operates through 63 branches in six States and Territories of Australia (Bluntish, 1991: 50). During the early years, growth was slow and the group based their operations around the Adelaide metropolitan area and created a small additional number of branches in

South Australia. By the end of the 1970s the group had made significant developments in their Sola Optical activities, and the National Health Insurance Act of 1972 assisted the national growth of professional optometry and laid the foundation for considerable company expansion in the 1980s (the corporate and support management structure and the South Australian Regional activities are outlined in Appendix I).

Optometry is the main business of the Laubman and Pank organization, and involves: eye examinations and prescriptions for individual customers and the dispensing of visionary aids (in contrast, an ophthalmologist is a medical practitioner specializing in the treatment of eye disease and eye surgery). Trained optometrists are employed to examine eyes and the visual function of clients, and to prescribe glasses, contact lenses or other visionary aids. In addition, an optometric assistant or 'dispenser' will assist the optometrist in dispensing optometrist's spectacle prescriptions. Dispensers may also deal with prescriptions. The Laubman and Pank Group is also involved in the manufacture and supply of lenses, spectacle frames and contact lenses through their laboratories set up under the organization Tescol Pty Ltd (see Appendix I).

Optometry has a long history that predates its rise to professional status in the 1970s. Traditionally, optometrists have distanced themselves from the commercial side of the business and adopted a paternalistic attitude towards their clients (Bluntish, 1991: 45). Today, both the consultative aspect with clients (examination and discussion) and the dispensing of optical devices (the retailing element) are central to professional optometry. The withdrawal of restrictive advertising legislation, changes in codes of ethics, increased competition and the need to satisfy customer expectations have all influenced Laubman and Pank's decision to adopt a service excellence programme throughout their Australian operations.

Quality management at Laubman and Pank

A dedication to excellence in our service to every client. This means that we must be totally committed to ensuring that each client feels they have received the best possible service, would want to return and would recommend us to others.

(Laubman and Pank Document, 1991)

In establishing quality excellence at Laubman and Pank the corporate vision outlined above has been defined, and seven principles for achieving this objective have been identified. These are seen to consist of the following needs:

1 To listen and react immediately to the needs of clients.
2 To provide more autonomy and responsibility to employees at all levels in the organization.
3 To provide the necessary resources.
4 To select the very best staff and provide the necessary training.
5 To measure, acknowledge and reward the achievement of individuals in relation to the corporate vision.
6 To be professional and commercially responsible.
7 To exercise a social responsibility to the community.

Between 1989 and 1991 the company has attempted to introduce Total Quality Management (TQM) in the form of a Service Excellence Programme (SEP). The programme was introduced without the aid of consultants, and by August 1991 the Adelaide Branch Manager was recommending that the programme be re-implemented through the use of external consultants with the aim of achieving service excellence and developing a: 'sustainable competitive advantage that our competition will find difficult if not impossible to emulate' (Bluntish, 1991: 64). Before analysing senior management evaluations of the programme, a brief account of quality management in Laubman and Pank is provided.

There is a long history of quality management at Laubman and Pank, with the main emphasis being placed on quality assurance techniques and the setting of laboratory jobbing quality standards (for example, both spectacle and contact lens manufacture are based on documented Australian Standards). However, the move towards Total Quality Management (TQM), in the form of a service excellence programme is a new development that was taken up by the organization in the late 1980s. With the growth in the company's core business (ophthalmic practice) and the selling of Solar Holdings to Pilkington, a large number of new employees and branch outlets have been acquired, including Trevor Henderson Optometrists and the creation of a new laboratory facility in Adelaide:

> So when we started again, we had to then start with a whole new batch of people to bring into the culture of the organization, which up to that point had consisted of people who'd been with us for many years. And I'm sure you'd appreciate the sort of problems when you're digesting, if you like, a whole lot of new people who didn't

know anything about us, into the culture of the organization ... We
had been embarking on an expansion programme apart from that, with
the purchase of other branches and establishing our own branches
around South Australia and, of course, Western Australia.

(Senior Management Interviews, 1991)

Following the growth in the size of the company there has been a need to
accommodate comparatively large numbers of new employees into the
organization. Under such circumstances, past traditions and operating
assumptions could no longer be taken for granted. A number of the senior
management group viewed TQM as a natural extension of the founding
philosophy of Laubman and Pank. However, the shift away from
historical conventions and traditional recruitment strategies should not be
underestimated:

We really don't view what's happening now as really a specific
programme, but rather a continuation of the philosophy which has
driven this organization right back in those early days. Certainly, it
sometimes gets a bit more emphasis and a bit more of a push, but it's
part of our general philosophy. And that philosophy manifested itself
in particular in the late 1940s when we made shares in the
organization available to anybody who wished to purchase them. And
that has continued right through, of course, until this day.

(Senior Management Interviews, 1991)

Although the history of Laubman and Pank continues to influence the
present culture of the organization, the parochial management style
associated with 'the traditional family business' is no longer deemed
appropriate either to managing the internal dynamics of the company, or
to the development of marketing strategies for the more commercial and
competitive optical business. Changes in legislation, customer
expectations and external competition have all played a part in shaping
the strategic decision-making process. In practice, there remains some
tension within the organization, particularly when traditional beliefs are
called into question by the exigencies of competitive business market
developments. As the Chief Executive Officer recalled:

While we could still rattle along holding together our approaches on
standards, ethics, performance, quality, it wouldn't be too long before
that was going to become increasingly difficult – a sort of straw
breaking the camel's back analogy. So it was then we decided to
create two new positions: one was marketing development; the other
was human resources. And at about that time service excellence and
Tom Peters had just happened to rear their ugly heads ... What Tom

> Peters was saying appealed to me, because I could sense that we were growing up out of a whole new group of people because of those acquisitions. It seemed that we were going to have to do something if the nucleus people – the South Australian-based people – if they were going to remain comfortable with the way the public was treated elsewhere in the organization.
>
> (Senior Management Interviews, 1991)

The Chairman of the Board who recounted that echoed this view of the history of TQM:

> Your starting point would be when [Human Resource Manager] came on the staff, which is three or four years ago, and then we started talking openly about service excellence as a specific thing. But, as I say, it really was, as far as I'm concerned, an extension of what's been happening all along. But we now have a greater urgency, I suppose – a greater emphasis on that – because of our geographic spread and the problems associated with a lot of new people coming in.
>
> (Senior Management Interviews, 1991)

The senior management group believed that service excellence could be used as the vehicle for reuniting an increasingly disparate organization (as a result of rapid expansion) into a more integrated business exhibiting a common set of beliefs and values. Moreover, the development of a culture based on employee involvement and company identification was seen to support the continuation (and re-emergence) of belief systems associated with the historically smaller optometric operation of Laubman and Pank pre-1980. In other words, the collaborative 'family business' atmosphere could be created and maintained within the larger and more geographically dispersed optometric business of the 1990s. Unlike previous quality schemes, this change programme centred on the development of a culture that would act to unify and integrate employees throughout the Laubman and Pank Group. As such, considerable attention has been given to setting up the programme and to ensuring that service excellence is maintained.

The job of implementing service excellence was given to the newly recruited manager of human resources. As he recalled in relation to the programme:

> In terms of service excellence, my role has been one, I guess, of bringing the concept to the organization . . . About three years ago I formally brought the concept here, and we've adopted it and have been implementing it ever since. I guess we will be for quite a while.
>
> (Senior Management Interviews, 1991)

The programme developed from an initial conversation between the Chairman of the Board of Laubman and Pank and the Managing Director of the State Bank of South Australia, where the benefits of TQM in service organizations were debated. The State Bank had invited Karl Albrecht over to help them set up and develop an implementation strategy for the implementation of TQM in their organization (see Dawson and Patrickson, 1991), and many of the ideas derived from this visit were openly discussed. Moreover, during the selection interview for the position of Human Resource Manager (HRM), the current HRM was asked whether he was familiar with TQM and later asked whether he was acquainted with the work of Karl Albrecht. As the HRM recounted:

> The Chairman came back and said, 'Hey, have you heard of Karl Albrecht and some of the work he's doing?' I said, 'Yeah, for the last two or three weeks I've been involved in putting ideas together.' So I didn't have to convince the chairman of the need . . . Then I took the senior management group away for a weekend and introduced them to the concepts and prepared a training programme in 2½ days, and it took off from that point.
>
> (Senior Management Interviews, 1991)

Once the programme had been started, there was little further reference or attention given to the State Bank quality initiative. As the HRM commented:

> I was very keen, right from the outset, to introduce something that we could work to that was home-grown, if you like, for Laubman and Pank. Our culture has been very much one of doing things ourselves, and both the chairman and the CEO were really confident that I could put it together. But basically we had the raw material; we had the ideas; it was just a matter of putting it together in a package that would suit us. So there were some benefits from doing it internally. I think there's also some shortfalls, in the sense that I think we could've got further in a shorter period of time using some external people. Because, unfortunately, someone coming in from outside seems to have a bit more credibility and command, I guess – more instant respect. Someone internally, they're under the spotlight themselves . . . I'm only human: if I fall down in an area; if someone wants some excellent service from me, and for some reason I don't deliver it, then instead of me being judged the package is being judged; whereas an external person, obviously, hasn't got that. They're not working here every day. They're bringing in ideas and implementing them. Whatever they do in their own work environment is not on display. Anyway, that's basically how it started, and I generated the training package.
>
> (Senior Management Interviews, 1991)

The NEM combined the ideas of Albrecht and Zenke (1985) and Peters and Waterman (1982) in making a presentation on what constituted excellent companies. Emphasis was placed on the importance of the client (both as an 'internal' and 'external' customer) and the need for continual improvements to meet changing customer expectations:

> I just tried to say, 'Look, it really just gets back to the client. In everything we're doing we should be focussing on how well we deliver that service, both to the internal client and the external client.' So I can't say I've introduced anything magical. It was really just drawing together the elements that are beautifully presented by Albrecht and Peters and Waterman. They're the source of my material.
>
> (Senior Management Interviews, 1991)

The session with senior management was developed with the objective of getting full support and agreeing on the 'vision' that the company should be aiming towards. A meeting was held at Victor Harbour in April 1989, and service excellence was forwarded as a means to ensuring that the company would be able to withstand competition, to grow effectively and place Laubman and Pank in the position of market leader. A statement of the company's vision was compiled at the weekend, and seven principles necessary to the achievement of that vision were outlined. Defining the message of service excellence and gaining the commitment of senior management was seen to be the first stage in the organizational process towards TQM. As the Chairman of the Board explained when discussing service excellence:

> The message, clearly, is that when you're talking of service excellence we're talking about everything that happens in the organization, not just the one-to-one relationship between a member of staff and a client. We're talking about the whole lot, and that's everybody who walks in the place; every piece of paper that goes out of the place; every contact that we as an organization have with anyone outside, in any shape or form, whether it's telephone, written word or anything.
>
> (Senior Management Interviews, 1991)

The focus of stage two rested on the delivery of this message to all Laubman and Pank employees. This involved considerable travel for the HRM and is still ongoing with the recruitment of new staff (although it should be noted that service excellent training is not done as part of the induction programme but rather three or four months after commencement of employment). The approach rested on clarifying what service excellence was all about and making staff aware of the importance of providing quality service to internal and external clients. The concept of internal customer–supplier relations was stressed, and the importance of quality service to the success and survival of the company was highlighted:

> The second stage was very much taking that message to the people once we had a chance to mull it over and agree that what we said was correct; agreed that that's where we wanted to go as an organization. Then there was a programme that, while we've only got 600-odd staff, it was a matter of they're spread all over the place, from Cairns to Kalgoorlie. So it was a matter of taking that message around to all the staff, which I did.
>
> (Senior Management Interviews, 1991)

Senior management assessment of service excellence

Senior management were generally positive about the benefits of the service excellence programme and did not view TQM as simply an operational technique for improving the organization and control of work, but as a management system that comprised a series of methods for encouraging employees to identify with a common set of values and beliefs. Whilst in theory senior management recognized the broader strategic significance of TQM for developing high-trust relationships and improving customer service, there was also a tendency to focus on TQM (particularly within the laboratory setting) as a scientific methodology for identifying and establishing documented procedures and quantifiable indicators. To a certain extent, this can be explained by the tendency for some senior managers to confuse quality assurance techniques with total quality management principles; typically however, senior management recognized and identified with the strategic significance of the cultural dimension:

> We changed such basic things as – we no longer refer to people now as 'patients'; they're 'clients'. The two hardest things we had to do was to get them to use the word 'client' and for the optometrists not to wear a white coat. The optometrists were equally as comfortable behind a white coat, and in some cases they confused those things with service excellence, whereas it wasn't. So if you didn't have a white coat to protect you, you had to be more professional with your client. The other thing was that to get the staff to believe that we

> really meant what we were about, we had to go over the top. We
> almost ran the risk of giving the shop away, because if there was a
> complaint, no matter what, we'd replace whatever was wrong.
>
> (Senior Management Interviews, 1991)

In changing the culture of the organization and moving away from
traditional conservatism towards a client-based culture, there have been a
number of other symbolic changes. These changes have been primarily
associated with dress codes and language; for example, first names are
now used throughout the organization in attempt to break down some of
the communication barriers between senior management and other
employees. Employee commitment and involvement was identified as the
keystone to TQM. Service excellence was viewed as a vehicle for
changing the culture of an organization and developing new work
practices based on the knowledge and understanding of the people
directly involved in daily operations. Senior management maintained that
it is only after attitudes have been changed that you can begin to replace
traditional methods with new working practices. Thus it was stressed that
attitudinal change should precede major system changes:

> It's a people thing: you've got to get attitudes changed. Then the
> system starts to flow and you'll see new work practices; you'll see
> new ways of doing things; you'll see paperwork cut out; you'll see all
> those things happening that streamline the operation. And you'll see
> people saying, 'Shit! That is not good enough, because I know the
> expectation of this section, of my boss, is that those glasses are not
> good enough.'
>
> (Senior Management Interviews, 1991)

Or, as another interviewee noted:

> It's frustrating, because it comes back to management; it comes back
> to people. There's nothing wrong with the machines that we've got;
> nothing wrong with the lenses that we buy in. It's all a people issue,
> and we still haven't really come to grips with that.
>
> (Senior Management Interviews, 1991)

Interestingly, whilst senior managers tended to agree that service quality
was also about managing cultural change, they tended to down-play other
senior managers' perceptions of the importance of managing people and
changing attitudes and beliefs. In part this can be explained by the history
of the company and the legacy of conservatism and tradition, which is
still perceived as the major shaper of senior management attitudes. In
other words, whilst there is a certain public agreement about the need for
a shift in the culture of the organization, there is also a belief that

conservatism still dominates senior management decision-making. As the Chairman of the Board indicated:

> We've got to reduce that level of conservatism without going overboard, so we'll be seen as more modern, more aggressive, more commercially orientated and more up-front generally.
>
> (Senior Management Interviews, 1991)

Following the introduction of service excellence, greater authority has been devolved to front-line staff in dealing with customer concerns and complaints. For example, if a customer returns to a Laubman and Pank retail outlet with a damaged frame, staff are now able to deal directly with the customer and have the authority to make up a new frame. Previously, these types of decisions would have had to be referred to the manager of that branch or the person responsible for the area of operation under question. As a senior manager commented:

> It was about giving the people right up-front the authority to make decisions that were going to cost us money, but if they perceived it to be to the benefit of the client that was okay. That was really, I guess, short-circuiting or bypassing a lot of the systems that we'd put in place. And really, to try and get through the concept that the extra effort was necessary to give the service that we were aiming to give.
>
> (Senior Management Interviews, 1991)

However, this change did present problems in that some staff were engaging in actions that went beyond the normal expectations of clients and resulted in additional costs for the company. A classic example was given of an incident where a customer had returned a pair of spectacles for minor repairs (costing just under $10) and was due to go on holiday to Cairns. The customer then went on holiday and indicated that he would be happy to pick up his glasses on his return. However, a branch employee sent a special courier up to the resort in Queensland, which cost the company $56 to deliver an $8 repair job. In this case, it was argued that the employee had over-stepped the bounds of reasonable service and was making decisions that were creating additional and unnecessary costs. Nevertheless, in recounting this story the senior manager stressed that whenever these situations arose it was important not to be overly critical of the 'offending' employee, but rather to 'counsel' him or her about appropriate actions and behaviours in working towards service excellence.

In terms of professional staff, there have been some problems in convincing optometrists to embrace fully the new client-based culture.

For example, in discussing the question of getting optometrists to accept change, one senior manager commented that:

> This is a pretty cynical view, but most of them come out of university and they can't wait to put the white coat on and become seen as a doctor, and wander around sort of making noises like, 'Mmmm, mmmm', and jotting down little notes that can't be read. When we took their white coats off them and when we told them that diagrams of dissections of the eye had to come off the wall and that they actually had to communicate with the client, they thought this was dreadful. There was such a reaction.
>
> (Senior Management Interviews, 1991)

Another branch level 'problem' arose in cases where staff began using the service excellence programme to hide the real causes for refunds:

> Quite often the reason for the refund that they might write down is 'service excellence' – nothing more, nothing less, just 'service excellence.' And that's a real problem, because (a) you don't know whether or not it really is service excellence or someone just covering their backside; and (b) it hides the real cause. It shows the symptoms but it doesn't show what the cause is, and unless you know what the cause is you can't do anything about it.
>
> (Senior Management Interviews, 1991)

In short, the introduction of service excellence to the retail outlets has taken a number of years and is still defined as being in its early stages of adoption. Senior management identified the need to maintain senior management support over a long period of time, and the need to invest adequate funds to ensure that the new service philosophy is further developed and refined. The senior management group also indicated that the focus on customer–supplier relations and the greater emphasis being placed on the supply of quality products had created some conflict between manufacturing and retail personnel:

> You had a set of people who were saying, 'These people are not supporting us in our desire to provide this better service and service excellence to the front line.' So it creates a lot of internal stress and you've then got to look at your whole system, because inevitably they're wanting, and a lot of ours were and still are, although we keep working at them, in being able to provide the back up.
>
> (Senior Management Interviews, 1991)

Numerous accounts were given of the problems of introducing service excellence into Tecsol laboratory operations (see also section on Adelaide laboratory). As one senior manager explained:

> The major area where we have some conflict and scepticism are in the
> laboratory areas. They are pretty much a service function, but their
> product goes directly to our own retail outlet and then to the client. So
> they're close enough that they can't really wipe their hands of it.
> Everything is still pretty much reflected fairly quickly internally. And
> certainly in recent times they've had some quality issues . . . In
> particular, I guess, there was a feeling that the management didn't
> care about the quality of the job going out. The more important thing
> was to meet the timetable rather than meet the quality standard.
>
> (Senior Management Interviews, 1991)

This situation has created tension between the retail and manufacturing
staff and has resulted in poor inter-organizational relations between
Tecsol and Laubman and Pank:

> Historically there's been friction between the Tecsol side of the
> company and Laubman and Pank. Tecsol has always been a service
> arm for Laubman and Pank, and it's my view that this has come about
> largely because of a necessary separation of many of the functions
> that Tecsol performs from Laubman and Pank. I mean, there is no
> logical justification that many of us younger ones can think of for
> having the supply function, which in fact only supplies Laubman and
> Pank as an arm of Tecsol. There is no logical reason why the
> laboratory which supplies Laubman and Pank should be a part of
> Tecsol. If it doesn't actually create the 'them and us' situation, it
> certainly doesn't discourage it when it does arise. And, of course, it
> does arise.
>
> (Senior Management Interviews, 1991)

Another 'obstacle' that has emerged has been middle managerial and
supervisory resistance to change. In the view of one senior manager, this
was a consequence of the traditional emphasis placed on technical
knowledge as the authority base for supervisors. As a result, laboratory
supervisors were well placed for dealing with contingencies and directing
staff in the day-to-day control of service operations. However, by placing
greater emphasis on the knowledge of operative staff in correcting and
adapting process operations, the traditional authority base of the
supervisor has been undermined. Although attempts are now being made
to redefine the function of middle management, not enough attention has
been given to this problem and supervisory resistance has resulted:

> We've had a philosophy of our managers still retaining a large chunk
> of technical work, and when they've got a bit of free time from that,
> managing the staff. Very, very slowly we're wearing that away,
> saying that we want professional managers. We want a laboratory

> manager who needs to know a bit about lenses and the technical side
> but, above all else, his major skills have to be in people management:
> to be able to motivate leading hands and so forth.
>
> (Senior Management Interviews, 1991)

Consequently, there is a need to redefine supervision and make the
expectations of the position clear not only to supervisors, but also to
operative staff and the senior management group.

Training was identified as a key ingredient to the successful introduction
of a service excellence programme, and it was suggested that this is often
an area that can be overlooked. On this issue, the Chief Executive Officer
indicated a requirement for customized training packages that would
fulfil the needs of different groups (geographically, demographically and
occupationally):

> Different people in different regions and different degrees of
> sophisticated markets: different age groups, demographics, income
> levels, require subtle differences in the way that they're approached.
> That means that the staff residing and working in those places need to
> have that bias built into their training. So it's not just a matter of
> twelve disciples rushing out into the scrub to give the word. So I
> guess they're the things that I've found to be interesting challenges
> because they're difficult to measure whether you're doing it right or
> whether you're doing it wrong.
>
> (Senior Management Interviews, 1991)

Supervision and training were therefore seen as major factors that could
facilitate or inhibit the successful management of TQM. As the Chairman
of the Board indicated:

> Unless it works at the level immediately above the operator level it
> isn't going to work at all; it doesn't matter what senior management
> do. I think that's a lesson well learned.
>
> (Senior Management Interviews, 1991)

In evaluating how successful the introduction of the service excellence
programme has been in Laubman and Pank, the senior management
group argued that the programme had proven more successful in some
areas than others, and that the programme was still in its 'infancy'. One
senior manager, in assessing the pros and cons of TQM, argued that:

> The positive side is that we have given people better signposts, and
> they can see themselves moving in the right direction. A number of
> them get a fairly big kick out of it. The down side is really the other
> side of the coin: frustration if something isn't done right;

disappointment, wondering whether you're the only one who's really trying to do things right or whether you're not, whether anybody really cares, or whether anybody really notices you.

(Senior Management Interviews, 1991)

In reflecting on the implementation of service excellence, the manager of human resources noted that:

I guess if you look back at that, if you want to critically analyse what we've done, my initial comment was that it really shouldn't have been me leading that; it should have been the CEO. I think if you can look objectively at what we've done all the way through, I would have preferred the CEO to be up-front. He doesn't have to do all the legwork, but has to be the person driving it. And in our case he hasn't been, for all sorts of reasons. If you look at Jan Carlson's work with Scandinavian Airlines, it's one that obviously comes out very quickly. He was up-front, leading it right from the start. People knew that he was committed to a basic change of direction.

(Senior Management Interviews, 1991)

Finally, in evaluating how close the organization is to embracing fully a new service quality culture, the Managing Director of Laubman and Pank responded:

I reckon halfway. Certainly, we've got significant improvements: there's no doubt about that – big improvements. But I think I'd be kidding myself if I said we were there. I know we're not there, because I'm out and around the branches and with our people all the time, and I constantly see areas where I can see that we're falling well short of what we want to be doing. But I do think we're a lot better than we were two years ago. So we've taken a quantum leap forward, and I reckon we're probably halfway there.

(Senior Management Interviews, 1991)

Laboratory manufacturing and service excellence

The Adelaide laboratory was an area viewed by senior management as being in need of change. The problem of poor management relations and the issue of quality and service excellence have become the focus of senior management attention. As one interviewee commented: 'The rest of the group tend to perceive laboratory-manufacturing people as a different group of people, and they are, to some extent'. In this section, these issues are appraised through an examination of five main areas:

1 The management and organization of Tecsol laboratory operations.
2 The introduction of a service excellence programme to laboratory manufacturing.
3 The development of a workers' participation committee for improving employee involvement.
4 The relationship between the conventional quality assurance system and the service excellence programme.
5 The effects of service excellence on the work of laboratory staff.

Tecsol Pty Ltd is made up of five divisions: ophthalmic laboratories, contact lens laboratory, supply, hearing centres, and the industrial division. The laboratories act as the manufacturing arm for Laubman and Pank, although there is also a wholesale operation connected with the contact lens laboratory (i.e. Tecsol sell contact lenses and lens solutions). Supply deals with the purchasing and distribution functions for the Laubman and Pank Group (essentially it acts as a distribution agency). The hearing centres are effectively straight retail operations dealing in hearing devices, and the industrial division provides industrial hearing and visionary aids and is also currently doing some consultancy work with VDUs (i.e. how to use VDUs safely without causing eye strain). As a senior Tecsol manager commented:

> Our only client, really, is Laubman and Pank. So those three divisions, other than a small amount of wholesale where we do go outside, are really just running on behalf of Laubman and Pank. Whether they're a division of Laubman and Pank or whether they're a separate company, it doesn't really matter. It just so happens that they've set it up as a separate company: Laubman Tecsol. So each of those is set up in national divisions, and the national manager then reports through to me. When I say 'national', we operate in three States, and they would normally have a manager in each State supporting to them: Queensland, South Australia and Western Australia. There are small operations in the Northern Territory and Victoria, but they're basically controlled through South Australia. That's the basic structure, if you like.
>
> (Senior Management Interviews, 1991)

The Managing Director of Tecsol Pty Ltd did not view these structural arrangements as problematic, although he did indicate that there might be some difficulties that arise from operating with separate boards of directors. Nationally Tecsol employs approximately 120 employees, and almost half of those are employed within the central laboratory in Adelaide. Although there are currently only small regional edging facilities, this is changing, with greater emphasis being placed on shortening customer delivery times. Consequently, Tecsol is now putting edging facilities in strategic branches. In discussing the more capital intensive (machine-based) grinding operations, the MD Tecsol noted that:

> If it's a grinding job, that's when they have to come in here [Adelaide], because there aren't enough urgent grind jobs to justify the initial capital expenditure in Perth and Queensland, so they send it here. The problem that causes, of course, is the turnaround time. You've got a day getting here and a day back again. But, fortunately, I think most people are prepared to wait three or four days for their glasses. So the one-hour service isn't an issue. Basically – we need to do what Laubman and Pank want us to do. In other words, if they want us to provide a faster service, then we've got to try and provide that in terms of the laboratories.
>
> (Senior Management Interviews, 1991)

In relation to the service excellent programme, the MD Tecsol argued that there are two main things that have come from the programme. First, to improve turnaround from an initial order to the customer delivery of the end product. Second, to reduce the level of faults and to ensure that a quality product is manufactured. The MD noted that in terms of quality, Tecsol have had problems in the contact lens area. Optometrists who have questioned the quality of the products being manufactured have highlighted these problems. The main indicator for poor quality has been the number of rejects and reworks sent back to the laboratory by the retail outlets. Although, as the MD explained:

> I'm told that that's a problem right throughout the industry. A lot of times you can't find out how the contact lens is going to go on the patient until they actually fit it. The manufacturing process is done, but if it doesn't work it's got to be sent back and reworked or remade. Now, that's a problem in the industry, but they're saying our quality hasn't been good. So that's the perception the optometrists have had. Rightly or wrongly, we've had to respond to that.
>
> (Senior Management Interviews, 1991)

At the end of 1991, Tecsol embarked on a three-month review of the contact lens laboratory. This involved thorough review of operations in terms of procedures, maintenance of equipment, staff, staff training, management and so forth. The intention was to assess the future strategic direction of the company and to determine whether they require a facility to make any type of lens requested, or whether they should concentrate operations on the main areas of demand and leave the specialist work to another facility.

One way in which they are trying to improve the efficiency of the laboratory is to relocate to one area rather than operating from three separate floors, which has proven to be inefficient. For example, the work of two and sometimes three employees involved running jobs backwards and forwards between various facilities at different locations. So the intention was to move everybody under one roof so that there would be one facility on one floor, which it is hoped will improve morale and significantly improve the efficiency of the laboratory. The MD of Tecsol felt that service excellence has largely been targeted towards the optometric side rather than the laboratory side, and that TQM issues in manufacturing are only just beginning to be addressed:

> From the ordinary worker's point of view, I don't think they've really seen any change. I think most of the changes have really been from the retail point of view. I think, to be fair, though, we have made a lot of changes to respond to service excellence, but they mightn't necessarily see it that way. I don't think it's really been explained to them that well. This gets back to my earlier point. They're a very important part of the process, and I think that we've tended – of course, we're an optometric company – to concentrate on the optometric side, and maybe leave some of the manufacturing staff out of it.
>
> (Senior Management Interviews, 1991)

In discussing the history of service excellence, many employees commented that when it first started it was the 'buzz word' that everybody used. However, within two years the concept had become 'stale' and employees were beginning to criticize and question the programme. By the third year of the programme, views towards service excellence had 'mellowed' considerably and a number of limitations of the programme were identified:

> Where service excellence is occasionally falling down is where you go out of the guidelines because you try to be nice to the customer, but you're not doing your research into the item hard enough, and therefore not making sure that what you're promising to the client can be achieved.
>
> (Adelaide Laboratory Interviews, 1991)

Initial employee contact with service excellence took the form of a two-hour session that summarized the main objectives of the programme and outlined the importance of worker participation. The Human Resources

Manager organized these introductory sessions, stressing the importance of a client-based culture and how there are both internal and external customers. The sessions were fairly relaxed, and were appraised as being 'successful' in getting the message across about the meaning of 'service excellence' and the implications for the Laubman and Pank Group. As an employee recalled:

> They presented it to us at a special evening. I think we did a three-hour film night and presentation of the whole programme – what was expected, how it was expected – which was quite good. I mean, you know so much but there's always more that you can learn, I feel, anyway. And I did pick up a lot that night.
> (Adelaide Laboratory Interviews, 1991)

Some employees were required to attend the service excellence session after work on a Friday evening. The timing of these sessions was criticized and it was argued that most people wish to get away on a Friday evening and are therefore unlikely to be receptive to new ideas. A number of employees also criticized the accompanying videos for being 'too American', and questioned their relevance to the Australian market:

> It was so American, and I personally believe that Australians don't like that sort of hoo-ha. They like to go in a clothes shop, have a look around, not be harassed, and I think people tend to get a bit scared off when someone comes up and is hovering around the whole time, trying to make conversation.
> (Adelaide Laboratory Interviews, 1991)

In general, interviewees agreed with the philosophy behind the programme (which sought the involvement of everyone in the provision of quality services to customers), but believed that it would take decades to achieve such an objective and that it was questionable whether senior management would be prepared to wait that long:

> It's only my personal opinion – I think I'd be correct in saying that I don't believe that the organization is prepared for the length of time it takes from step A to your final achievement of goals.
> (Adelaide Laboratory Interviews, 1991)

It was also pointed out that such a long-term strategic change – which required that every element of an organization adapt to the new philosophy – was likely to develop at a different pace in different organizations and departments:

> We've all got our own little problems; we're all going to advance at different rates. I think that's where the problem is at the moment –

> we're all advancing at different rates in the organization. Some
> achieve a lot more, others don't achieve very much at all, but we're
> all going in the same direction – I think that's the important thing.
> (Adelaide Laboratory Interviews, 1991)

In assessing the effects of service excellence on Tecsol operations, the
most significant change was seen to have occurred in the 'image' of the
company. There was increased employee awareness about the future
strategic direction of the Laubman and Pank Group and the attempts that
were being made to make the Group more competitive and commercial.
In the opinion of one employee, there remained a lot more that could be
done to sell the image of the company:

> I'd like to carry it even further. Like, all our staff should be wearing
> T-shirts at home on the weekends with Laubman and Pank written on
> the back; caps for the kids – baseball caps, Laubman and Pank: it's a
> free plug. These are the sort of things I think that we should be doing.
> (Adelaide Laboratory Interviews, 1991)

Typically, employees were in favour of change programmes that would
improve the image of the company and supported the transition from an
old and established conservative company to a more modern and
competitive business. In the words of one employee:

> We had to sort of go out, wash our face, freshen up and look a bit
> more yuppie – sell ourselves. We weren't selling ourselves enough.
> (Adelaide Laboratory Interviews, 1991)

On the question of service quality and employee involvement, it was
noted that some staff do not want to get involved:

> There's a lot of staff who don't want to be involved in anything, but
> come here and then go home without any involvement.
> (Adelaide Laboratory Interviews, 1991)

This was seen to create problems when setting up voluntary groups to
discuss shop-floor concerns:

> It's difficult to get the people onto a committee. Most don't want to
> be. Those who want a committee seem to be the radical group: the
> ones who are outspoken and want tremendous change to occur. That's
> the danger: it's not balanced because it's not compulsory, it's
> voluntary.
> (Adelaide Laboratory Interviews, 1991)

This problem was seen to be evident in the setting up of a Workers'
Participation Committee (WPC). The committee was created in response

to an anonymous employee attitude survey, which was circulated in May 1991. The survey was described by some employees as enabling individuals to 'go-to-town' and put all their frustrations down on paper:

> Of course, on the survey they don't even answer the question: they put what they want there. 'Listen' – just big letters, right across the form: 'Listen'. Because I was able to read them. 'Sack management; you'll get results.' 'Get rid of Joe Blow' – really heavy stuff – real heavy; brilliantly presented, brilliantly fabricated – excellent. So, of course, it goes to the board. They read it. My God! I mean, they read that information. What's their perception? . . . Anyway, to cut it all short, it came across very bad. We looked very bad, anyway. So, let's go along with what they want us to do. So, of course, they implemented a worker participation committee.
>
> (Adelaide Laboratory Interviews, 1991)

For some staff, the results from the survey created a great deal of anxiety and stress that was still present at the time of our interviews. It was felt that senior management over-reacted to the survey, and as a consequence the current WPC is causing as many problems as it is solving. As the manufacturing manager commented:

> See, people in Australia, they all think it's the management's responsibility. If anything goes wrong, that's their problem. Let's all laugh about it: it's pretty funny. They don't have the accountability; they don't want the accountability. They say they do, but they don't. If you start giving them the accountability they start to have all these harassment problems amongst themselves, and they fight among themselves, and bickering occurs, which is occurring at the moment.
>
> (Adelaide Laboratory Interviews, 1991)

Middle management argued that whilst employees talk about wanting more responsibility, in practice if you reduce supervision many employees do not want to organize themselves. It was claimed that there is a need for supervision that can often be overlooked when discussing problems and suggesting change strategies. The supervisor is the front line of management, and as such must absorb and deal with a lot of shop-floor concerns and aggravations. In being the first line of formal authority, supervisors also tend to be blamed for problems or conflicts that emanate from the shop floor. In the view of one supervisor, this had been exacerbated by the formation of WPC, which had bypassed supervision:

> It was all good fun initially, you know, some of these people would have had years of frustration, and they were able to get them all out. It

was all good fun in a way, because both parties, even management, were able to sit back and listen and, 'Oh, is that why you behaved that way?' and 'Is that why this is happening?' – you know. Six weeks down the track it was going too fast. They were coming up with trivial issues and everything was an issue. You know, 'We'll raise that', and away it went . . . But where you've got a machine that's running and you're relying on how many minutes in an hour or day, that machine stops because someone says something that wasn't said two years ago. You're losing production time. Let's put dollar value aside. Let's forget dollar value. I'm looking at it from the urgency of that job. The client's waiting out there for their job and we promised them – we committed ourselves. What you have is a situation where the machine stops. We'll catch up with it, but their issue is number one; their participation's number one; you've got to listen to those issues. You don't want them to get the feeling that you're not interested. And of course you've lost the contract; you've lost what we're here to do.

(Adelaide Laboratory Interviews, 1991)

From a supervisory perspective, it was claimed that more time should be spent listening to supervisors who are dealing with problems on a day-to-day basis and that more effort should be made to ensure a balance of opinion from the shop floor. As one supervisor commented:

The only time you should raise an issue to the board that's going to be written up in the minutes is when the leading hand has been notified, and managers say, 'We're not doing anything about this.' Then they've got the right to raise the issue. But they've got to give courtesy first to the leading hand and to the managers to handle that problem or issue that they've raised.

(Adelaide Laboratory Interviews, 1991)

There was a view among some staff that concerns were no longer being raised with supervisors and that the WPC had resulted in reduction in communication between supervisors and employees on the shop floor. The WPC was viewed as providing a forum that served to erode the position of supervisor, and in so doing increased tension on the shop floor. Moreover, the removal of people from the shop floor to attend meetings was seen to increase pressure on those employees who remained:

The main thing is if you're pulling people out of the production environment that area stops and somebody's got to work a bit harder to get that person covered. So there's a lot of pressure on people.

(Adelaide Laboratory Interviews, 1991)

In discussing the problem of supervision and the consequence of the WPC, one technician commented that:

> It's certainly not easy to be a manager or a supervisor. I mean, I wouldn't want to be. Sure, the pay might be better but I don't know, you certainly lose friends. They've tried out quite a few chaps in the labs for supervisory sort of positions, but the same thing always happens. You know, they were one of the boys and now they've got to start giving a few orders and directions, and it never goes down too well. It ends up with them just getting totally frustrated and chucking it in, and getting back to being one of the boys again. You can't seem to be a supervisor and be a nice guy as well.
>
> (Adelaide Laboratory Interviews, 1991)

The WPC was also questioned by those not involved. It was argued that the committee was too quick to accept single perspectives and views of problems, had too much decision-making power, and was likely to make changes that were not necessarily for the good of all. The committee gets together once a fortnight and is chaired by the managing director. In the words of one employee:

> I think it's very important that the managing director knows a little bit of what goes on and not just gets ideas from one person because they think that person's giving them all the information. I think you've got to take somebody from the right, from the left, and hopefully somebody from the middle, and then make a decision on it, and not just go to one side. Because there are always at least two sides to a story.
>
> (Adelaide Laboratory Interviews, 1991)

It was also suggested that the committee was not functioning effectively and that there was an outstanding problem with the internal dynamics of the group:

> We decided that a committee would be the right way to go, so that they could air their views or if they felt that was too restrictive, on a one-to-one communication basis then they could have a discussion on that. Unfortunately, it's just not the right group we've got there. It's very much an intimidating group.
>
> (Adelaide Laboratory Interviews, 1991)

Thus the WPC was set up with the intention of improving employee involvement on the shop floor and tackling the issues raised in the anonymous attitudinal survey. The committee was intended to complement the service excellence programme and tackle particular problems associated with employee relations within the Adelaide laboratory. However, after a few weeks supervisors felt undermined believing that the committee was dealing with trivial issues that should have been raised directly with themselves. Moreover, other employees felt that there was a lack of balance in the views of shop-floor members and that the issues being raised did not necessarily reflect the 'real' concerns of all employees. In short, the WPC in tackling the problem of poor employee relations has created other interpersonal problems, particularly among supervisory staff.

On the question of changes in work tasks and the service excellence programme, it was generally claimed that the programme had done little to change the nature of work. Many employees claimed that they were providing 'excellence' in service and that the programme merely highlighted what they were already doing. For example, an ophthalmic repairs mechanic commented that:

> Well, I personally think repairs have always given service excellence. Even though I'm there by myself at the moment and we've got stacks and stacks of work, I refuse to let my quality slip just for the sake of getting a couple of extra jobs a day out. But we don't get a lot of reports back. We get the odd thank you note or complimentary phone call from branches around the place. But I think we provide an excellent service.
>
> (Adelaide Laboratory Interviews, 1991)

In another interview an optical mechanic claimed that:

> To me it was a breath of fresh air, because I thought, here's me: I've been trying to tell people for years, sort of thing, and now at long last someone's up there cracking a whip and saying, 'Yes, that's what you're all going to do now.' So in a way it sort of brought, I felt, everyone – or tried to bring everyone more closer to the standards that I would like. It's a little bit like living in a middle class social environment and bringing the lower class a little bit higher up. It's hard saying that, but that's the way I felt I can identify with it.
>
> (Adelaide Laboratory Interviews, 1991)

From the perspective of laboratory personnel, the service excellence programme had only brought about minor, if any, changes to work operations. A number of staff did not feel it was possible to attribute quality improvements to the service excellence programme, and questioned the programme's applicability to their existing quality assurance system. For example, one of the problems with improving quality was seen to stem from the poor or delayed feedback on items that did not meet customer expectations. It was argued that it is very difficult to trace faults if you do not receive immediate feedback. In some cases, it was claimed that it could be as long as six months before comments about poor products were received. As one of the laboratory employees explained:

> If you said to me, 'Here are the three lenses', I can say, 'Okay'. I can check each and every one of them; then I know exactly what's going wrong. But you just telling me they're wrong I'm going to say, 'What's wrong?' If you can't say, 'Right', then I don't know why. And if I don't know why I can't really do anything about it. So feedback from other people here is an extremely important thing, and that should be right through the organization.
>
> (Adelaide Laboratory Interviews, 1991)

In operating to preset standards, Tecsol have been using a quality assurance system for a number of years. The national manager of the ophthalmic laboratories explained that they have been manufacturing to the Australian Quality Standards for over a decade, and currently review standards annually. In addition to these fairly broad based standards, the laboratories have also developed their own standards in response to requests by Laubman and Pank Optometrists:

> We've got our own what we call quality standards, not based on Australian Standards but what Laubman and Pank require. It's fairly tight. That's been tightened every year. Every twelve months there's a review on manufacturing quality standards as regards to Laubman and Pank. That's in consultation with Laubman and Pank so everyone agrees what that should be.
>
> (Tecsol Laboratory Interviews, 1991)

The manufacturing manager highlighted the problem of matching standards with service excellence. He indicated that whilst it may make sense to strive for a zero-defect manufacturing operation, in practice there is always a percentage of rework that can never be fully resolved as it is based on the subjective and changing target of customer expectations. A client's perception of what is an appropriate or 'expected' visionary aid may differ from a standardized product that fits a documented norm. Factors such as the position in which the client likes to wear spectacles and the evaluation of significant others (such as family members) can influence a client's attitude to a new optical purchase. As the manufacturing manager explained:

> With optics 90 per cent of your work is black and white and 10 per cent is in a grey area. That 10 per cent has to be adjudicated by somebody, by some person. That's evaluated by another senior person

in quality, and with either a senior person in manufacturing – in other words, a senior supervisor or foreman type person – myself. Then a decision is made: should it or should it not go out? There's a lot of stuff that shouldn't go, won't go. That's quite clear to see; that's easy to see. It's that grey area. In that grey area there's probably about 5 per cent that would actually go out, that's okay [inaudible]. This is where the disharmony occurs. You've got people who are adamant it's black and white and won't see the grey area.

(Tecsol Laboratory Interviews, 1991)

In this sense, the service quality programme is creating some tension between what is seen as realistic quality standards within the laboratories and the philosophy of zero defects. This is made even more difficult to communicate, given the confusion and belief that the measurement of quality standards is fairly straightforward in manufacturing and that therefore targets should be easier to achieve. However, it fails to account for the nature of the product, which in order to satisfy customer requirements must be able to accommodate subjective and unknown data. As a result, the retail arm will tend to blame laboratory work and the manufacturing operations claim that these are unrealistic expectations and reflect a misunderstanding of the relationship between product manufacture and client satisfaction. Furthermore, it was also suggested that by over-emphasizing standards in an attempt to ensure defect-free products, turnaround time can become a secondary issue. For example, if a product is rejected because it fails to reach standards beyond those expected by a customer, then by delaying the delivery of the product the problem of customer dissatisfaction may arise in a situation where it need not have occurred. Thus, there would seem to be a need for a balance between product delivery time and quality, and a recognition that a customer's assessment of a product may change for subjective reasons.

Finally, in assessing the success of TQM the manufacturing manager commented that:

Successful areas? I would think that turnaround times have come down from, say, what used to be a five to seven-day turnaround to clients is down to a two-day turnaround. That's an amazing achievement. Quality standards have definitely improved. Costs have come down, waste has come down dramatically in a lot of areas, and our labour costs have come down, and we review our procedures far more often than we used to.

(Adelaide Laboratory Interviews, 1991)

Service excellence and competitive optometric practice

> I think they're trying to make it more retail oriented; whereas before it was, you know, a profession. But, of course, we are retailers as well, because we are selling frames, and there is a profit to be made on them. If you don't have profit you haven't got a business. So I think they are now emphasizing a lot more on the retail side of it as well: to be professional but being able to sell.
>
> (Branch Level Interviews, 1991)

In the optometry and retail area of Laubman and Pank there has been a movement away from a professional practice that undervalued the marketing and selling function towards a more retail-oriented business that provides a professional service. Whilst some tension remains between retail and optometry, there is an increasing awareness of the importance of selling products to customers. For the optometrists, this shift in emphasis has been accompanied by a change in dress codes and the replacement of the white coat with more general business attire. In conjunction with this 'symbolic' change there has been an attempt to replace the traditional optometrist–patient approach with one based on a closer consultant–client type relationship.

An optometrist described the change in the role and function of his job as follows:

> Optometry's always been – certainly, the way we've practised it here – it's always had an important retail component. Really, that's what it is. So there's been two phases of trying to hide behind superficial professionalism, with white coats, calling clients patients, putting on unnecessary airs and dignity. Most professions do that from time to time. And in the climate of society today, all professions have tended to become more humanized, more accountable. Their clients or patients expect to be told what's going on, in terms of medicine, dentistry, engineering, or whatever.
>
> (Branch Level Interviews, 1991)

However, the withdrawal of the white coat was not taken lightly by optometrists, who were anxious and wary of the response of colleagues practising either privately or in other organizations. Moreover, in assessing the programme and describing what optometrists would do if they were in the position of having to introduce service excellence, it was suggested that:

> Having to cope with new concepts upsets some people. They see the change and feel threatened. I think I would have concentrated less on

having total group training together, and tended to incorporate it into a general company philosophy that was ongoing on a day-to-day basis.

(Branch Level Interviews, 1991)

Optometrists generally viewed this new emphasis on selling products as largely the responsibility of front-line staff. For example, in asking for an initial response to service excellence, one optometrist commented that:

Initially I thought it was a bit of a joke. You know, I thought, 'Hell, hang on: they're giving us a lot of things to do which we can't implement.'

(Branch Level Interviews, 1991)

With the service excellence programme it is intended that an 'educated' customer interacts more closely with a 'team' of providers who aim to provide a 'quality service' that meets or exceeds the expectations of the customer. In practice, however, a division remains between the optometrists and other retail service staff. Although this may be explained by the professional standing of the optometrists, it was also reinforced through the commission-based payment system that applied to optometrists. This reward and recognition system simultaneously differentiated optometric practice from retail activities and down-played the role and function of other front-line staff:

Here the optometrists get everything (commission). We don't get anything from the jobs that we do, it all goes to the optometrists.

(Branch Level Interviews, 1991)

The clear divisions between optometrists and other branch level staff acted as potential barrier to teamwork and the development of good internal relations. Although some optometrists did develop strong links and work cooperatively with retail staff, this was not seen to be the norm. As one optometrist explained:

When [HRM] gave us a spiel up in the top room. Yeah, to me, having come from private practice, to hear service excellence I thought, 'Why do we need this? If we're in a job we shouldn't have to have service excellence pushed down our throat because you know it.' I mean, it's all part of private practice. I realized I wasn't in private practice, although David Pank said every optometrist here should run their show – their little area – as though they were in private practice, and I do here, which sometimes causes a few little ruffles because I like to see my patient and talk to my patient, and introduce my patient to the optical assistant to help them with the frame.

(Branch Level Interviews, 1991)

The move towards a more 'personalized' service has not been initiated by the service excellence programme, but reflects the different preferences of optometrists. In other words, TQM has done little to change the attitudes and behaviours of optometrists, who continue to practise in the manner to which they have become accustomed. For front-line staff this was seen to create a 'problem' that could be potentially alleviated through recruiting 'professional managers' to replace the 'professional optometrists' who acted as managers. The 'problem' was seen to rest on the fact that optometrists did not always behave in ways that were conducive to the development of service excellence. It was suggested that these idiosyncratic patterns of behaviour should be open to more scrutiny and control:

> I don't think I'd let the optometrists get a way with as much personal feelings as they do. Some optometrists can be a bit picky about what they do and how they treat their patients. Sometimes they're fairly greedy: you can tell. We think, 'If we were like that, we'd be out on our ear.' I think there should be more control.
>
> (Branch Level Interviews, 1991)

This situation was seen to reinforce the need for a manager, particularly within the retail outlets, who was not an optometrist, and was further highlighted by the rivalry between optometrists who sought to increase the supply of clients and improve their salaries:

> That's another problem. We really do think that [a particular optometrist] is doing the right thing, and yet there's jealousy: 'Why has he got so many clients? What are you doing to bring in so many clients? You must be giving him all the new clients', and things like that, whereas it's not true. These people are coming back and they want to see him. I feel that the optometrists can learn from that a bit, and yet they're probably seeing it the other way.
>
> (Branch Level Interviews, 1991)

Whilst some optometrists were seen to be 'practising service excellence', there were no other systems in place to reinforce this type of behaviour. According to a number of interviewees, client retention was achieved through developing close interpersonal relations with customers and working with other staff towards satisfying client needs. A teamwork approach was seen as being central to a client-oriented system of operation:

> We work best as a team. It's important that we work as a team and that we respect each other. If we didn't we'd find it almost impossible. In close quarters it's very important – almost essential – that we work as a team.
>
> (Branch Level Interviews, 1991)

The movement of clients between different staff was identified as an area where teamwork could be developed further in order to ensure an improved and more personalized service to the client. In practice, optometrists did not tend to spend time introducing their clients to other staff, but rather would leave the client's record on a shelf and return to other tasks. Although it was recognized that such 'personalized' service would not always be possible during busy periods:

> They [optometrists] just put their record on the shelf with a number
> ... In a way, you have to be that way to a degree, because sometimes
> we're that busy that people have to wait to see us, because we're a
> busy branch. But I think in the cases where we're not busy we're still
> using that system. I think that it shouldn't be like that.
>
> (Branch Level Interviews, 1991)

It was also noted that optometrists continued to use the word 'patient' when referring to clients (as did a number of other staff), and that the service excellence programme had not changed their job or their attitudes. As a professional occupational group, optometrists are able to maintain a degree of control and autonomy in their work. They also have the potential option of setting up their own practice. In the past, some optometrists have used their period of employment at Laubman and Pank to gain the knowledge and experience required to set up their own practice. However, as one optometrist stated:

> I think that, generally, the core of guys we've got now, give or take a
> few, are all pretty loyal and dedicated. I think they all quite enjoy
> their job. But I only see them once a year when we have our Laubman
> and Pank annual meeting where they all get together.
>
> (Branch Level Interviews, 1991)

Under existing work arrangements, the dominance of optometrists, poor remuneration packages for other employees and a 'top-heavy' organization structure were all seen to contribute to the problem of low employee morale on the shop floor. As one interviewee commented:

> I think the fact that they don't get a lot of money out the front, and yet
> they know very well that some of the hierarchy are quite well-
> established gentlemen of the world – quite wealthy fellows. I think
> that might disillusion them a little bit. It's not that they don't perform;
> they still do their job, but that would be a thing that they would make
> comment about. But, then again, I guess any worker who sees the
> boss drive his BMW in the car park, while he drives his second

hand Kingswood, knows that the boss is getting a lot more than him. I
don't know how you overcome that.

(Branch Level Interviews, 1991)

A second and related point raised by interviewees, was that there were
'too many chiefs and not enough Indians':

> There's too many chiefs and not enough Indians, and I think that's a
> case with a lot of big businesses. At least here they still do try to keep
> it more like a family structure. You know, the hierarchy are not
> unapproachable. So that's a good thing.

(Branch Level Interviews, 1991)

Once again this was seen to reflect the dominance of the optometrists and
resulted in difficulties for other front-line staff in knowing who they were
responsible for, who they should listen to and who they could ignore. As
one interviewee recounted:

> When you're beginning you have to decide who you're meant to
> listen to and who you're not meant to listen to; who you're meant to
> take the final answer from and what is the final answer. That takes a
> long time until you get the hang of it. I'd say it was a year in the job
> before I felt comfortable with my job, knowing exactly what I was
> meant to do.

(Branch Level Interviews, 1991)

Third, the pay system was seen to be out of line with the tasks and
responsibilities required of front-line staff. On this point one interviewee
commented that:

> I do like the job, but I don't think they accept the fact of what is
> involved with it. I think they do to a certain degree, but I think they
> should look at what I do and class it as such. This is my belief,
> because as you probably know here, it's shop assistants' wages.

(Branch Level Interviews, 1991)

Whilst another claimed that:

> I think the other thing is that we don't believe that we should be on
> the same rate as a shop assistant. We're doing a lot more – even on
> the optometric assistant level we're doing a lot more. We have to
> know a lot more than just being on a check-out . . . So I think there
> should be more incentive. I think they believe that they are giving us
> plenty of incentive, but I don't think the consensus is that that is the
> case.

(Branch Level Interviews, 1991)

Interviewees identified all these factors as inhibiting teamwork, restricting the branch level adoption of a service excellence philosophy, and contributing to low morale and disillusionment among retail staff. Moreover, in evaluating the service excellence programme, there was general agreement that whilst quality service provision was necessary to attract and retain customers, the programme had lost its momentum:

> I think it's all fallen into a big low at the moment, because nothing's happened from it and everyone's sort of sick of it. First everyone was all hyped up, but it's stopped, because there's never been anything happen from it.

(Branch Level Interviews, 1991)

There was some frustration among employees that the programme had not delivered what it promised and that a general failure by management to provide feedback to front-line staff had resulted in disillusionment with the programme – although it was stressed, that this did not mean that they did not continue to provide a quality service to customers. As one interviewee explained:

> To start off with, it looked good; but no-one ever followed it up. My biggest bug is that they gave us this big meeting about it – you know we had to sort of go up and learn all about it and everything – this kind of thing. I feel that most of it's commonsense. If you don't sort of look after people, they don't come back. But there's nothing to hype you up and keep you going. Management never come down and say, 'How's everyone going? Let's get going: we can do this, we can do that.' That's not done, so people just lost their interest, and said, 'Why should we bother?'

(Branch Level Interviews, 1991)

Two other concerns with the service excellence programme stemmed from the emphasis on the 'hard sell' and problems associated with the supply of poor quality products. On the first count, it was noted that retail staff tended to treat pensioners with more care than other customers, although it was recognized that they should focus more on the 'mature' client who is more likely to purchase the more expensive products. The second 'frustration' centred on product manufacture, as one interviewee commented:

> Because we are the front-line staff we're going to rely on the quality service of our manufacturers of the lenses and the frames. Otherwise we have to apologize for the company. And if they let us down, which does happen quite a bit, that's difficult. So that's where the frustrations lie.

(Branch Level Interviews, 1991)

These frustrations, problems and concerns of front-line staff were identified as causing dissatisfaction on the shop floor. As one employee put it:

> Morale is very low, but we all feel the same way: that if it were different we would love our jobs. Because I love the people; I love the industry. I think it's interesting; we're helping people; we're seeing people constantly – new, different people every day. And that's very interesting work. The hours are good for me; they suit me perfectly. It's just there are too many times I go home and say, 'I wish there was another job which was the same but with a different system.'
>
> (Branch Level Interviews, 1991)

Finally, in asking employees what they would do differently if they were in charge of the business, one employee commented as follows:

> I'd probably keep my finger on the pulse a bit more with the staff. I'd like to say keep the staff happy, or happier, but then you're always going to have somebody that's not happy. But I really think to make sure that their workplace is conducive to good professionalism, to make sure that they've got decent surroundings to work in, and also to make sure that their pay structure is better than it is at the moment. That's a big bone of contention. The staff here are on shop assistants' wages, and that creates a big bone of contention. Because, as they say, they're knowledge is more technical than shop assistants, so therefore they should be paid more than shop assistants, and rightly so ... I just wonder sometimes if perhaps they're a bit removed, or if the managing director's perhaps a bit removed from actually what is going on down on the floor.
>
> (Branch Level Interviews, 1991)

Conclusion: TQM in the Laubman and Pank Group

> If you're in manufacturing, I guess you can say, 'Hey, we're introducing a particular programme. We're going to have 99 per cent of our jobs leave our particular operation manufactured to our standards and on time for delivery', and you can measure that. In the service area it's more like a perception. It's very hard to say when you've done a job well. They talk a lot about the perceptions that the person you deal with walks out with: 'hey, that person was interested in me and I really feel good about going in there.' I think that's difficult to measure.
>
> (Senior Management Interviews, 1991)

There are a number of points that can be made in concluding this paper on the effects of service excellence on the organization and operation of the Laubman and Pank Group. For example, it has been shown how the language and culture of an organization is often closely aligned with the attitudes and behaviour of staff. In this case, in managing the transition towards a client-based culture the 'medical' white coat was replaced and it was decided that customers should be treated and referred to as 'clients' rather than 'patients'. In practice, however, the word 'patient' was still extensively used in discussing customer service, and consequently the expected shift in attitudes was not as extensive as originally envisaged. This highlights the cost and time involved in embarking on a programme that seeks to achieve a transformational change in attitudes, behaviours and working practices.

Whilst the data outlined in this document raise a number of issues that warrant further discussion and critique, these are not dealt with here. However, eight major lessons on managing the introduction of TQM in the Laubman and Pank Group are identified and outlined:

1 Introducing TQM is a continuous contextual process that requires the ongoing commitment of all levels of management. That is, the management of TQM is a dynamic process that is carried out within the context of other ongoing changes. For example, the historical legacy of divisions between manufacturing and retail operations cannot be ignored in the process of introducing TQM at work. Consequently, such factors as high levels of interpersonal conflict and poor patterns of communication are likely to bring about either a reduction in the general enthusiasm of staff and/or an increase in employee resistance to change.

2 The 'success' of TQM is dependent on all employees, from the receptionist to the managing director of the company. There is also a need regularly to reinforce the commitment of senior management through planned activities and organizational events, and to ensure that enough funds are available to support a continuing comprehensive programme of total employee involvement.

3 Getting employees involved and changing attitudes is a major keystone to TQM. It is important not to over-emphasize quantifiable results or to focus on short-term gains. Attitudinal change and the more general development of a culture of service excellence is the bedrock on which major system changes can later be achieved.

4 The introduction of TQM cannot be achieved overnight, but requires considerable planning and effort on the part of senior management if the scheme is going to be successful. This can be very frustrating,

especially in the first two years, when the general perception may be that 'you're getting nowhere' or 'nothing has changed'.

5 Strategies for introducing TQM may need to be modified at different stages during the process of change. It is not simply a question of establishing a programme, but of maintaining an interest and commitment to longer-term objectives. Different approaches are also likely to be required to convince different groups of employees. For example, some optometrists, in being professional tertiary-trained people, felt TQM wasn't necessary or applicable to them, and so time had to be spent convincing them otherwise. Although the process of changing the attitudes and behaviours of optometrists is likely to take time, it was identified as being a key factor in achieving teamwork and service excellence at branch level. The emphasis should not be on simply attracting customers, but also on retaining clients through the team provision of a quality service.

6 Appropriate training programmes were identified as being critical to any scheme that aims to bring about a whole scale change in service quality. These programmes should be customized to meet the needs and expectations of different groups and levels of staff.

7 Supervision is an element that is often overlooked in embarking on major change programmes. There is a need both to examine the job of the supervisor and how this is going to change with the involvement of employees in process improvements, and to involve supervisors in the process of adaptation. In short, the function of supervision should be clearly defined and supervisors should be engaged with, and trained in, the use of new service concepts, so that they may act as facilitators rather than inhibitors of change.

8 It is not always appropriate to measure the success of change through the identification of quantifiable benchmarks. Whilst quality assurance systems may be necessary in the manufacture of products to pre-specified standards, customers' expectations are not static but, rather, change over time. TQM sets out to provide a system to meet these changing expectations by taking into account the qualitative as well as quantitative dimensions of change.

Conclusion

An earlier version of the above company write-up was sent to Laubman and Pank, who provided comments; the version reproduced here is the one that has been agreed with the company and has been used as a source for book chapters and refereed journal articles.

Appendix III: an example of a processual case study used for teaching purposes

In using case study material for teaching purposes, the case is often summarized and presented in a fairly concise way that may 'hide' some of the more interesting, if rather detailed, findings. However, one of the main benefits of using case studies in which you have been actively engaged in fieldwork is that the more complex elements of the case can be brought out in class discussion. In the illustrative example used below, I draw on an early piece of longitudinal research into computers and change in British Rail marshalling yards. If case studies are to be used regularly for this purpose, then it is useful to have an introductory piece that draw attention to the typical characteristics of teaching case files and how the case study can best be approached and analysed by the student. Consequently, the first section in this appendix replicates some guidelines for case study tutorials, which were developed by Liz Kummerow and myself for a second-year undergraduate course that we ran at the University of Adelaide during the early 1990s. The second section (which some readers may wish to skip to) then demonstrates how a very large and detailed case study (see Dawson, 1986) can be summarized into a few pages for teaching purposes. Those who are more familiar with this example will know that the change did not go as smoothly as is indicated by the case. For example, there were major industrial relations issues raised in Wales that involved protracted negotiations. Senior management had to modify their strategy and develop a more participative approach, which involved the local shunting staff in managing the change process. Once students have a general grasp of the case, with these type of processual studies you can begin to build in details that complicate and muddy their initial analysis and understanding of change. It is also useful in stimulating further discussion and debate.

Guidelines for case study tutorials

Typically, case studies are derived from organizational research and consultancy and provide an opportunity to analyse organizational problems and derive possible solutions. They may take a snapshot of an organization at a particular moment in time, or discuss a particular issue or problem faced by a company. The processual case study is concerned with capturing processes as they happen, and this generally involves the collection of a large body of qualitative longitudinal data. However, elements from these more detailed studies can be summarized and used to shed light on the way people experience organizational life in particular settings and contexts. Today, case study analysis is used widely as a training and educational technique with students of management. Students are usually required to take the role of manager or other participant in the case, or of an external observer such as a management consultant or academic organizational analyst. Their task is to analyse the problem presented in the case. This may involve coming up with practical suggestions as to how to tackle the problem and/or the use of analytical tools, concepts and theories from lectures and reading material in order to interpret, understand and explain the events in the case. Case study analysis is seen to have a number of advantages over the more traditional tutorial method. For example, case study analysis involves students in active rather than passive learning; introduces managerial and organizational 'realities' into the educational process and enables students to apply analytical, conceptual and theoretical ideas to real-world situations, and helps students develop analytical and problem-solving skills required for effective management – or indeed any form of participation in organizations – in the real world (see, for example, Clegg *et al.*, 1999).

In using processual case studies for teaching, group work is highly recommended. One important advantage of analysing the case as a group is that it enables the particular situation/issue that is depicted in the case to be considered from a number of different perspectives. This helps to guard against 'tunnel vision' (perceiving issues narrowly, from a single perspective only), which often characterizes individual analyses of case study material. Working as a group has a number of additional advantages. It enhances students' communication skills and gives them some experience in dealing with the kinds of problems that develop in groups. Group work can also be seen to simulate real-world experience in that students (like decision-makers in organizations) must be prepared to defend their particular way of looking at, and dealing with, the presenting problem in the face of opposing perspectives and solutions.

Guidelines for analysing a case

In their review of the case study method, Selvarajah *et al.* (1991) suggest a standard procedure for students to follow in analysing a case. Five practical steps or stages are recommended, and these are described below:

Stage 1. Read the case quickly to gain a general impression of the situation and the kind of problem you think the organization is facing. You might find it useful at this stage to underline, highlight or annotate information in the case that indicates that a problem exists – for example, a statement that the firm is experiencing high labour turnover. The aim at this stage is not to prove that your initial impression is correct; it is simply to distinguish the essential elements of the case, from the non-essential elements. Ask yourself: 'What sort of organization is this?', 'What problems does its management appear to be facing?'

Stage 2. Read the case study questions carefully and, if there is a choice, decide which you will attempt. Make sure that you understand exactly what each question is asking you to do. In this respect it may help to underline key terms in each question. It is important that you understand the meaning of these key terms and can distinguish between terms such as 'analyse', 'discuss' and 'evaluate', which are often mistakenly taken to mean the same thing (see Selvarajah *et al.*, 1991: 11 for a glossary of terms that are often used in case study questions).

Stage 3. Read the case again very thoroughly, perhaps several times. These subsequent readings will provide you with a more complete understanding of the case, and may also reveal additional key information that was not apparent to you on your first reading. Look for evidence that will help you to answer the questions you have been set. By the end of Stage 3 you should have a good understanding of the main problems the organization is trying to confront, and you should be aware of the sorts of analysis, recommendations and/or decisions that you will make to deal with these problems. Some additional guidelines to assist you in your second and subsequent readings of the case include:

(a) Do not consider the organization in isolation, but take into account aspects of the broader context (the economic, social, technical and political environment) that may be detailed in the case.

(b) Try to gain an understanding of the various facets of the organization's internal environment. Research has shown that people tend to view organizations only from their own perspective, so that, for example, marketing people see marketing issues as paramount, accounting people focus on financial issues, and production people on production problems. As indicated above, one of the advantages of analysing the case as a group is that these different perspectives are more likely to be given consideration.

(c) Be careful in appraising facts and opinions. Facts about a firm can be distorted if they are not considered in the context of other environmental factors such as economic conditions, competition, strengths and weaknesses of the market etc. Also, facts that initially seem impressive can sometimes be deceptive. For example, at a first glance a firm's current performance indicators may look positive, but when they are evaluated in the context of the previous year's performance they may indicate a decline. It is also important to consider the source of facts that are presented in the case. For example, company documents such as annual reports and media releases often present an overly positive image of the company, which may not be shared by shop-floor employees. You should also be careful when evaluating opinions expressed by the key characters in the case. Organizations often comprise competing interest groups and members of these different groups can have quite different perspectives on issues and problems that face the organization. An industrial relations issue, for example, is likely to be viewed quite differently by a senior manager than by a union official.

(d) Don't accept everything that you read at face value, but question the statements that people make and form your own opinions about them.

(e) While you will probably identify a number of alternative courses of action, or proposals, for solving or analysing the problem presented in the case, you may be required to recommend only one. In this instance, it is often useful to look back through the case for a statement of the organization's objectives. Knowing the objectives of the firm can provide a useful guide to your choice of a course of action.

Stage 4. Plan your answer. Some useful guidelines to assist in this stage are:

(a) You must be able to cite evidence from the case to support your arguments and recommendations. Evidence may consist of facts, figures (where relevant – e.g. a chart showing the organization's structure, graphs showing trends in sales, profit, turnover etc.), statements made, and views expressed by the characters in the case. As indicated above, however, you must be careful in appraising facts and opinions since the way in which they are presented in a case can sometimes distort their meaning and disguise the subjective bias of the author and/or the characters in the case.

(b) It is legitimate to draw inferences about matters that are not explicitly stated in the case. However, you should always be able to justify such inferences by drawing on case material. Engaging in 'flights of fantasy', where no support or justification is given for the points you make, is not permissible.

(c) It is important that you apply your knowledge of the theories you have learned in your study of management to the evidence you have assembled. Your ultimate goal is to make some concrete and practical recommendations or analytical statements, which have theoretical rather than just intuitive credibility. Vague conclusions, such as 'the jobs of the workers have to be enriched', or 'Fred has to change his leadership style', are not sufficient for this purpose.

Stage 5. Write your final answer, being sure to include all of the tasks that you have been set. Be selective in your use of quotations or opinions expressed in the case. Do not simply paraphrase what you have read in the case; this approach will not provide a satisfactory answer. Try to express your ideas in your own words and address the issue in a concise and relevant manner.

The British Rail case study: learning from the past?

In 1971, British Rail (BR) decided to invest 13 million pounds (1971 prices) in a new computer system to improve the performance of its freight operations. Having considered a variety of options, including the possibility of developing a system 'in-house', BR decided to purchase software already developed and proven in railway freight operations in North America. The system in question was known as 'TOPS' (Total Operations Processing System).

The decision to computerize was based on two factors:

1 The severe economic crisis facing British Rail's freight business due to competition from road haulage and the decline of the industries that were traditionally the railway's principal source of freight revenue (coal, iron and steel).
2 The identification of inefficiencies in the day-to-day supervision of freight operations stemming from inaccurate and out-of-date information about the whereabouts of freight resources – empty wagons, locomotives and freight trains.

The computerization of freight operations control

Prior to computerization, information on the disposition of freight resources and the operating situation was reported through an hierarchical structure, consisting of supervisors in local marshalling yards, who reported to divisional control rooms who in turn reported to regional control rooms. Operations as a whole were overseen by a central control room at BR headquarters in London. The principal methods of communicating information were 'manual', involving either telephone or telex reports of such things as the numbers of empty wagons 'on hand' in a marshalling yard, or the 'consist' of a freight train *en route*. Much of this information was inaccurate, not least because of the manipulation of information by marshalling yard supervisors. For example, empty wagons were frequently in short supply, and in order to satisfy the daily requirements of local customers, supervisors under-reported the number of wagons 'on-hand' and over-reported the number of 'empties' required.

This resulted in a gross over-supply and under-utilization of resources. In 1971 there were well over half a million wagons on the BR network, only 80 per cent of which were accounted for in daily reports from supervisors. Similar problems were involved with locomotives, and these, along with empty wagons, were frequently 'hidden' in remote sidings by supervisors in order that they could respond to unexpected changes in local requirements. As a result, although a vast amount of information was being passed day-to-day on the disposition of freight resources, very little of this bore any relation to the reality of the operating situation at 'ground' level. Moreover, there were inevitable delays in passing information on by 'manual' methods. In the context of 'time-sensitive' railway operations, much of this information on the whereabouts of resources was invalid by the time it reached its destination. As a result, senior operations management were simply unaware of much of what was happening and spent most of their time in a 'reactive' role, attempting to establish what had happened and why.

The economic circumstances of the freight business meant that a solution to the problem of supervising freight operations had to be found if rail freight was to remain competitive and in business. The TOPS system offered a potential solution. Each local marshalling yard was to be equipped with an on-line terminal linked to a mainframe computer at BR headquarters. Marshalling yard staff would be required to provide information to 'TOPS clerks', who would input information via the local terminals. This information provided a 'real-time' picture of the operating situation in any particular area. Because the information was communicated by electronic means direct to a central computer and could be easily accessed, the 'inbuilt' delays and inaccuracies inherent in the old 'manual' reporting system could be avoided. Furthermore, because the TOPS system kept tabs on each individual wagon, locomotive and train, it was impossible to 'hide' resources as had previously been practised. Moreover, because the system could cross check reports from local terminals almost instantaneously, any attempt to input misleading information was rejected by the computer.

The implementation problem

The decision to computerize the control of freight operations involved considerable uncertainty and risk. There was no guarantee that the system would arrest the decline of the freight business and every possibility that the implementation of the system would run into difficulties, with the risk of delays and the escalation of the costs of the project. Despite the advantages of buying-in an already proven technological innovation, successful adoption of the new technology still depended on solving a number of technical, personnel, industrial relations, and managerial problems. The situation was summed up in 1981 by one senior freight operations manager in BR, who described TOPS as BR's most speculative investment since the Beeching Report and restructuring in the 1960s.

Given the critical economic position of the freight business, there was considerable concern at Board level that computerization should be completed within a four-year timescale and within budget. The scale of the project was enormous. In technical terms, it meant adapting the TOPS software to suit BR's operations, providing a network of computer terminals in 150 locations around the country, installing a new mainframe computer centre, and upgrading BR's existing telecommunications system. In personnel terms, there was the major task of educating all levels of freight operations staff, from shunters to headquarters management, about the capabilities and use of the system, and of providing specialist training for the staff who would make day-to-day use of the system. In industrial relations terms, it meant gaining the acceptance of the new technology by the rail unions in a climate that had previously proved resistant to rapid change. Finally, there was the question of how the introduction of the new technology should be managed. Should traditional practice be followed, where each specialist department was allocated responsibility for the aspects of the project that concerned them (e.g. computing to Management Services, retraining to Personnel etc.) and each BR region be given the responsibility for the management of change in its own local areas, or should a new approach be tried?

The 'task force' approach

It was the risk of delay through inter-departmental rivalries and regional/headquarters conflict that was most feared by management. Despite nationalization, geographical identities remained strongy rooted in the organizational culture, and at corporate level functional specialisms jealously guarded their areas of expertise. There was every possibility that the whole project would founder on the rocks of inter-management squabbles. However, the BR chief executive gave the project high-level support and appointed a senior operations manager to head up an implementation team. Given the high stakes involved, other departments made no effort to take responsibility for the various aspects of implementation, and in the ensuing vacuum the project manager was able to assemble a 'task force' in the form of a cross-functional team that assumed complete control of the entire project. Computing, telecommunications and operations specialists were seconded from their departments, whilst the training function and regions were virtually bypassed altogether. Instead, a number of operations staff and a year's intake of graduate trainees were co-opted to form a team that would act as a mobile training force, travelling around the country to retrain staff. The 'task force' was presented to the rest of the organization as a '*fait accompli*' and, with the support of the Chief Executive, set about bending normal rules and procedures and upsetting the traditional customs of the organizational culture with a view to the introduction of the TOPS system without delay.

Creating a 'culture of change'

The two principal non-technical tasks facing the 'task force' were in gaining the acceptance of the new technology by staff and management, and convincing the unions of the need for rapid change. In relation to the first task, the initial step was to create within the implementation team itself an almost unbounded enthusiasm for and identification with the achievement of change. The team was run on almost militaristic lines, and a number of devices, including a special 'TOPS logo', a 'TOPS tie', a 'TOPS newsletter' and a package of training graphics featuring a character called 'TOPS Cat', were employed to foster a corporate identity for the project. In the words of one of the task force members, 'if you weren't fired with enthusiasm for the project, you were fired from the project!'. Faced with such commitment backed by high-level management support, local personnel saw little opportunity or point in resisting change. Where they did, the project team ignored any protestations and carried on regardless. The use of the mobile team proved a masterstroke in providing a training package that could combine classroom theory with 'hands on' experience on the job. Any resistance to the new reporting procedures required for computerization by the staff – many of whom had spent years working by traditional methods – were more readily overcome.

In terms of the trade unions, there was no opposition in principle to the computerization, not only because the introduction of TOPS promised to save the jobs that would be lost if the freight business went to the wall, but also because it involved the creation of new jobs – at least in the short term. Whilst consulting with the rail unions from a very early stage, management studiously avoided entering into any time-consuming national negotiations over extra payments for using the new technology. Furthermore, no attempt was made by management to develop the potential of the TOPS systems for keeping tabs on train crews. It was certain that the 'Big Brother' connotations of such a use would have brought vigorous union opposition, in particular from the train drivers' union ASLEF. As a result, union leaders were 'won over' to the system and were happy to cooperate in its speedy introduction. Indeed, national officers of the unions were instrumental in resolving some of the small localized disputes that did occur during the implementation programme. In retrospect, the view of many national officials was that if management had introduced such a system sooner, much of the market that had already been lost might have been saved.

Technological change and organizational innovation

The TOPS computerization project was completed on time and within budget in October 1975. A far more efficient utilization of freight resources was achieved and operational control considerably improved. In particular, it became clear that management for the first time had an opportunity to play a 'proactive' role in the planning and control of freight operations. As one operations manager put it, 'we now had a production line we could control'.

Case study questions

1 What would you identify as the critical factors that contributed to the successful implementation of the TOPS system?
2 What were the advantages and disadvantages of the 'task force' approach?
3 How important is context and culture in understanding change?
4 Are there any general lessons that can be learnt from this case study on the process of organizational change?

Conclusion

This appendix illustrates how these more detailed longitudinal processual studies can be used for teaching change at undergraduate and postgraduate levels. They can be used to discuss and draw out some practical dimensions to change, as well as being used to address conceptual issues and the more complex dynamics of understanding change processes.

⚉ Bibliography

Alvesson, M. and Willmott, H. (1996) *Making Sense of Management: A Critical Introduction*, London: Sage.

Bacharach, P. and Baratz, M. (1962) 'Two Faces of Power', *American Political Science Review* 56: 641–651.

Badham, R., Couchman, P. and McLoughlin, I. (1997) 'Implementing vulnerable socio-technical change projects', in McLoughlin, I. and Harris, M. (eds) *Innovation, Organizational Change and Technology*, London: International Thomson Business Press.

Baldry, C., Bain, P. and Taylor, P. (1998) '"Bright satanic offices": intensification, control and team taylorism', in Thompson, P. and Warhurst, C. (eds) *Workplaces of the Future*, London: Macmillan Business.

Barley, S. (1990) 'Image of imaging: notes on doing longitudinal field work', *Organization Science* 1(3): 220–247.

Becker, H. (1973) *Outsiders: Studies in the Sociology of Deviance*, New York: Free Press.

Beckhard, R. (1969) *Organizational Development: Strategies and Models*, Reading, Mass: Addison-Wesley.

Bloor, G. (1999) 'Organizational culture, organizational learning and total quality management. A literature review and synthesis', *Australian Health Review* 22(3): 162–179.

Bloor, G. and Dawson, P. (1994) 'Understanding professional culture in organizational context', *Organization Studies* 15(2): 275–295.

Boje, D. (1991) 'The storytelling organization: a study of story performance in an office-supply firm', *Administrative Science Quarterly* 36: 106–126.

Boje, D. and Dennehy, R. (1993) *Managing in the Postmodern World: America's Revolution Against Exploitation*, Dubuque: Kendall-Hunt.

Bryman, A. (1988a) *Quantity and Quality in Social Research*, London: Unwin Hyman.

Bryman, A. (ed.) (1988b) *Doing Research in Organizations*, London: Routledge.

Buchanan, D. (1994) 'Cellular manufacture and the role of teams', in Storey, J.

(ed.) *New Wave Manufacturing Strategies: Organizational and Human Resource Management Dimensions*, London: Paul Chapman Publishing.

Buchanan, D. and Badham, R. (1999) *Power, Politics, and Organizational Change: Winning the Turf Game*, London: Sage Publications.

Buchanan, D. and Boddy, D. (1992) *The Expertise of the Change Agent: Public Performance and Backstage Activity*, London: Prentice-Hall International.

Buchanan, D. and Preston, D. (1992) 'Life in the cell: supervision and teamwork in a "manufacturing systems engineering" environment', *Human Resource Management Journal* 2(4): 55–76.

Buchanan, D. and Storey, J. (1997) 'Role-taking and role-switching in organizational change: the four pluralities', in McLoughlin, I. and Harris, M. (eds) *Innovation, Organizational Change and Technology*, London: International Thompson Business Press.

Buchanan, D., Boddy, D. and McCalman, J. (1998) 'Getting in, getting on, getting out and getting back', in Bryman, A. (ed.) *Doing Research in Organizations*, London: Routledge.

Burgess, R. (ed.) (1982) *Field Research: A Sourcebook and Field Manual*, London: Allen & Unwin.

Burnes, B. (1992) *Managing Change: A Strategic Approach to Organizational Dynamics*, London: Pitman.

Burnes, B. (1996) *Managing Change: A Strategic Approach to Organizational Dynamics*, 2nd edn, London: Pitman.

Burnes, B. (2000) *Managing Change: A Strategic Approach to Organizational Dynamics*, 3rd edn, London: Pitman.

Burns, T. and Stalker, G. M. (1961) *The Management of Innovation*, London: Tavistock.

Campbell, A. (1969) *Maori Legends*, Wellington: Seven Seas Publishing.

Chapman, J. (2000) *Fragmentation in Archaeology*, London: Routledge.

Child, J. (1972) 'Organization structure, environment and performance: the role of strategic choice', *Sociology* 6(1): 1–22.

Child, J. (1997) 'Strategic choice in the analysis of action, structure, organizations and environment: retrospect and prospect', *Organization Studies* 18(1): 43–76.

Child, J. and Smith, C. (1987) 'The context and process of organizational transformation', *Journal of Management Studies* (24)6: 565–593.

Clark, J. (1995) *Managing Innovation and Change: People, Technology and Strategy*, London: Sage.

Clark, J., McLoughlin, I., Rose, H. and King, R. (1988) *The Process of Technological Change: New Technology and Social Choice in the Workplace*, Cambridge: Cambridge University Press.

Clegg, C., Legge, K. and Walsh, S. (eds) (1999) *The Experience of Managing: A Skills Guide*, London: Macmillan Business.

Collins, D. (1998a) 'Il a commencé à penser avant d'avoir rien appris. A processual view of the construction of empowerment', *Employee Relations* 20(6): 594–609.

Collins, D. (1998b) *Organizational Change: Sociological Perspectives*, London: Routledge.

Collins, D. (2000) *Management Fads and Buzzwords: Critical–Practical Perspectives*, London: Routledge.

Creswell, J. (2002) *Research Design: Qualitative, Quantitative, and Mixed Methods Approaches*, 2nd edn, London: Sage.

Dalton, M. (1959) *Men Who Manage*, New York: Wiley.

Dawson, P. (1986) 'Computer Technology and the Redefinition of Supervision.' Ph.D. Thesis, University of Southampton.

Dawson, P. (1987) 'Computer technology and the job of the first-line supervisor', *New Technology, Work and Employment* 2(1): 47–60.

Dawson, P. (1991) 'From machine-centred to human-centred manufacture', *International Journal of Human Factors in Manufacturing* 1(4): 327–338.

Dawson, P. (1994) *Organizational Change: A Processual Approach*, London: Paul Chapman Publishing.

Dawson, P. (1996) *Technology and Quality: Change in the Workplace*, London: International Thomson Business Press.

Dawson, P. (2001) 'Contextual shaping in the origination, implementation and uptake of manufacturing cells', *Integrated Manufacturing Systems* 12(4): 296–305.

Dawson, P. (2003) *Understanding Organizational Change: The Contemporary Experience of People at Work*, London: Sage.

Dawson, P. and McLoughlin, I. (1986) 'Computer technology and the redefinition of supervision: a study of the effects of computerization on railway freight supervisors', *Journal of Management Studies* 23(1): 116–132.

Dawson, P. and Palmer, G. (1995) *Quality Management: The Theory and Practice of Implementing Change*, Melbourne: Longman Cheshire.

De Vaus, D. (2001) *Research Design in Social Research*, London: Sage.

Dey, I. (1993) *Qualitative Data Analysis: A User-Friendly Guide for Social Scientists*, London: Routledge.

Dunphy, D. and Stace, D. (1990) *Under New Management: Australian Organizations in Transition*, Sydney: McGraw-Hill.

Easterby-Smith, M., Thorpe, R. and Lowe, A. (2001) *Management Research*, 2nd edn, London: Sage.

Elger, A. (1975) 'Industrial organizations: A processual perspective', in McKinlay, J. (ed.) *Processing People: Cases in Organizational Behaviour*, New York: Hold, Rinehart and Winston.

Felstead, W. J. (1979) 'Qualitative methods: a needed perspective in evaluation research', in Cook, T. and Reichardt, C. (eds) *Qualitative and Quantitative Methods in Evaluation Research*, California: Sage.

Ferlie, E., Ashburner, L., Fitzgerald, L. and Pettigrew, A. (1996) *The New Public Management in Action*, Oxford: Oxford University Press.

Flick, U. (2002) *Introduction to Qualitative Research*, 2nd edn. London: Sage.

Frost, P. and Stablein, R. (eds) (1992) *Doing Exemplary Research*, California: Sage.

Gabriel, Y. (2000) *Storytelling in Organizations. Facts, Fictions and Fantasies*, Oxford: Oxford University Press.

Gill, J. and Johnson, J. (1991) *Research Methods for Managers*, London: Paul Chapman Publishing.

Glaser, B. G. and Strauss, A. L. (1967) *The Discovery of Grounded Theory*, Chicago: Aldine.

Gouldner, A. (1965) *Wildcat Strike*, New York: Free Press.

Gray, G. and Pratt, R. (1991) *Towards a Discipline of Nursing*, Melbourne: Churchill Livingstone.

Guth, W. D. and MacMillan, C. (1989) 'Strategy implementation versus middle management self-interest', in Asch, D. and Bowman, C. (eds) *Readings in Strategic Management*, London: Macmillan.

Hamel, G. (2000) *Leading the Revolution*, Boston, Mass.: Harvard Business School Press.

Hamel, G. and Prahalad, C. K. (1994) *Competing for the Future*, Boston, Mass.: Harvard Business School Press.

Handy, C. (1986) *Understanding Organizations*, Penguin: Harmondsworth.

Handy, C. (2001) *The Elephant and the Flea*, London: Hutchinson.

Harrison, N. and Samson, D. (1997) *International Best Practice in the Adoption and Management of New Technology*, Canberra: Commonwealth of Australia.

Hildebrandt, E. and Seltz, R. (1989) *Wandel der betrieblicher Sozialverfassung durch systemische Kontrolle?* Berlin: Edition Sigma.

Hinings, C. (1997) 'Reflections on processual research', *Scandinavian Journal of Management* 13(4): 493–503.

Hodder, I. (1982) *The Present Past*, New York: Pica Press.

Hodder, I. (1986) *Reading the Past*, Cambridge: Cambridge University Press.

Huczynski, A. (1993) *Management Gurus: What Makes Them and How to Become One*, London: Routledge.

Jackson, B. (2001) *Management Gurus and Management Fashions*, London: Routledge.

Jacobs, A. (1983) 'Film and Electronic Technologies in the Production of Television News: A Case Study in the Introduction of Electronic News Gathering in an ITV Company.' Ph.D. Thesis, University of Southampton.

Johnson, M. (1999) *Archaeological Theory: An Introduction*, Oxford: Blackwell.

Johnson, P. and Duberley, J. (2000) *Understanding Management Research: An Introduction to Epistemology*, London: Sage.

Kamp, A. (2000) 'Breaking up old marriages: the political process of change and continuity at work', *Technology Analysis and Strategic Management* 12(1): 75–90.

Kanter, R. M. (1983) *The Change Masters: Innovation for Productivity in the American Corporation*, New York: Simon and Schuster.

Kanter, R. M. (1990) *When Giants Learn to Dance: Mastering the Challenges of Strategy, Management, and Careers in the 1990s*, London: Unwin Hyman.

Kanter, R. M., Stein, B. A. and Jick, T. D. (1992) *The Challenge of Organizational Change: How Companies Experience It and Leaders Guide It*, New York: Free Press.

Kantrow, A. (1987) *The Constraints of Corporate Tradition: Doing the Correct Thing, Not Just What the Past Dictates*, New York: Harper & Row.

Kelly, D. and Amburgey, T. L. (1991) 'Organizational inertia and momentum: a dynamic model of strategic change', *Academy of Management Journal* 34(3): 591–612.

Knights, D. and McCabe, D. (1998) 'Dreams and designs on strategy: a critical analysis of TQM and management control', *Work, Employment and Society* 12(3): 433–456.

Knights, D. and Murray, F. (1994) *Managers Divided: Organization Politics and Information Technology Management*, Chichester: John Wiley & Sons.

Kotter, J. (1996) *Leading Change*, Harvard: Harvard Business School Press.

Kotter, J. (1997) *Realizing Change*, Harvard: Harvard Business School Press.

Langley, A. (1999) 'Strategies for theorizing from process data', *Academy of Management Review* 24: 691–710.

Leavitt, H. J. (1964) 'Applied organizational change in industry: structural, technical and human approaches', in Cooper, W. W., Leavitt, H. J. and Shelly, M. W. (eds) *New Perspectives in Organizations Research*, New York: John Wiley.

Lodge, D. (2001) *Thinks . . .*, London: Secker & Warburg.

McLoughlin, I. and Clark, J. (1988) *Technological Change at Work*, Milton Keynes: Open University Press.

Morris, J. and Wilkinson, B. (1995) 'The transfer of Japanese management to alien institutional environments: editorial introduction', *Journal of Management Studies* 32(6): 719–730.

Odin, J. (2001) 'The performative and processual study of hypertext/postcolonial aesthetic', University of Hawaii at Manoa (www.thecore.nus.edu.sg/landow/post/poldiscourse/odin/odin/7.html).

Onions, C. (1973) (ed.) *The Shorter Oxford English Dictionary*, Oxford, Clarendon Press.

Orlikowski, W. J. (1992) 'The duality of technology: rethinking the concept of technology in organizations', *Organization Science* (3)3: 398–427.

Orton, J. (1997) 'From inductive to iterative grounded theory: zipping the gap between process theory and process data', *Scandinavian Journal of Management* 13(4): 419–438.

Palmer, I. and Dunford, R. (2002) 'Who says change can be managed? Positions, perspectives and problematics', *Strategic Change* 11: 243–251 (www.interscience.wiley.com).

Panteli, N. and Dawson, P. (2001) 'Video conferencing meetings: changing patterns of business communication', *New Technology, Work and Employment* 16(2): 88–99.

Parry, K. (1996) 'The case for using grounded theory to research the leadership process in organizations', Management Chapters, University of Southern Queensland.

Parry, K. W. (1998) 'Grounded theory and social process: a new direction for leadership research', *The Leadership Quarterly* 9(1): 85–105.

Pettigrew, A. (1973) *The Politics of Organizational Decision-Making*, London: Tavistock.

Pettigrew, A. (1985) *Awakening Giant: Continuity and Change in ICI*, Oxford: Basil Blackwell.

Pettigrew, A. (1987a) 'Context and action in the transformation of the firm', *Journal of Management Studies* (24)6: 649–670.

Pettigrew, A. (ed.) (1987b) *The Management of Strategic Change*, Oxford: Basil Blackwell.

Pettigrew, A. (1990) 'Longitudinal field research on change: theory and practice', *Organization Science* 1(3): 267–292.

Pettigrew, A. (1997) 'What is a processual analysis?', *Scandinavian Journal of Management* 13(4): 337–348.

Pettigrew, A. (2002) *Leading Organizational Change: Frameworks and Findings from Warwick Research 1985–2002*, Report for the Office of Public Sector Reform, Cabinet Office, London.

Pettigrew, A. and Fenton, E. (eds) (2000a) *The Innovating Organization*, London: Sage.

Pettigrew, A. and Fenton, E. (eds) (2000b) 'Integrating a global professional services organization: the case of Ove Arup Partnership', in Pettigrew, A. and Fenton, E. (eds) *The Innovating Organization*, London: Sage.

Pettigrew, A. and McNulty, T. (1995) 'Power and influence in and around the boardroom', *Human Relations* 18(8): 845–873.

Pettigrew, A. and Whipp, R. (1991) *Managing Change for Competitive Success*, Oxford: Blackwell.

Pettigrew, A., Ferlie, E. and McKee, L. (1992) *Shaping Strategic Change: Making Change in Large Organizations. The Case of the National Health Service*, London: Sage.

Pfeffer, J. (1981) *Power in Organizations*, Boston: Pitman.

Pfeffer, J. (1982) *Organizations and Organization Theory*, Cambridge, MA: Ballinger Publishing Company.

Polanyi, M. (1962) *Personal Knowledge*, London: Routledge.

Polanyi, M. (1983) *The Tacit Dimension*, Cambridge, MA: Peter Smith.

Porter, L. W., Crampon, W. J. and Smith, F. J. (1976) 'Organizational commitment and managerial turnover: a longitudinal study', *Organizational Behavior and Human Performance* Feb.: 87–98.

Preece, D. (1995) *Organizations and Technical Change. Strategy, Objectives and Involvement*, London: Routledge.

Preece, D., Steven, G. and Steven, V. (1999) *Work, Change and Competition. Managing for Bass*, London: Routledge.

Procter, S. and Mueller, F. (eds) (2000) *Teamworking*, London: Macmillan Business.

Quintanilla, J. and Sanchez-Runde, C. (2000) 'New forms of organizing through human resource management: the case of Fremap', in Pettigrew, A. and Fenton, E. (eds) *The Innovating Organization*, London: Sage.

Riley, M., Roy, C., Clark, A. *et al.* (2000) *Researching and Writing Dissertations in Business and Management*, London: Thomson Learning.

Ropo, A., Eriksson, P. and Hunt, J. (1997a) (eds) 'Special issue: reflections on conduction processual research on management and organizations', *Scandinavian Journal of Management* 13(4), 331–503.

Ropo, A., Eriksson, P. and Hunt, J. (1997b) 'Reflections on conducting processual research on management and organizations', *Scandinavian Journal of Management* 13(4): 331–335.

Roy, D. (1967) 'Quota restriction and goldbricking in a machine shop', in Faunce, W. (ed) *Readings in Industrial Sociology*, New York: Meredith Publishing Company.

Ruigrok, W., Achtenhagen, L., Ruegg-Sturn, J. and Wagner, M. (2000) 'Hilti AG: shared leadership and the rise of the communicating organization', in Pettigrew, A. and Fenton, E. (eds) *The Innovating Organization*, London: Sage.

Schein, E. H. (1985) *Organizational Culture and Leadership*, San Francisco, CA: Jossey-Bass.

Schlesinger, P., Sathe, V., Schlesinger, L. and Kotter, J. (1992). *Organization. Text, Cases, and Readings on the Management of Organizational Design and Change*, Homewood, IL: Irwin.

Selvarajah, C., Petzall, S. and Willis, O. (1991) (eds) *Management Case Studies*, 3rd edn, Melbourne: Longman Cheshire.

Silverman, D. (1985) *Qualitative Methodology and Sociology*, Aldershot: Gower.

Starkey, K. and Pettigrew, A. (2002) 'Andrew Pettigrew on executives and strategy: an interview by Kenneth Starkey', *European Management Journal* 20(1): 20–25.

Strauss, A. and Corbin, J. (1998) *Basics of Qualitative Research: Grounded Theory Procedures and Techniques*, 2nd edn, Newbury Park, CA: Sage.

Trezise, P. and Roughsey, D. (1991) *Gidja*, Brisbane: Angus and Robertson.

Turner, B. A. (1988) 'Connoisseurship in the study of organizational cultures', in Bryman, A. (ed.) *Doing Research in Organizations*, London: Routledge.

Van de Ven, A. and Huber, G. (1990) 'Longitudinal field research methods for studying processes of organizational change', *Organization Science* 1(3): 213–219.

Van de Ven, A. and Poole, M. (1995) 'Explaining development change in organizations', *Academy of Management Review* 20: 510–540.

Venugopal, V., Suresh, N. and Slomp, J. (2001) (eds) 'Manufacturing cells: design, implementation and analysis', *Integrated Manufacturing Systems: The International Journal of Manufacturing Technology Management* 12(4): 230–325.

Wagner, R. and Sternberg, R. (1986) 'Tacit knowledge and intelligence in the everyday world', in Klemp, G. and McClelland, D. (eds) *Practical Intelligence*, Cambridge: Cambridge University Press.

Whipp, R., Rosenfeld, R. and Pettigrew, A. (1987) 'Understanding strategic change processes: some preliminary British findings', in Pettigrew, A. (ed.) *The Management of Strategic Change*, Oxford: Basil Blackwell.

Whyte, W. (1948) *Human Relations in the Restaurant Industry*, New York: McGraw-Hill.

Whyte, W. (1955) *Street Corner Society*, 2nd edn, Chigaco: University of Chicago Press.

Whyte, W. (1984) *Learning from the Field*, Newbury Park, CA: Sage.

Wilkinson, B. (1983) *The Shop Floor Politics of New Technology*, London: Heinemann.

Wilson, D. (1992) *A Strategy of Change: Concepts and Controversies in the Management of Change*, London: Routledge.

Woodward, J. (1958) *Management and Technology*, London: HMSO.

Woodward, J. (1980) *Industrial Organization: Theory and Practice*, 2nd edn, Oxford: Oxford University Press.

Index